Richard B. (Richard Burleigh) Kimball

Saint Leger

A Romance

Richard B. (Richard Burleigh) Kimball

Saint Leger
A Romance

ISBN/EAN: 9783744770798

Printed in Europe, USA, Canada, Australia, Japan

Cover: Foto ©ninafisch / pixelio.de

More available books at **www.hansebooks.com**

A ROMANCE.

" Quicquid agunt homines, votum, timor, ira, voluptas,
Gaudia, discursus, nostri farrago libelli."

BY

RICHARD B. KIMBALL,

AUTHOR OF " ROMANCE OF STUDENT LIFE," " UNDERCURRENTS," ETC.

NEW YORK:

GEORGE P. PUTNAM, 532 BROADWAY.

1862.

At the age of twenty-three years I find myself upon the threshold of two worlds. The PAST summons the thousand incidents which have operated to determine me as a responsible being, and presents them before me, with fearful vividness. The PRESENT seems like nothing beneath my feet. And the FUTURE, no longer a shadowy dream, throws open its endless vista, and whispers that I must soon enter upon all its untried, unknown realities. Here I am permitted to pause a moment, ere I commence upon that new existence which ends only with the INFINITE.

I have finished my life upon earth. The ties which connect me with the world have parted. I have to do now only with eternity. Yet something which I may not resist, impels me to retrospection. I look back over my short pilgrimage, and feel a yearning which I can not restrain, to put down a narrative of my brief existence, and to mark the several changes which have come over my spirit, in the hope that the young, with whom I chiefly sympathize, may profit by the recital.

But what will this avail to youthful spirits, flushed with the glow of health, secure in their fancied strength, determined on enjoyment? To them the world is everything. Alas, they know not that the world will reward them with infamy, if they trust alone to it! Yet it is to such I make my appeal. I would arrest them, before they cease to have sympathy with every saving influence, because of their habitual opposition to it.

But I will not anticipate the moral of my life. Let this be gathered from the record of it.

BOOK 1.

—Οὐδὲν ἔμπεδον, αλλ' ὅπως ἐς κυκεῶνα πάντα συνειλέονται, και ἐστι τωὖτὸ τέρψις
ἀτερψίη, γνῶσις ἀγνωσίη, μέγα μικρόν, ἄνω κάτω περιχορεύοντα, καὶ ἀμειβόμενα ἐν τῇ
τοῦ αἰῶνος παιδιῇ.

Lucian, Vitarum Auctio, 303.

—Where nothing was fixed, but, as in a mixture, all things were confounded; where pleasure and pain, knowledge and ignorance, great and
small, were the same; where all things up and down were circling round in
a choral dance, and ever changing places as in the sport of eternity.

Saint Leger.

I.

The Saint Leger family have resided in Warwickshire for a long period. My father, who was fond of tracing genealogies, affirmed that the estate upon which we lived was bestowed upon Bertold Saint Leger by Richard the lion-hearted, for the conspicuous services which he had rendered that monarch in his war with the Saracen. How such an uninterrupted possession had been maintained for so long a time, and through every successive revolution, my father did not explain. The task might have proved difficult. At any rate, it was well to rest satisfied with an account which appeared every way authentic. Be this as it may, our family was certainly an ancient one.

My grandfather, Hugh Saint Leger, by his marriage with a lady of large fortune, became possessed of the valuable estate which joined Bertold Castle, and was considered one of the wealthiest gentlemen in Warwickshire. This large patrimony fell to my father, who was an only child.

Bertold castle was a singular, grotesque-looking pile, half ancient, half modern, in its appearance. Up to the time of my father's marriage, it remained as it had stood for generations. The castle was built upon the very brink of the Avon, and its foundations were deeper, it was said, than the bed of

the river. The old moss, which covered its walls, extended
down into the stream, so that the castle seemed to rise directly
from the water. Many were the dismal stories which were
told of dungeons far under ground, of secret passages, beneath the bed of the river, communicating with the other side,
and of cruelties practised upon the unhappy prisoners confined in them in days of yore, and especially in the time of
the famous Guy, Earl of Warwick, of whom my ancestor was
a firm adherent. It was said, too, that the spirits of these
unfortunate persons still haunted the neighborhood, and made
the green banks of the Avon their place of meeting. The
low murmur of the stream, as it swept gently under the walls
of the castle, was said to be the voices of these spirits, as they
breathed their lamentations over the waters which had been
the only witness of their sufferings. I speak of nursery tales
and neighborhood gossip, not of course credited by the enlightened, but which served to fill my infant mind with terror
and awe. And as this sketch is intended to give the history
of my mental, as well as of my external life, I dwell with the
more minuteness on those things which first affected it most
powerfully.

On my father's marriage with a daughter of one of the noble families in Warwickshire, the castle was almost completely
metamorphosed. His pride would not permit him to throw
down a single stone of the stanch pile which had stood so
long a tower of strength for his ancestors; while the improvements of the age required a mansion more in accordance with
its refined and peaceful spirit. It was consequently resolved
to add to the pile a splendid modern structure, which was to
become, par excellence, the residence of the family. The old
dining-hall and the state-rooms were however allowed to remain in all their sombre grandeur. The library was not quite
dismantled; but all of the handsomer books were re-

moved into the new room, built for that purpose. Enough nevertheless remained to save it from utter neglect, although the dusty cobwebs around the walls gave evidence of the slight attention it received.

The older servants saw with dismay the preparations for enlarging the establishment; looking upon it as a virtual abandonment of the "Old Castle." This was considered a bad omen, and to augur the termination or downfall of our house. A prophecy was quoted relative to the dreaded event, now about to take place, which was said to be of great antiquity :

> "When ye Saint Leger shal marrie a virgyn fair,
> Shal build a new castel both wondrous and rare,
> Lett him warnynge tak, for ye last of his race
> Shal hee meet in yt castel, face to face."

My grandfather held this prophecy in high veneration. He was wont to say, " With so plain a warning in view, the Saint Legers would stand an unbroken name for countless generations." The consequence was, that nothing was done to the old castle, except what came strictly under the denomination of repairs. Improvements were not thought of. At length, Hugh Saint Leger was gathered to his fathers, and the great gong of the castle struck his requiem amid the weeping and lamentation of relatives, servants, and retainers; for he was a man of many virtues; both generous and kind, though stern in his manner, and possessing somewhat of the haughty bearing of the preceding age.

My father was educated at a more enlightened period, when improvements waxed rife; when distinctions began to soften, and changes to be thought necessary. He affected to disregard the prophecy which had been always so religiously believed. He maintained that the old castle was built mainly with a view to defence, in case of attack; that it possessed great conveniences for a garrison, but comparatively few for

a family residence; and while he revered it as the home of
his fathers, regarding with just pride the frowning battlements,
which had resisted every assault, still he maintained that there
could exist no reason why improvements should not be made,
which might accord with the present state of things. The
"addition" was consequently resolved upon. My father was
particular always to give it that name, secretly deciding, perhaps, that by so doing he avoided the letter of the prophecy.
The new mansion was built. My father married. Years
rolled happily away. He was blessed with three promising
children; and everything went on joyously and well. My
own recollections are of my home in the improved state I
have described. From the old servants however I learned at
an early age the existence of the prophecy, and the fearful
construction which superstition had given it. Little was said
openly; but the deprecatory air, the sombre, melancholy look,
which two or three of the old crones, who had become super-
annuated in our service, constantly wore, were always a sore
interruption to our childish sports. Did we meet them while
full of the elastic, happy, feeling which children so much
enjoy, it was always: "Poor children! God preserve ye:
Who knows what ye may come to! God send ye an easy
death!" and the like.

My brother—I had but one, and he was my senior—seemed but little affected by these prophecies of evil, while upon
my own mind they produced a chilling and lasting effect.
Like the insect that flutters nearer and nearer the flame which
is to prove its destruction, I used to steal away and hold daily
conferences with these old creatures; and hour after hour
was wont to be entertained with stories of the bloody wars in
which old Bertold Saint Leger figured; of the exploits of the
famous Guy of Warwick; and of my brave grandfather,
Hugh Saint Leger, the last worthy of the race, as they were

pleased to style him; always concluding however, by quoting the dreaded prophecy, and assuring me that I was doomed.

These lessons, so often inculcated, began to produce their impression. Somehow I took to myself the whole force of the prediction, regarding my brother and sister as exempt from its influence.

The result was, that in my very childhood I became serious and thoughtful. Life, in its spring-time, was losing every charm. The world looked no longer joyous and gay.

I had begun to suffer.

II.

STRANGE season of childhood! marked by cloud and sunshine; full of light-hearted pleasures and fresh griefs; yet how fraught with consequences when the new-created being, ushered into life, commences upon immortality! Precious season, when every new object makes an impression, and every impression is indelible! And what fearful issues hang upon each! issues which reach through time, and peradventure into eternity.

III.

IN order to present a proper narrative of my life, I should give some account of those who exercised most influence upon it. My father was in many respects a singular man. He possessed in a great degree the stern nature of my grandfather, which was nevertheless considerably modified by a natural urbanity of manner, which old Hugh Saint Leger never manifested. He had a warm, generous heart, and was devotedly attached to his wife and children. Although a younger brother, I never could perceive any difference in the treatment of his sons. He was equally affectionate toward both,

yet never familiar with either.   His urbanity was manifested
in social life with his friends and acquaintances ; but when
any one sought his intimacy, a repulse was certain.   Yet he
was neither haughty nor overbearing.   Pride he certainly
possessed ; yet it seemed a just and honest pride, rather than
the vain conceit of a weak mind.   From his children he not
only expected obedience, to the letter, but he never suffered
his commands or wishes to be questioned.   I well remember
once unconsciously asking him why, I must do some act which
he had commanded, and the withering sternness of his re
sponse as he re-echoed the command, without deigning any
explanation.   In justice I should add, that his requirements
were reasonable and proper, although to a wayward child
they might seem otherwise.   In his religion my father was
strict and devoted.   He hated with a pious indignation, and
early instilled in the minds of his children an abhorrence of
the Romish church.   Frenchmen were another aversion, and
it was with difficulty that he could bring himself to treat one
with civility.   Possessing in the main sound views, he entertained violent prejudices, which it was impossible to change.
He was not ambitious, except for his children.   He omitted
nothing which might insure to them every advantage, as well
in education as in personal advancement.   For them he labored and planned.   No expense was too great, no sacrifice
too large.   But if my father was ready to do all this, much
did he expect in return.   What he thought we could accomplish, we were compelled to accomplish, no matter though
the task were difficult, nay overwhelming.   No excuse was
accepted.   In vain we sometimes pleaded that our companions were not tasked so heavily.   With something like a sneer,
he would reply, "If you ever wish to be anything, do not
talk about what others do, but set your mark away beyond
them all, and when once the mark is fixed, let there be no

drawing back. *Try*, and the thing will be done." And try we did, until it seemed as if no labor was half so hard as ours. Yet after all, we generally fulfilled what was required, and had the satisfaction of making glad a parent's heart.

I do not think I could have borne so cheerfully all that my father imposed upon me, had it not been for my mother. What a world of feeling and tenderness is in that name! Though still living, let me pay her the tribute which I can not withhold. I should think my duty but half accomplished, did I omit to record what I owe to her. In disposition she was angelic. I think I never saw her ruffled in temper, or discomposed. She was mild, yet dignified, and possessed a sweetness of manner which was perfectly fascinating. Above all, she was devotedly pious, and it was her first care to instil into the minds of her children a love for sacred things. Morning and evening did I lisp my infantile prayers to her, and it seemed as if she sent them up for me to God.

"Come, William, it is high time to be up, if you wish to go out with Roger to the Park, across the Avon, and see the new rookery. The sun is up long before you. Do not you hear the larks singing? It will soon be breakfast time, and Roger can not wait."—"Dear mother, I am so sleepy."—"You are! and how long has my son been in bed? Eight hours, and sleepy yet. You must not become a sluggard."—"Mother, mother, I want to whisper to you; I forgot my prayers last night. You were away, and I fell asleep without saying them."—"My son, you should be careful never to forget them. You should remember who keeps you alive, and makes you so happy; and you should always put yourself under His care before you sleep. But God will forgive my little boy, for he was very tired last night."—"Mother, let me say my prayers now." All this comes upon me with the freshness of first ideas. And it is just what my dear mother

said to me—I remember it so distinctly. Day after day she
would impress some religious truth upon my mind, and so
kindly, so tenderly, that it would have melted an older heart
than mine. How she loved me: how she loves me still:
perhaps with a difference in the feeling too.

IV.

To my mother I came with my troubles; to her I repeated
all my grievances, save *one*. I never could name to her what
sat heaviest at my heart—the belief that I was doomed. Often did she perceive that something afflicted me; and most
soothingly did she attempt to discover the cause; but my
tongue refused to do its office, if I desired to tell her; and
my only relief was in tears. My mother sometimes thought
that my fears were of a religious nature; and she would accordingly attempt to comfort me by the merciful promises of
the Scriptures. But in vain. The prophecy haunted me.
And to the one of all others who might have afforded me consolation I could not speak of it.

My brother Hugh was more than five years older than myself, and of course was rather a protector than a playfellow.
He was a noble boy; kind in his nature, quick in his
feelings, forgiving and generous. We loved each other
fondly. Evil betide the one who dared offer indignity to me
when Hugh was present! He took a pride in defending me,
and fancied himself a man, as he fought battles and achieved
victories in my behalf. He was intelligent and apt in his
studies, though not of a thoughtful turn. He had a fine
voice, prepossessing manners, and a rapid flow of language, together with a commanding energy of character, which over-
came every obstacle.

My little sister was a general favorite; and though in great danger of being spoiled in consequence, yet by the judicious government of both parents, she was preserved from such an unhappy fate. She was like her mother in disposition, and being educated at home, under her immediate direction, it was no wonder that the resemblance daily grew stronger.

I will mention one more, and our family are all told. There resided with my father a maiden aunt, many years older than himself, who had always lived at the castle. She was a younger sister of Hugh Saint Leger, and had occupied one room in the old castle for many years. This was a small but neatly finished chamber, on the river side, commanding a fine view of the Avon, and the country beyond.

This singular woman, at the time of my birth, was at least sixty. In appearance she was tall and commanding. Her hair was perfectly white, and she wore it short over her head. She had gray eyes, which sparkled with the brightness of youth, and retained all their original quickness of vision. Her habits were peculiar. She required but little service, although one of the old crones I spoke of was always in attendance upon her. With the family her intercourse was singular enough. She rarely came to the table, and never sought the society of any one; yet when addressed, she would mingle freely in conversation, showing remarkable accuracy in matters of history, and especially in chronology. She spent most of the time either in her own apartment, musing and reading, or in wandering along the banks of the Avon, plucking a flower here and there, or picking up small pebbles on the shore; talking to herself the while, with great earnestness. The usual occupations of her sex she never engaged in for a moment. I know not if she knew the use of the needle. She rarely retired to rest until the night was far spent, and seldom rose before mid-day.

As may be supposed, such a person produced upon my

mind a lasting impression. When a child, she was a mystery to me; and as I became older, she was no less an enigma. She appeared to have no sympathies; yet she seemed, judging from her acts, to be attached to us all. If I deemed myself slighted by any of the servants, I had only to tell Aunt Alice, and without investigation or question, the offender was subjected to the severest reproof. If I was ill, I found my way to Aunt Alice's apartment, and received every attention which it was in her power to bestow. Nothing asked of her was refused, and she never tired of our importunities. Yet in all this, no feeling, no sympathy, was manifested; all was cold—without heart, without life. Yet she was roused to anger by the slightest opposition. Seldom indeed did she meet with it, but when she *did*, the storm and whirlwind were fit emblems of her wrath. These paroxysms lasted but for a brief space; and in the exhibition of them there was the same want of feeling, of vital passion, as in her calm moments. Passionless; possessing nothing like affection in her heart, with no apparent ties on earth; she seemed to regard everything around her like shadows on the wall: they came, they went—but they were shadows still, while she remained the same. Often have I crept close to her, as she wandered out on some of her long walks, and listened to the conversation she was holding with herself. This was sometimes in a foreign language, of which I knew nothing. When she spoke in our own tongue, her subject was generally of things long past, of which I could understand but little. I could perceive that she often kept up an imaginary conversation with two, and sometimes three persons, with great volubility; and I could in consequence very rarely make out a connected link of what was said.

Again I would steal unnoticed into her room, and listen as she recited strange events of history, which made my young blood run cold, and my heart beat so violently that I was glad to discover myself, and ask some favor at her hands. At last I came to spend a great deal of time in her apartment; and Aunt Alice would relate to me, in the same passionless style, long-forgotten stories of our house; marked passages of history relating to it; and a minute and almost tedious narrative of historical events, relative to any subject I chose to start. These were always free from the ordinary gossip with which lovers of the marvellous are apt to lard their stories, and therefore produced the stronger impression. Of course Aunt Alice was familiar with the prophecy to which I have alluded; but she only spoke of it as an historical fact, and by no persuasion or artifice could she be induced to give an opinion of its application; neither would she listen to any from another person; so that my morbid fears found no relief from her. Treated with marked respect by my father and all the family; allowed to have her will in everything; this remarkable woman lived among us like a spirit from another world. She came and went unquestioned; continued year after year, pursuing the same round of strange employments; solitary and soulless; having apparently no sympathy with her sex, no feeling with her kind.

V.

I HAVE always been disposed to deny that our early days were intended to be our happiest. True it is, that most look back to them with pleasure, mingled with feelings half of regret, half of sadness, that they are passed. The reason of this is, that those days are free from the anxieties which mature life is sure to bring. The man, pressed down with business, loaded with care, even though his coffers are filling with wealth, looks back upon his childhood as a green spot in his existence, while all around is drear and desolate.

And if business engross him not, if he knows nothing of the drudgery of acquiring riches, but lives for his own pleasure and amusement, how soon these pall upon him—then he, also, sighs for the careless, thoughtless, happy feelings of early days, when time needed no destroyer, and the hydra-headed monster Ennui found no place of attack.

Is it a wonder that such as I have mentioned, the slave of pleasure as well as the slave of toil, should look away across the dreary waste of years, and seek to recall the past? But it is too late: youth will not come back, and they have no talisman to compel it to return :

> " Non enim gazæ, neque consularis
> Summovet lictor miseros tumultus
> Mentis ; et curas laqueata circum
> Tecta volentes."

When I hear friends conversing together of " good old times," closing their conference with, "Ah, well! those were happy days, sure enough; the happiest part of our lives, if we had but known it :" I feel persuaded that they have made but a poor use of existence. What! has God made us with such rich preparatives for true enjoyment, such noble powers of mind and sense, and yet designed us to retrograde through life? Yielding us a few hours of questionable happiness at first, to be succeeded by days of weariness or wo? It is not so! Who would be contented always with such happiness? Who does not know that it is but the pleasure of animal existence; an existence gay indeed as the bird's, and like the bird's thoughtless too?

The man who wisely employs himself about things imperishable, must grow happier each succeeding day in time, and so on through the period beyond, which we call eternity. The goodness of God ordains this; the wisdom of God proclaims it.

My own childhood was peculiarly thoughtful; and the thoughtful child must of necessity be unhappy. Too young to understand the great mystery of existence, everything in life seems strange and inexplicable. A heavy burden hangs at the heart of such, and I felt its full weight. My greatest relief was in active exercise; for although not addicted to the ordinary sports which children love, I was fond of exposure and fatigue; and my constitution being robust, I could indulge in these without danger. Yet I was solitary, even in my associations. In hunting I took peculiar delight. At the early age of ten, I was the owner of a small gun and shooting apparatus; but I never took pleasure in scouring the country after a pack of hounds, in company with a score of noisy sportsmen, pursuing to the death a poor fox or hare. There was no excitement to me in leaping ditches, clearing hedges, or in a scamper across the plain; but I loved to take my gun, and without even the assistance of a favorite pointer, make my way to the great forest which lay across the Avon, before the sun rose, and spend the whole day in traversing it.

Not that I was eager for the reward of the sportsman.   Many a time has the woodcock crossed my path unscared, and
often have I lowered my piece, raised against the life of the
timid hare.   I defy you, reader, to go out betimes into the
green-wood, and catch the inhabitants just waking from their
slumbers, and commence your bloody work, without some
qualms of conscience against taking life so early in the day.
The night, however, generally sent me home with a well-filled
bag.

The wild-cat was often to be found in the most extensive
forests.   This animal was in size considerably larger than the
domestic cat, while its teeth and claws were tremendous.
With these creatures I waged a war of extermination.   This
was not carried on without risk, certainly.   Yet I loved the
hazard, and felt no hardship in the toil.

But after all, when the excitement of the chase was over,
thought was once more in the ascendant.   My father (erro-
neously perhaps) determined to give his children a private
education, affirming that public schools and universities were
alike destructive to mind, manners, and morals.   So at home
we were kept, and furnished with erudite teachers, who knew
everything about books and nothing about men.

I had in all this abundance to foster the unhappy feeling
which burned within.   Thought, how it troubled me—and I
had so much to think about.   But beyond all, the great wonder of my life was, " What life was made for ?"   I wondered
what could occupy the world.   I read over the large vol-
umes in the old library, and wondered why men should battle it with each other for the sake of power, when power
lasted but so short a time.   I wondered why kings who could
have done so much good had done so much evil; and I wondered why anybody was very unhappy, since death should so
soon relieve from all earthly ills.   Then I felt, there was some

unknown power busy within me, which demanded a field for labor and development, but I knew not what spirit it was of. I wanted to see the world; to busy myself in its business, and try if I could discover its fashion, for it was to me a vast mystery. I knew it was filled with human beings like unto myself, but what were they doing, and wherefore? The *what* and the *why* troubled me, perplexed me, almost crazed me. When I came to learn something more of the world; and it was a strangely important crisis in the affairs of man; the world seemed like a mad world, and its inhabitants resolved on self-destruction. How I longed to break the shell which encased this mystery. I felt that there was a solution to all this : but how was I to discover it? Not that I was kept so perfectly secluded; I had often accompanied my father to London; I had seen much of the outside form and fashion of the world, but I did not get into it. I had so educated myself, that I could not. The pageant passed ever before my eyes, a pageant still. I had no friend to clear up my difficulties, for these were difficulties I never mentioned. Firm in the idea that some fearful destiny hung over me, and believing that it was connected with this general mistrust of all I saw, or read, or heard of, I kept these feelings to myself, and thus lived two lives at the same time. Had I but told my mother, how readily might I have been relieved. Had my instructors at the first attempted to gain my confidence, and sought the reason of the premature anxiety which brooded around my young heart, even then I might have forgotten these first fearful impressions ; but it was now too late. The habit was formed, and it could not undergo an easy change. Have not many who read this page exclaimed, at one time or another, " Would that I could rid myself of my early impressions ! Would that I could overcome this fostered propensity of my youth !" Too late ! too late ! I warn ye ; for impressions are never effaced from the young mind; a rooted propensity never eradicated, beyond danger of evil. Reform may come, it is true; reason may show the folly and the sinfulness of yielding to fancied images of ill; repentance may bring forgiveness after it; and the soul be happy in the assurance; but

> ——" There the action lies
> In his true nature:"

and though repented of, and forgiven, there it must lie for ever!

Thus I continued, until my sixteenth year; when an incident occurred which gave a new direction to my life

VI.

OFF the coast of Scotland, but far out into the Atlantic, lie, as all well know, the outer range of the Hebrides, a cluster of rude islands, made up of rough rocks, wild mountains, deep and unsightly valleys, while toward the ocean their rocky cliffs assume a form of peculiar grandeur. Here the storm-king holds perpetual revel. Here the elements continue, without intermission, their incessant strife. The deceitful eddy, the fearful whirlpool, the perilous strait, are here. Here too are dark caverns, across whose entrance the waves beat continually; while the tops of the threatening cliffs are lost in gloomy clouds, and against their bases, roll with its restless heaving, the everlasting sea.

These islands, although so near to England and Scotland, have retained all the simple and homely manners of a ruder age. It is probable that the dangers of the seas, and the horrors of the tempests which prevail there, were sufficient to deter any from venturing thither, unless urged by a peculiar necessity. Barren rocks and a bleak climate presented no great inducements to the rapacity of the bucanier, or the ambition of the conqueror. Yet the people were by no means left undisturbed in their unenviable possessions. Each island was originally governed by its own chief. But it is related that Harold Harfiger, the light-hair-ed, in A. D. 870, pursued thither several petty princes, whom he had driven out of Norway, and who had taken refuge in the Hebrides, whence they made descents upon his territories His attack was successful. These pirate-chiefs were put to death, and all their followers either slaughtered or dispersed. On regaining their ancient seats, Ketil, the flat-nosed, was sent by Harold with a large fleet to subdue them. This he easily effected, and then openly declared himself independent, assuming the title of Prince of the Hebrides. The islanders continued, under Ketil, to be little else than rapacious pirates.

After his death, the kingdom of Man was formed out of them. The islands then became tributary to Norway, and were governed by princes sent from that country. They af-terward shook off the yoke; or according to some, were ceded by the king of Norway to the king of Scotland, about the year 1263. Still the government was in the main an independent sovereignty; for the warlike chiefs who ruled there, although nominally under the Scottish crown, were too far removed from the power that might compel obedience, to regard it with much awe.

These chiefs were descended from Somerled, of Argyle, the ancestor of the great clan of the Macdonalds; and so in-dependently did they exercise their authority, that they took upon themselves the regal title, and assumed the name, of " The Lords of the Isles."

These chieftains continued without intermission, and with various success, to make furious inroads upon the main land; where, after devastating to a considerable extent, they would be driven back to their island-homes: there they would, for want of other occupation, make war upon each other. This troublesome state of things continued into the present cen-tury. For after the commotions in England and Scotland

were allayed, the heads of the island-clans (to whom had been
allowed an importance which they did not deserve, and which
only served to foment insurrection) broke out in rebellion.
This was speedily put down.   The act of 1748 for abolish-
ing heritable jurisdictions was passed, which destroyed for ever
the power of these petty tyrants.

The inhabitants of the Hebrides were, at the time I speak of
them, in the main fishermen, hardy and robust, from constant
exposure to the vicissitudes of ocean-life.   Sheep and black
cattle were raised in some of the islands in considerable
quantities.   The soil was owned by one or more lairds, to
whom the occupant paid a small rent from its productions.
But little attention was paid to its cultivation, the stirring life
of the fisherman being much preferred to the quiet and less
exciting occupation of agriculture.   No country or region,
of all that I had heard or read, made such an impression upon my imagination as the stormy Hebrides.   Not from
anything peculiar in the history of the inhabitants ; not from
any childish fancy or association by which they were impressed upon my mind ; it was simply their natural position ; so
near to all that was beautiful in scenery, yet so wild and rugged ; so near to the great commercial marts of Christendom,
yet so repulsive in their aspect that no adventurous trader
from other lands ever ventured there.

I never could think of these islands as inhabited, but delighted to regard them in gloomy grandeur, companions of
the tempest and the storm ; a spot where Nature might triumph over the arts, and schemes, and contrivances of man.

I ought, however, to mention that Aunt Alice was the first
who led me to think of them.   Whenever she indulged in
historical details, of which I was very fond, she generally
made mention of the Hebrides.   There was evidently some
secret connected therewith which she did not wish to discover,
and I never presumed to inquire about it.

My mother was nearly related to the noble family of the Venachoir, in Argyleshire. Some of my cousins of that fam ily had passed a considerable portion of the sporting season at Bertold Castle, and we were all invited to visit Glencoe the following summer. As the year came round, the invitation was renewed. My brother had no relish for the visit, as he began to take an active part in the affairs of the day. In short, he was becoming a thorough man-of-fact; such a one as society, with its irresistible and enslaving influence, makes and moulds. He was full, to be sure, of ambitious hopes and brilliant expectations, in which certainly there was little room for disappointment ; but these hopes and expectations were such as belong to the man who trusts all to this world, and who seeks and receives his recompense from it. Let me not do injustice to my brother. He was to me the same kind brother still. He was whole-souled and generous; but he had committed himself to a certain course. The chains of conventional form and habit were fast fettering his spirit, and the natural man was becoming the artificial slave.

A ramble in the Highlands, though attractive enough to a youth who knew nothing about law, politics, and public speeches, and cared less, was the last thing my brother would think of undertaking. It would break off his plans for present action, and interfere with his schemes. In brief, he did not wish to be brought back to the natural and the romantic, having put on the armor of earthly strife, and engaged in that restless action which belongs peculiarly to it. He had not, be it understood, become hackneyed in the contests of the arena; all was new, exciting, and alluring. His brow was unclouded; his heart beat hopefully, and his mind was as yet free from the selfish considerations which after-life presents.

To me the invitation opened a world of enjoyment. I was an admirer of natural scenery. I yearned for some change that should serve to give a new direction to my thoughts. I longed to mix with the world, not as an actor in its scenes, but as a student of its mysteries; to divine its va- -ious forms and phantasies, if indeed I might discover their meaning. I would fain oppose myself to its ever-shifting, endless changes, and ask how and why they occurred. The time had arrived when the Man began to develop, and some sphere, place, opportunity, was absolutely necessary for natural growth. The *direction* had been already given, it was of the dark and sombre cast; yet I had not quite for- gotten how to enjoy.

I was sixteen. Our friends in Scotland were pressing in their invitation. I asked and obtained permission to pay the visit. How happy the thought of striking out into life made me ! my heart seemed fresh again.

VII.

It was the month of June. I had finished the little preparations necessary for my tour, which I had determined to make alone; not even accompanied by Thomas, a faithful servant, who had from my childhood been devotedly attached to me, and who was always my companion and ready assistant in every adventure where I required his aid. So alone I was permitted to go. I farther determined to take the mail-coach in preference to a more secluded though imposing means of conveyance. My mother dismissed me with gentle cautions as to my general conduct while away, entreating me to be careful of myself; not to forget my daily devotions, if I expected the protection of Providence, and to be sure to let her hear from me often.

My father gave me letters of introduction to various families of distinction in the different towns through which I was to pass, and a well-filled purse, with directions how I might replenish it if necessary. Aunt Alice had not spoken to me on the subject of my excursion; but on the morning of my departure she put in my hands a small parcel, and immediately turned away. I had not then time to examine it; so I placed it carefully in my portmanteau, intending to open it when more at leisure.

The " Fly Dragon" royal mail-coach passed through Warwick about ten o'clock. Proceeding thither in our own carriage, I had not waited many minutes before it made its appearance. I chose an outside, and secured the seat of honor next to the " whip." Several passengers got on at Warwick

There was the usual show of idle, do-nothing fellows around
the door, increased by a number of lazy grooms and lacqueys,
to whom the arrival and departure of the royal mail were the
principal events in their existence. The horses were pran-
cing, impatient of delay. By each, stood a groom ready to
lift the blanket that covered the animal, when the signal
should be given. "All right?" asked the coachman; "All
right!" responded the guard; "All right!" echoed the
groom; and away flew the horses, leaving the four attendants with arms outstretched, each having retained his
blanket.

What glorious excitement filled my bosom, as we coursed
along! The balmy breath of the morning; the sweet fra-
grance of the hedge and of the field; the bracing air, added
to the newness of my situation, made me feel like a new creature. My identity was almost gone; hope, and the various
emotions that hope gives birth to, swelled my bosom; I felt
a thousand new ideas springing up within me. Just then I
could have shouldered the universe, so strong did I feel, or
"put a girdle round about the earth in forty minutes," I felt
so fleet. What can equal the energy of untried youth!

Among the passengers that took the stage-coach at Warwick was a young man, apparently about one-and-twenty
years of age, who in several ways attracted my notice. He
was rather tall and slender, of an Italian cast of features,
with long dark hair, piercing black eyes, and beard trimmed
after the peculiar style of the Prussians. There was nothing
English in his appearance. Much to my surprise, however,
he spoke the language without the slightest accent, and seemed perfectly familiar with the ordinary customs of the country, and with the localities we passed. He conversed with
considerable freedom with those who sat by him, though they
were evidently acquaintances of the road. His servant, a sinister-looking fellow, of foreign appearance, occupied a back

seat, and had charge of divers sporting implements, which betokened a relish for the chase in the master. Yet the latter was not a person to be suspected of such a propensity, or of belonging to such gentle craft. In spite of myself, I felt an instinctive antipathy to the stranger; and the more I tried to dispel it, the stronger it became. He had apparently been long abroad, and from the suspicious glances cast ever and anon around him, was evidently accustomed to scenes of danger, perhaps violence. Still there was nothing of the frank, open bearing of the soldier in his manner, but rather the wily caution of the intriguer; and I wondered the more that one so young should bear such marks upon his brow.

At one of the stopping-places, the stranger alighted, and on regaining his seat, his body came almost in contact with mine; and as he bent over to pass me, my eyes glanced involuntarily into his bosom, where I beheld a stout leathern belt, in which were thrust a dagger and a brace of pistols, so disposed as ordinarily to be concealed from view by the vest and the light mantle worn over it. At that moment the stranger's gaze met mine; as if aware of the discovery I had made, he gave a scornful smile and took his place. Half ashamed at seeing what I certainly could not help observing, and piqued at the assumption of the stranger, whom I had by this time put down for one no better than he should be, I settled into a moody silence, considerably unlike the buoyant feelings which signalized our starting.

I did not long maintain this feeling, but entered into conversation with Walter, the "whip," a veteran roadster, now some fifty years old, whom I had known since my childhood. He had for many years been in the service of a family who were on terms of intimacy with us, and had afterward left them for the more lucrative employment of the road. Of course I recognised him at once on mounting.

"The young Master Saint Leger travels alone, I see," said Walter, in an inquiring tone; "nothing amiss, I hope?"

"Nothing," I replied; "I am just going to shake hands with the world, and prefer an *incog.* to a formal introduction."

"And that's the way to make the most of the acquaintance, if you are wise, and the shortest route to send you to the devil if you are foolish," answered Walter, confidently.

Remembering that my old acquaintance was somewhat of a moralist, I felt like giving him his bent, and asked: "How is that, Walter?"

"Why," replied he, "if the young Saint Leger should drive into the world with a load of introductions to all the high-born and honorable, the rich and the noble, he might be courted, and flattered, and fooled, till he would become as great a fool as any. But if he would know where he stands, and the road he travels, let him take his first start without any help, just as you are going to do, I hope, and then he will find out what he is good for, and what his friends are good for; but, young man, if this is done merely to throw off the restraint of the governor's presence, and the proper curb of experience and good advice, why then, as I said before, you will soon be posting to the devil, and all the governors and friends in the world can't hold you up."

I was struck with the homely soundness of Walter's speech, and told him that I fully agreed with him; but that the present excursion was to be a short one, and that nearly all my time would be passed with my relatives.

"So much the more need, then, of making the most of what time you have; we shall be at Oxford presently, and there 'The coachman leaves you, sir,' " said Walter, touching his hat, and mimicking the tone used when the customary shilling is expected. "Now take my advice; stay a day there instead of hurrying on to London. Old Nancy, the housekeeper—I suppose she is alive yet—will only look a day longer for you, and that will harm nobody. You have been in Oxford a hundred times, no doubt. You have seen all the fine buildings and the grand colleges and halls; so you need waste no time about them; just stop at the 'Hen and Chickens' instead of going to the 'Angel,' where you will be recognised, and served accordingly. But at Mother Christy's all you have to do is to sit still and see the world. Depend upon it, 'tis the only way."

Walter's advice to me was most opportune, for I was just in the mood to receive it; not from any wish to escape proper restraint, but I longed to break over, for a time at least, the bounds which my birth and the rules of society imposed, that I might say to my fellow: "Man, we meet in common together. God made us both. What say you? what are your thoughts, your impulses, your sympathies?"

I assented at once to Walter's proposal.

Just then we stopped to change horses, and most of the passengers alighted. I was somewhat tardy in getting up, and on mounting found, greatly to my surprise, that the foreign-looking stranger had taken my seat, and was coolly looking the other way, as I thought, purposely to avoid me. In a very civil though determined tone, I suggested to him that he had my place. He pointed with a careless air over his shoulder, and remarked that there were plenty of seats above. His contemptuous manner set me completely on fire. The blood boiled in my veins, I was so angry; and taking a step toward the stranger, I exclaimed, "You may take your choice, either to vacate my seat instantly, or be pitched off the box."

What might have been the end of the controversy I can not tell; for Walter promptly interfered, saying ·

"Patience! patience! Master Saint Leger. The young man is foreign-bred, and does n't understand the custom of the English road. So I must tell you, sir, that seats on o stage-coach are like beds at an inn; and as you make your bed, so you must lie in it, you know."

"A plague on your roads, your customs, and your impertinence!" said the stranger, addressing Walter, but resuming his old seat at the same time; "for the present I bear with all three. As for my young master there, I have no desire to quarrel with him unless he forces me to it. His fangs are not grown yet, and I dislike to have too great an advantage."

"With all submission," retorted Walter, "I would advise you to seek no matter for quarrel with a Saint Leger, for though the cub may not know his own nature till he is roused, you will find enough of the tiger there before you have finished. These are peaceful times, letting alone the cursed Frenchers across the water. We have done with feuds, and quarrels, and bloodshed, since the time I was a baby, I may say; but I will uphold, till I see the difference, that a Saint Leger is a Saint Leger so long as a drop of old Bertold's blood remains, which they say is having its last run, but of that I do n't pretend to know."

During this harangue, the stranger's countenance had settled into its usual contemptuous expression which seemed for a moment excited at the mention of my name, for he muttered, half to himself, without appearing farther to notice the coachman: "Saint Leger! strange enough too; we shall see." In the meantime, I maintained a determined silence, quite ashamed at the violence of my passion, and fully resolved not to embroil myself in a disreputable controversy with an unknown adventurer. My thoughts, in the meanwhile, were none of the most pleasant. All my wise philosophy had vanished. Where, I asked myself, were the strong yearnings to make acquaintance with humanity? where the desire to meet my kind on common ground; to know men; to know myself? A moment of foolish excitement had dispersed all; and I felt that I was but a child. After a time, however, my

natural equanimity began to return. I reflected that I had to
school myself if I expected to pass profitably through life,
and that every incident must serve to teach me something.

The stage-coach rolled rapidly on. We had passed the old
town of Woodstock, and the splendid palace and park of
Blenheim, and were in sight of Oxford. The country in the
vicinity is enchanting. The day was fine; the season the
loveliest in all the year; and as we approached this famous
seat of learning, the sun, which had enriched the landscape
with its declining rays, sunk gently out of sight, leaving behind a canopy of gorgeous clouds, which were full of change-
ful beauty, as each succeeding hue threw a new aspect over
the scene.

How my young heart enjoyed what was before me! How
like a very paradise it seemed! I lost for the moment the
thought of everything earthly; of everything unpleasant,
and gave myself up to this new influence. My revery was
broken by Walter, who exclaimed: "I have been waiting
for you to speak first, but I see Master Saint Leger is not
disposed to make free with his tongue. So I will just say,
that I suppose I was fairly enough to blame for not sending
that jackanapes to the seat which belonged to him, when he
had the impudence to take yours. But to tell you the truth,
I wanted to see your mettle, my boy, and by St. George and
the Dragon! I came near rousing more than we could have
carried. I do believe you would have thrown him under the
wheel if I had not stood between; and what a scandal that
would have been to his majesty's royal mail! You saw,
though, I gave him a settler. But it did do me good to see
your blood up; not that I counsel brawls and swaggering
and all that; no, no; Walter Roland is a peaceful man; but
it requires a man of spirit to be a man of peace and no
coward."

"I feel ashamed of such a sudden show of passion," replied I, "and I candidly acknowledge it; for that stranger, whom I can not help disliking, might not have been aware of the affront put upon me."

"He not aware of it!" exclaimed Walter, with a grin. "Hush!" said he, speaking in a lower tone. for fear of being overheard, and making what was intended to be a very significant gesture from one side of his face; "I have seen *him* before, or my circumspection goes for nothing."

"Seen him before? why what do you mean?" inquired I.

"Nothing," answered Walter, "except that you will probably see him again, and that he knows as much of the rules of the road as either of us: not a word more, for he is watching us. You will part company at Oxford, and here we are already; just over the bridge, then two squares, and we are safe at the Hen and Chickens."

There was the usual blast of the guard, the usual bustle of attendants at the inn, the usual questions and the usual answers. The "Fly Dragon" threw off her passengers, and forthwith rolled away to her resting-place.

I remained quietly at the Hen and Chickens, a respectable inn, frequented by the regular "traveller," men of counting-house importance and the like, but of a stamp entirely different from the Cross, the Star, and the Angel, which were in high repute.

I had at least the satisfaction of feeling that I was not known. I observed that the stranger seemed astonished when I ordered the porter to take in my luggage, but nothing was said, and I was heartily glad to be rid of his presence. At the door a pretty, rosy-cheeked chambermaid asked if the young gentleman would be shown to his room. I assented; and after shaking off the dust with which the ride had encumbered me, I proceeded to the traveller's-room and ordered refreshments. I had ample chance to look around me. Here were seated several mercantile men, some engaged in conversation, others over their port, or reading their newspapers. Two or three mawkish-looking young fellows were talking largely about the Newton races, which had just come off; and a small knot of town's people were discussing in a corner divers subjects over sundry flagons of ale. I took a seat near the window, to command a view of the passers-by. The twilight continued far into the evening, and tempted out the most recluse; now a student from one of the colleges would pass with cap and gown; next came tripping by some tradesman's daughter, dressed for an evening out; then the sturdy laborer, covered with dust and sweat, going home after his day's toil to meet his wife and children, and be refreshed; some servant girls, in their Sunday's best, were talking and laughing very loud, as they sauntered along the pavement, watched by three or four young men, who might have been students, though they had doffed the garb of the college; carriages rolled along the street; the hackman was soliciting a fare; and the beggar was whining out the customary petition; while occasionally the rigid, unearthly sound of a passing Israelite would startle me with its never-ending, "Clothes! old clothes!" The very town was agog that evening. Presently a Frenchman made his appearance with two little dogs which he had taught to stand, the one upon the shoulders of the other (each upon his hind legs), while the by-standers, by offering inviting morsels, first to one and then to the other, endeavored to disturb their equilibrium. The poor animals, although evidently very hungry, maintained their position, casting ever and anon longing looks toward the tempting bribe, and then despairingly toward their master, who only scowled at them, shook his head, and muttered, "Dé donc!"

After the performance was over, requisition was made for pennies and sixpences, according to the liberality of the donors. The old man could speak no English be-

yond the " var' good," " tank-ee," which he used most gen-
erously, whether his suit was favored or rejected.   As he approached me, cap in hand, leading his little dogs, I thought
I could discover traces of deep feeling under the air of
mendicant entreaty which he assumed.   A strong sense
of pity came over me; and as he passed, I dropped into his
cap a half-crown piece : *" Dix mille grâces — ah, mon Dieu !"*
exclaimed the poor fellow; and then, as if remembering himself, repeated with great energy, three or four times, " Var'
good; tank-ee, tank-ee !"

As the old man turned away, after receiving the contributions, I walked up and addressed him in his own tongue.   Had
I cast a handful of guineas into his cap, it would not have
had half the effect that was caused by a few familiar words
in his native language falling upon the poor creature's ear.
He stopped, clasped his hands together, lifted his eyes to heav-
en, and poured out a torrent of exclamations, blessings, and
thanks, as if it were by some direct interposition of Providence that I had crossed his path.   After this was over,
Pierre, for that was the old man's name, informed me that he
was valet to the Marquis de ——, a distinguished nobleman
of France; that his master, having fallen under the displeas-
ure of the government, was obliged to fly his country, with
his wife and only child, a beautiful girl, seventeen years of
age; that, by the assistance of humble friends, they had found
their way to the seaboard, and thence on board an English
vessel, bound for London, where they landed about two
months previous; that the marquis was too proud to make
any application to his English friends for relief; that madame
was in delicate health, and that the whole charge devolved
upon Mademoiselle Emilie, who took care of her mother,
sang and played for her father, and wrought at embroidery
every leisure moment, from the proceeds of which a considerable sum was weekly realized.   Pierre, in the meanwhile,

fulfilled his usual duties as valet to the marquis, to which were added those of steward and cook.

Beside this, whenever an opportunity allowed, and as Pierre confessed, without the knowledge of the family, he stole away with his two little dogs, which had been trained to innumerable grotesque feats to please his young mistress in happier days, and exhibited them in the manner I have described. The additional sum derived in this way was absolutely necessary to support the household, although they occupied a miserable little hut in the suburbs of the town.

I was deeply affected with Pierre's narrative, which was detailed with great effect, in a most forcible manner, but resisted his earnest entreaties to accompany him home, believing that the natural pride of the marquis would overcome any other feeling he might have in seeing a stranger, no matter under what circumstances. So, pressing a guinea upon poor Pierre, who went into another fit of ecstasy on the occasion, I bade him adieu.

Here was a new train given to my thoughts, and for the first time in my life, *sentiment* came into play. As I walked slowly toward the inn, I revolved Pierre's story over and over; every word that he told me of the unfortunate family was full in my mind. But the thought of the young girl, so devoted, so cheerful, so persevering in her efforts to provide for her parents, in this their hour of adversity and distress, was uppermost in my thoughts. How I regretted that I had not accepted the invitation of the valet, and thus obtained an interview. I will see her yet, I exclaimed; I will show her that an Englishman can sympathize with her, and she will understand my feelings. I had wrought myself up into a fever-heat of enthusiasm by the time I reached the inn. Around the door were collected another group, intent upon the mummeries of an old gipsy, who, bent nearly double with age and pretended infirmities, was soliciting fortunes from the by-standers.   The old creatuie was apparently well known, and consequently, although there were numbers ready to listen to her predictions, few cared to be the subject of them.   As I came up, the hag cast her black eyes upon me, which were still bright and piercing, and exclaimed, " Here is a fine youth, that I warrant me never has had his hand crossed by old Elspeth.   Try a sixpence, now, and see if you do n't have a fortune with it."   I do not know what devil prompted me to assent to this appeal.   I knew the gipsy habit well, and had a thorough contempt for the jugglery; but the crowd gave way, and the old crone hobbled up to me; almost without my knowing it, she had my hand.   First, she crossed it with a " silver sixpence"—of course of my bestowing. "A strange hand!" muttered she; " I must cross it again with a silver shilling; it must needs be, young master," she continued earnestly.   I was prepared for this, and as I had commenced I determined to go on; so the silver shilling was produced.   Another cross followed, and again old Elspeth was in a quandary.   " Indeed, I can say naught," she muttered; "my tongue is strangely tied.   God wot what it means; but if I had a half-crown piece to get the right angle with, you would hear something worth knowing."   By this time the attention of the crowd was attracted, for the fortune-teller's demand was exorbitant, even for a gipsy.   Determined to end the scene, which was becoming anything but agreeable to me, I put a half-crown in her hand, and said, " Take what you will, only have done with this foolery."   The old creature took the money, without paying any notice to my remark, crossed my palm with it carefully several times, till she seemed to have struck upon the right line, then stopped, drew herself up till her form was erect, and looking me full in the face with her keen sharp eyes, she uttered slowly:

> "When y⁰ Saint Leger shal marrie a virgyn fair,
> Shal build a new castel both wondrous and rare,
> Lett him warnynge tak, for y⁰ last of his race
> Shal hee meet in yᵗ castel, face to face."

Had every possible calamity of earth been at that moment announced as about to happen to me, I could not have been more completely overwhelmed.

All the gloom of my life-time gathered around my heart; nothing could exceed the blackness of darkness that succeeded. But pride, that pride which afterward supported me under so many emergencies, came to my relief. I forcibly withdrew my hand from the hag, and turned quickly away, exclaiming as I left her, "Pshaw! I have heard that doggrel a thousand times before; if this is all you have got to say, it is hardly, as you promised, worth the knowing."—"If you have heard it before, heed it now! heed it now!" quoth the crone. "Ah! ah!" continued she, "give but one golden guinea, and old Elspeth will reveal wonderful things—fearful things—and perhaps a way to get by the doom." I had by this time reached the door-way; without noticing this last appeal, I turned neither to the right nor left, but sprang to my chamber, locked and bolted the door, and threw myself upon the bed, in a state of frenzy and despair.

VIII.

In this situation I slumbered long and heavily; yet, in my slumber, I was conscious of a great weight, which hung like an appalling calamity over me, just ready to fall. Sleep is wonderful; but at times it comes so strangely over the senses, locking up some, unlocking others, and giving to them such unusual vigor and acuteness, that we are perplexed and baffled in forming any rules for this universal but mysterious phenomenon. I can even now distinctly remember the miserable, unhappy slumber of that night. The appearance of the room; the bed and curtains; the window overlooking a garden; the very chairs and table, stand directly before me, just as they appeared when I opened my eyes the morning after the incidents I have narrated, and saw the sun streaming in through the casement, which had not been closed during the night. The sight of everything made me heart-sick —home-sick. Every article in the room which looked cheerful and inviting the day before, now appeared sad and sombre. I started from the bed and threw up the window. The air of heaven was no longer fresh, but sultry and oppressive. I glanced into the little garden. The shrubs and plants and flowers looked lonely, and I pitied them. I next unlocked the door of my chamber and went down to the public room. It was early; too early for the appearance of any but the servants of the house, who stared at me as if I had made a mistake. I went to the street-door and looked out upon the scene of the last night's occurrences. There was the spot where stood the old Frenchman and his dogs; and here, close by the door, that accursed gipsy had gone through with her mummeries. Neither the one nor the other was now there. All was quiet, save the occasional jolting of heavy market-wagons, or the monotonous call of the milkman.

I could endure this no longer: "What, oh, what will become of me!" I exclaimed aloud. The sound of my own voice had a salutary impression. I reflected a moment; I thought of my mother and her kind counsel. I returned to my room, took my Bible from my portmanteau (for my devotions were neglected the previous evening), and sat down, determined to be calm. Uttering a short prayer to my MAKER, I opened the Holy Book. I turned unconsciously to the Epistles, and commenced reading the fifth chapter of the

First Epistle General of JOHN. I read on to the sixteenth verse, which is as follows:

"If any man see his brother sin a sin which is not unto death, he shall ask, and he shall give him life for them that sin not unto death. There is a sin unto death; I do not say that he shall pray for it."

On reading this verse a tremor seized me. Sweat in large drops stood on my forehead; my limbs trembled, and I was so utterly unnerved that I dropped the book, and sank back into my seat. Here then was the solution of the whole mystery. Here was an explanation of all that seemed strange before. I was indeed the doomed of Heaven, and there my condemnation stood recorded. Could I gainsay it? Could any one gainsay it? The awful words were written, and stood forth in letters of fire. I took up the Bible again, but dared not open it for fear that place should meet my eye. How I longed to read it over once more, and see if I had read aright! Presently a new idea struck me: perhaps the English version was incorrect, or bore too harsh a construction, or was open to explanation. I hastily drew from my pocket a small Greek Testament, which I usually carried, turned eagerly to the verse, and read the latter clause·

$$\text{ἔστιν ἁμαρτία πρὸς θάνατον οὐ περὶ ἐκείνης}$$
$$\text{λέγω ἵνα ἐρωτήσῃ.}$$

Hope, which had been kept alive for the time, was completely lost, as I examined critically the words of the original Greek. There could be no doubt as to their literal signification. Indeed there was nothing on which to raise a question. To be sure, I half started a doubt about the reading of ἐρωτήςη; but I was familiar with the language, and knew that ερωταω answered to the Latin *interrogo, oro*, and the rendering of that was unimportant to me so long as the first part stood so clear:

" There is a sin unto death !"

I groaned aloud. I was alone, and dared not even ask my
God to have mercy on me.

I am aware that this narrative may appear insignificant to
the reader, but to me it is invested with an importance com-
mensurate with what I suffered. I know too that many will
exclaim: "What folly;" "victim of his own imagination;"
"nervous excitement;" "monomania," and the like; but if I
can not reply satisfactorily to such, I will hope that there are
others who understand that imaginary evils are the worst
that can fall upon man; that nervous excitement is more to
be dreaded than any other; and that the narration of what
has actually happened may prove of some benefit to others
who may run the risk of like suffering. Be it understood
also, that my misery was such as no person, though possessing never so great strength of mind, but trained as I had
been, could throw off. No matter what my reason told me ;
no matter how strong were the dictates of judgment and
common sense; I could not get rid of the terrible conviction. The fact that no human being knew of my agony, not
even my mother, added to my wretchedness. I felt like a
wanderer upon the face of the earth.

It is curious how such kind of suffering levels all distinction in our feelings toward others. That morning I was
eager to get a courteous look from the most ordinary traveller at the inn; I was anxious to speak and be spoken to;
and yet intercourse with any one made my heart still heavier.
I wondered if those I saw had not some secret sorrow. Could
they be happy and unconcerned as they appeared? Suddenly I thought of *Emilie;* and the thought gave me a new impulse. I longed to see her—I determined I would see her.
But how could I find my way to her humble dwelling, or
what apology should I give, if I found it, for the intrusion?

As I have before remarked, the story of Pierre gave (for the first time in my life) scope to *sentiment;* and it now seemed about to prove an antidote to my present distress. Not that this last was extinguished: it was only quieted. But quiet is a great relief sometimes.

Emilie! it was a word of enchantment. Could I leave without seeing her? Should I not watch for the coming of the old Frenchman to give his daily exhibition, and then accompany him home? I hesitated, notwithstanding this appeared an easy way to accomplish my object. What, after all, could I say to her, or how should I address the marquis? "No, no," thought I; "not now—not yet." I will remember her, but we meet not in this way. When I am something more than a puling child, she shall see me—shall know me; at present, adieu! I was now in haste to leave the town, and took accordingly the early coach for London. I secured an inside; there were but two other passengers with me; I scarcely noticed them. Retreating into one corner of the coach, I became absorbed in reflections of varied character. Passing through (unconsciously to me) a beautiful region, after some four hours, the wheels struck upon the pavements of the metropolis. I was soon at my father's mansion in Russell Square, and found old Nancy anxiously expecting me. The kind creature had lived from a child in our family, and had been successively promoted, until she was intrusted with the charge of the town house. It was early in the afternoon, and feeling no fatigue from my journey, I made preparations for a saunter about the city. London was just then a scene of extraordinary excitement. The quarrel between the colonies of North America and the parent state was so far advanced as to oe almost beyond hope of reconciliation. Besides, the king and his particular adherents seemed determined to reduce the colonies to submission at

any sacrifice; while the Rockingham party, who had obtained an honorable fame by the acknowledged integrity and
high character of their illustrious leader, maintained that any
farther attempt to bring back the colonies to obedience would
be only attended by loss of men and means, and expose the
country to the successful attacks of foreign foes. This party
was in favor of acknowledging the independence of the new-
styled United States of America. The Earl of Chatham had
been for some time in strict retirement. It was well known,
however, for his eloquence had forcibly proclaimed the fact,
that the earl opposed the wretched policy which had placed
the government and her American dependencies at variance.
He had glowingly depicted the unnatural war; had alluded
with scorn and indignation to the employment of "hireling
troops and merciless savages," and had thundered his denun-
ciations against the authors of this inhuman policy. But his
eloquence was in vain. The war continued, till by the interference of France, the result to a calm observer appeared
doubtful. The Rockingham party were in favor of a cessa-
tion of hostilities, and of acknowledging the independence of
the United States. And it so happened that the Duke of
Richmond had given notice of an address to the throne to that
effect, which was to be debated on the very day I arrived in
London. This I learned from the first journal I took up at
a coffeehouse, which I entered shortly after leaving Russell
Square. It was rumored also that Chatham would appear in
his place in the house of lords and oppose the address. His
pride for his country had overcome every other consideration; and though he objected strongly at the outset to the
policy by which government had been guided, yet now that
issue was taken, and a foreign power had dared to side with
the rebellious colonies, he would consent to yield nothing;
not an inch of territory, not the slightest privilege; until those

colonies were taught submission ! It may easily be imagined that I felt a great desire to be present on so remarkable an occasion.

I had not, as I have observed, taken any interest in the every-day politics of the time. The notorious profligacy with which they were managed, and the unblushing venality which pervaded office, from highest to lowest, made me turn disgusted from the study of present legislation. But Chatham I had always admired; even in his foibles, I almost venerated him, for I believed him pure. My father was a strong adherent of WILLIAM PITT, and, unlike many of the friends of the great commoner, he did not turn against him because his sovereign had granted him a peerage. This night the great man was to speak. I had never seen him, and it might be the only opportunity I should have, of witnessing that surprising eloquence of which I had heard so much. Without farther delay I hastened home, dressed, and proceeded to Westminster. By the courtesy of the Duke of ——, I procured admission to the house of lords, just as they had assembled.

I glanced eagerly around, but could see no one who answered to the description of the earl. The house was full, and the ordinary business was going forward. I thought at first that I had been misinformed, or that the public rumor was unfounded. Still there was an evident looking for something to come. Expectation seemed to wait upon every word, every motion, however insignificant. There was something in the very atmosphere which told of the approach of a scene. The common-place business went on; motions were made and carried; and so far, everything was of course. At length the ordinary routine was over. The Duke of Richmond rose to move the proposed address to the throne. At the same moment, a slight confusion was noticed near the entrance leading to the chancellor's room. The confusion

increased; when the Earl of Chatham appeared, supported
by his son and son-in-law, and made his way with great difficulty to his seat. How different did he look from the picture in my imagination. Where was the erect form, the
commanding air, the fearful frown, the noble bearing, for
which Pitt was so remarkable? Alas, how changed! he was
emaciated and sallow; his wig covered nearly all of his face;
his limbs were closely wrapped in flannels, in consequence
of gout, and his whole form appeared worn out by continual pain.

The house was hushed to a death-like stillness. It seemed as if respiration would disturb its repose. At length
the Duke of Richmond, who had paused until the earl
was seated, commenced the debate. The duke's speech
was sensible, and to the point. He took a full survey of the
causes which led to the war; of the policy of the mother-
country toward the colonies, and of the subsisting relation of
things; and concluded by showing most forcibly, that no
benefit could possibly be expected by a further prosecution
of hostilities.

When the duke had taken his seat, CHATHAM slowly rose.
Expectation now reached its highest point. Every eye was
strained, every ear excited. Breathless, I leaned forward to
catch the first tones of his voice. But I could hear nothing
save a low, inarticulate muttering, of which I could not understand a syllable. My heart sunk within me, out of sympathy for the man upon whom "senates had waited" so
submissively. I could not bear to feel compassion for *him*.
The same anxious attention, the same solemn death-like stillness continued. By degrees the earl's voice became less
incoherent, and his words, spoken slowly and with difficulty,
could be distinguished. It was evident that he was reviving
as he advanced. One great idea seemed to be at his heart,
and that was a sense of the degradation which had come upon

his country. As this idea became gradually developed, his voice assumed its natural tone; his eye once more gleamed with its ancient fire; his form despite of disease and age, dilated, and PITT stood up, commanding and impressive. There he rose, in proud elevation, his left foot advanced, his right firm, his left hand clenched and resting upon his hip, his body slightly bending forward, and his right arm extended, his hand open downward, with a half-menacing, half-deprecatory air.

"My lords," exclaimed the earl, "where is the majesty of the throne? where the dignity of this noble house? where the power of the legislature? where the honor of England? Gone! lost! shamefully yielded up to a hereditary foe, who boasts of her power to humble us in the dust; ay, boasts of it; proclaims it at foreign courts, and taunts us with it at our very doors. I call upon the noble duke to bear me witness, that none deplored the unhappy differences with America more than I; that none opposed the obnoxious measures taken to subject and oppress her, more than I : but, my lords, the die once cast; the honor of the nation at stake, and rebellion, aided by the most odious of foreign interference, lifting up its head to brave the lawful and salutary restraint of government, there is no longer room for debate. When the question is degradation at home and abroad, or war, let us have war! War with all its horrors, all its evils, all its iniquities, but not dishonor. Ay, let us suffer anything, all things, rather than disgrace and ignominy!"

It was said that some parts of Chatham's speech on that memorable night equalled the best efforts of his best days. Certain it is, that for several minutes he showed no signs of debility, or any loss of his natural vigor. But in a short time his strength failed; his mind appeared to wander from the subject of debate; and his voice again fell so low as scarcely to be audible. In this he way he continued, occasionally

rousing himself for the moment, but again relapsing into a
low and indistinct tone.

The earl sat down. Deep silence pervaded the house.
There was a sadness upon the spirit of every one present, for
every one felt that the great man had spoken for the last time.
There was little inclination to proceed with the debate.
After a long pause, the Duke of Richmond rose, and in the
mildest manner defended his own opinions. During this
second speech, Chatham, upon whom all eyes were still turned, appeared nervous and impatient. The duke closed;
Chatham immediately rose, as if to reply; but he uttered no
word. He appeared to be struggling with his strong emotions. Suddenly he placed his hand upon his heart and fell
back into the arms of his friends. The earl had been struck
by apoplexy.

A scene of confusion ensued, which it would be impossible
to describe. The excitement was intense. The earl was
immediately conveyed away, and the house broke up. I left
the place, and drove to Russell Square, deeply impressed
with the solemn scene I had just witnessed. It had done me
great good. It brought my mental energies into action, and
drove away the mists which like a foul miasma had poisoned
my soul. I had now something to think of, which was real
and practical. I had read of greatness, and here was its end!
My mind was carried away with the reality. I found there
was no pomp, parade, nor circumstance, in bare truth. I began to reason more clearly: I turned my thoughts inward,
and asked myself if I had anything to *do ;* and my conscience
troubled me when I tried to answer the question. Full of
these ideas, I lay awake nearly the whole night, revolving in
my mind the events of the previous evening. How strange
the constitution of youth! I had quite forgotten the distress
of the preceding day—I had forgotten Emilie.

IX.

I REMAINED in London but four days ; and each successive day brought a change in my feelings. The salutary impulse given to my spirit by the scenes I had witnessed in parliament, soon yielded to the old disease. The sight of the crowd, the bustle and noise and tumult of the metropolis wearied me, for after the first excitement was over, my mind was ill at ease. Have you not at different periods felt a sense of misery steal over you, without being able to account for it? Have you never awaked in the morning, feeling an unhappy sensation at your heart—a sort of half-smothered pang—which you could not shake off, but which you could not explain? I do not stop to examine the cause of feelings which the experience of most will at once recognise. I have at present to do simply with narrative, reserving such reflections for a future chapter. I was now every way unhappy. It seemed as if the elastic spring of childhood had resisted and resisted the insidious approach of the fiend, until no elasticity remained. If, therefore, I ceased to feel as acutely, I also suffered less acutely; but so much greater the danger that my disease should pass the limit of recovery. Prayer was no relief to me—so I ceased to pray, altogether. Yet I was only sixteen! I felt many years older; and my frame, owing to the vigorous exercise to which I had subjected it, was already well developed. I was tall, well formed ; and as I before remarked, athletic ; yet the mental anxiety which I had endured gave a thoughtful expression to my countenance, quite at variance with my natural buoyancy of feeling. I say

that I had ceased to pray.   But I could not give up my hold
upon sacred things without remorse, while I felt that I was
only more miserable by thus putting off the evil day.   It appeared that nothing remained for me but to lay hold of the
world, and give myself up to it; not in wickedness, nor in
excess, but " till I might see what was that good for the sons
of men, which they should do under the heaven all the days
of their life."   The world seemed a world to enjoy : that is, if
one could bring it to pass, and I resolved to try.

I had begun to answer my old question about the *what* and
the *why*.   Yet the answer gave me no satisfaction.   Enjoyment? pleasure? gratification?   The sounds were empty
ones; yet I determined to listen to them.   Within five days I was
thus metamorphosed.   Three separate incidents had thrilled
my soul, and were all working together; Emilie, the spectacle in the house of lords, and those fearful words of holy
writ.   Although the last seemed to have lost their effect upon me, they were perhaps in reality more powerful than either
of the former.   A vague ambition to know and be known,
was kindled by my visit to Westminster, but this soon yielded
an equal place to the recollection of the young French girl.
But the three, considered as mere incidents, were shortly
banished, although all exercised a latent but powerful influence over my coming destiny.

X.

Four days I had been in London.   The fifth saw me on
my route toward Scotland.   Though miserable enough, I was
determined.   What there might be of happiness in the world,
I was resolved to know ; and I threw myself, without further
thought, upon the trial.   I reached Edinburgh in safety.   This
was my first visit to Scotland, and I stopped two or three

days to view the interesting objects within the town. I proceeded next to Glasgow and Stirling. As I advanced into the Highlands, my admiration gradually increased at the wonders of nature which I beheld on all sides. The lofty mountains, the deep and dark glens, relieved often by delightful valleys, produced an impression of grandeur never before excited in my breast. The beautiful lochs enclosed within the recesses of the mountains, crowned with every variety of verdure, had the effect of enchantment upon my enthusiastic mind. How I gloried in that Highland tour! Oh, Nature, Nature, in thy deep solitude, what heart of man can retain a feeling of evil! what imagination can conceive a thought of sin!

I had reached Inverary, a small neat town, at the head of Loch Fyne, the capital of the Western Highlands. This brought me near the end of my journey: for Glencoe, the seat of the Earl of Venachoir, was situated in the beautiful valley of that name, about thirty miles distant. Here I determined to take horse. I procured a strong and serviceable but not very fleet nag, and refusing the aid offered by mine host of the Three Herons, of a stout, sandy-haired, bandy-legged urchin, called Swankie Benjie, to act as guide, I departed, after many injunctions that "I maun gang the right gate, or mickle waur wad it be for me." As I was particular to take minute directions about my course, I felt that I had a pretty good knowledge of the route, and was therefore the less intimidated by this caution. Leaving the town, I struck at once into a part of the Highlands more grand and impressive than anything I had yet beheld. As I advanced, new and unexpected objects presented themselves. Now, as I climbed the side of a mountain, there would suddenly burst on my view a silvery sheet of water, full of picturesque beauty, reposing quiescent and unruffled in the very heart of the old hills. On one side the rocks were piled upon each other, forming precipices which it was frightful to behold; deep chasms or ravines lay far below me, at the bottom of which flowed small streams of water; and these, after winding and turning around the bed of the mountain, found their way into some loch or river. Again I would emerge into a long valley, diversified with fine woods and rich pasturage, equal in beauty and fertility to any region I had ever beheld. The air was cool and bracing; and as I spurred on my horse, my heart beat full within me once more, and I felt what support real solitude, Nature's solitude, could bring to the soul.

As the day declined, I approached Glencoe. The spot was famed for its picturesque beauty. The sun was just melting away into the small but beautiful loch in the vale of Glencoe, when I came in sight of the castle. It was a fine antique pile, situated at the head of the loch, and commanding a view of the delightful valley beyond; while on either side a range of lofty mountains extending beyond the sight, cast their dark shadows far across the vale, and gave to the scene an air of gloomy magnificence. I pushed on with what speed I could; and spurring my horse into something between a pace and a gallop, I soon reached the entrance to the park which surrounded the mansion. The ponderous gate stood open, as if to invite the traveller to enter. A small but strongly-built tower stood on each side, commanding the entrance, and the road wound through the grounds, turning in every direction before it reached the castle. The walk I had just entered bore frequent marks of horses' hoofs fresh cut into the gravel; and as I proceeded, I heard sounds of laughter and frolic, at no great distance, while the thick foliage by which I was surrounded prevented a view of the merry-makers. In a moment, however, I emerged from the thick seclusion of the wood, and came in sight of the castle, which was directly before me. Around the portico were gathered a company, of both sexes, on horseback, apparently just returning from an excursion. I felt the awkwardness of my situation; travel-worn as I appeared, upon a dull horse, which was now thoroughly jaded from his day's labor. But there was no alternative: so I pushed on. My pride was always my protector. Although a weakness in my character, it supplied the place of a severer virtue. My approach was not unobserved; and as soon as I came near enough to be recognised, one of the party dashed forward, galloped rapidly up to me, and exclaimed: " Cousin William, upon my word, you have come at last! Welcome to Glencoe."

"Thank you, thank you, dear Hubert," said I; "I am right glad to get here, I assure you. Let me tell you in advance how I love the Highlands. What a glorious country!—what——"

"Stay," said Hubert, interrupting me, "till you and I have had a grand hunt over ledge and rock, through the moor and across the mountain, glen, and morass. None of your gentle park-hunting, such as you find among the woods of Warwickshire! Wait till we have had a hunt, such as *I* call a hunt, and then admire as much as you like. But come (for we had not advanced a step) come; yon group will think I am keeping you all to myself. We have this moment returned from a ride of four hours; you have arrived just in time, for we are all as hungry as wolves, and you will be none the worse for breaking your fast, which I dare say has lasted since the morning. Come on."

" Not just in this plight : look at my horse;" said I, throwing myself off, and pointing to the animal, which exhibited decided signs of the discipline I had subjected it to. "Excuse me for not venturing into your company under too many disadvantages."

Hubert laughed at the appeal, but immediately dismounted. " Well, you shall have your own way," said he; " Charlie will see to the nags. Now come along." And thrusting his

arm within mine, we proceeded to the mansion. " Pray, tell
me," I asked, "before we get any nearer, who you have
there ?" "Nobody," replied Hubert, with nonchalance; "just
our own family, and a friend or so."

" Your family, then, have marvellously increased of late.
You have two sisters and a brother : but there are some half
dozen mounted."

" Well, then, Mr. Englishman, if you must know, the
young man in front is the young laird of Glenross ; the lady
on the gray horse, is his sister : they have only joined us for
the ride. The youth behind, whose face you can not see, is a
forty-fifth cousin of yours and mine : at least my father says
so. He is from foreign parts, I believe ; he has spent nearly a
week with us, and will stay as much longer as he pleases.
My sisters and my brother Frank you know without an introduction."

The party dismounted as we approached. My cousin
Frank came forward, and again I was welcomed to Glencoe ;
while his sisters advanced and greeted me with the greatest
cordiality. I was then formally presented to the young laird
of Glenross and to his sister. There remained but the " forty-fifth cousin" to be disposed of; he had lingered behind the
rest, giving some orders to his servant, so that I had not as yet
caught a glimpse of his features. But as Frank called out his
name, he approached, and my old stage-coach acquaintance
from Warwick — the foreign-looking stranger — stood before
me. I was taken by surprise, but I was not confused. My fel-
low-traveller, on the contrary, seemed aware in advance, of my
presence, having no doubt recognised me at my first approach.
He appeared under some restraint, which he endeavored to
conceal by assuming an openness of manner quite at variance with what I believed to be his real character.

" Count Vautrey, this is my cousin, William Henry Saint
Leger," said Frank : " Saint Leger, Count Vautrey !"

The count bowed politely, or rather with assumed politeness.

"I think we have met before," said he, attempting something like good humor, while a half-malevolent smile struggled for expression on his features; "and if I owe you an apology, I will make haste to tender it, pleading for excuse my ignorance of the masquerade coach-dress, and supposing, from your familiarity with the whip, that you were some near friend of his, especially as you stopped at the quarters he recommended."

"I accept your apology," replied I, in a similar tone, "with the same readiness that I allow your excuse : so let the matter be put at rest. If I discussed ethical subjects with old Walter, or passed a night at the Hen and Chickens, it has neither lowered my standard of morality nor weakened my self-respect."

Farther speech was interrupted by the appearance of the Earl of Venachoir and lady, who received me with warm greetings, and extended the proffers of true Scottish hospitality. Without more ado we entered the mansion, when I obtained leave to retire a few moments to adjust my dress, previous to appearing in the dining-hall. This done, I hastened to join the company, who were just ready to set down to a most bountiful repast. I need not describe the entertainment. It is enough to say that it was just such a one as your sportsman loves—where a preference is decidedly given to the substantials, and which delights the appetite of the traveller, sharpened by hard riding, long fasting, and lean fare. It was cheerful and lasted well into the evening. Indeed, I did not wait to the conclusion—claiming the privilege of a weary man, to retire early. Accordingly, when the ladies had left the hall, and the young laird announced that he must depart—adding, by way of apology, that his sister was under his protection—I also took leave, and found the way to my apartment. This was a moderate-sized room in a wing adjoining the northwest part of the castle, connected with the main building by a long corridor, or hall, and it was evidently of modern construction. The room on one side looked out over the silvery loch upon which the castle was built, upon the other, the high range of mountains frowned fearfully down. I threw open the casement and let the air have free passage through the apartment. My breast was filled with singular emotions; my ideas were confused, my brain troubled. "Count Vautrey—Count Vautrey," I repeated: "the name is familiar to me; a distant relative, too?" But soliloquising on the subject brought no nearer the solution; yet the name awakened a train of associations, confused and indistinct, but which carried me back to infancy, and then, running still farther on, became lost in that unremembered world of fresh images, fresh ideas, and fresh wonders—the first days of human life. Feeling thus, I retired, and after wearying myself in endeavors to become satisfied of something, at length sank into a sound slumber.

XI.

FRANCIS MONCRIEFF, Earl of Venachoir, was of ancient lineage, and one of the most distinguished men in Scotland. He was full cousin to my mother (her own and the earl's mother were sisters), and in consequence of their having no other cousin, the relationship was the more cherished; so that their children were taught to regard each other as near kinsfolk. The earl was about fifty years of age. He had a commanding figure, and a face expressive of firmness and decision; and his ample forehead betokened thoughtfulness and benevolence. He was known throughout the country for his prudence and integrity. Ever firm in adherence to his king, his mild and liberal views, added to extensive influence, had done much to conciliate those of his countrymen who had engaged in an unhappy and fruitless contest against the crown. He stood high in the esteem of his sovereign and of the court, and was respected as well as feared by the most audacious cateran. The countess, his wife, was a daughter of the house of Argyle, and in her youth was famed far and near for every attraction of her sex. She had been educated in France, and it was in that country that the earl, then Francis Moncrieff, met by chance the haughty daughter of the great duke. Whether the foundation was there laid for his future successful suit, I can not say; but it is certain, the lady frowned upon every lover until young Moncrieff appeared, and he was never known to pay devoirs to any save his future bride. She was about five summers younger than the earl, and did the honors of the castle with a grace I have never seen excelled.

Of the children, Francis was the eldest. He had only passed his majority by a year or two. He inherited the sedate and dignified manner of his father, and at an early age was called by the rest of the family the young philosopher. He was uniformly courteous, and although living in a country where it was difficult always to sustain such a character, nevertheless preserved it. Margaret, the next, was nineteen. She had grown up, elegant, sensible, and unaffected, without the romantic notions one would suppose a young lady might imbibe in the Highlands. There was a quiet reserve in her manner, which might be mistaken for *hauteur*, but a farther acquaintance would convince one of the error. Her education was received at home; both the earl and countess being of opinion that the fashion in Scotland of sending the youth upon the continent for mental training was injurious to the interests of the United Kingdom, as they were sure to imbibe strong prejudices against England, which it was all-important now to put at rest. My cousin Margaret possessed a mind of no ordinary cast. She was neither carried away by the circumstance of her birth, nor elated at what too often excites the female heart, the constant adulation of the other sex; and, as I have said, possessed too much sense to be spoiled by flattery or led away by mere tinsel. Hubert came next in age, being something more than a year older than myself. He was a daring, head-strong youth, alike fearless on every occasion, and with all the courage and hardihood of a true highland chief. I always loved him as a brother. Not a shadow of selfishness ever crossed his heart. Open, straight-forward, and resolute, he scorned an intriguing, crafty spirit. Passionate perhaps he might be termed; but if in error, there was none so quick as he to acknowledge it. He was short and muscular, and his forehead was expansive and profusely covered with light brown hair. Ella, the youngest, was a perfect fairy. She was nearly sixteen, just old enough to be very romantic, and to be very full of fun and frolic. She had good sense, too; but as she was situated, did not find it always necessary to tax this somewhat praiseworthy quality. She bade fair to be a great beauty and a great wit; and in the incipient exercise of her vocation, manifested so much real kindness of heart, that, in spite of petty caprices and a mischief-loving spirit, she was a general favorite with all who visited the castle.

The reader has now an idea of the family in which for a short season I was to be domesticated. It should be remembered that I speak of them as they appeared in their intercourse with each other. The world might have formed a very different opinion in many respects; for the Venachoir were of a haughty lineage as well as noble, else one of the house could never have mated with a daughter of MacCallum More. How much the world would have been mistaken in the estimate, I leave for those to determine who have so often felt the injustice of its censure and the shallowness of its praise.

XII.

I was awakened in the morning by a loud knocking at my door, which was continued until I was fain to shout that I was neither asleep nor deaf, and to demand what was wanting.

"Thanks for a response at last!" exclaimed a voice which I knew to be Hubert's. "Here I have been making a tumult for at least five minutes, and not one word could I get from you. I was going to take a run across the glen after moorfowl, and if you care to go along, we have no time to lose. The sun will soon be peeping over Ben Cruachan, and then it will be too late."

"I will not detain you three minutes," I exclaimed; and hurrying on my dress without ceremony, I proceeded to join Hubert, whom I found in the court-yard, almost impatient at my delay.

"Good morning," said he; "you have rested well, I hope, and are ready for a little ramble before you sluggards are out of their beds. Excuse my rousing you, but I knew you would like the excursion."

We mounted our nags forthwith, attended by Christie, an old huntsman, who enjoyed the sport with a keen relish, and a small boy to take care of the horses when we should dismount. We had some half-dozen miles to ride before reaching the glen, but I was perfectly recovered from the fatigue of the previous day, and felt invigorated by the fresh breath of the morning. Would I could depict the glories of early dawn in the highlands! The bracing atmosphere, so pure, so invigorating; the awful silence of the old hills, and the stillness of the valley; the beauty of the ever-varying scenery.

now most enchanting in repose : all these can never be ade-
quately described, even when they are realized. We rode
on for a time in high glee, putting our horses to the jump,
and then checking them into a slower pace. As we turned
down a rugged path, which brought us close to each other, I
leaned over toward my cousin, and said : "Hubert, pardon
my abruptness, but pray tell me who *is* that Count Vautrey?"

"I sometimes think," responded Hubert, slowly, "that he
is the devil. If I am mistaken, I beg pardon of the evil
one."

"No jesting, I beg of you, because I am concerned to
know," I replied. "Tell me what you meant by saying he
was our forty-fifth cousin, and what does he at Glencoe, and
how can he claim your hospitality?"

"A pretty set of questions I am to answer, and all to be
done fasting !" quoth Hubert. "I detest genealogy, so you
must apply to Margaret. You know there is a French cross
in our line far back; Heaven send us no more specimens of
it ! What he does at Glencoe you will soon see for yourself.
I can not discover that he does anything except talk nonsense
to Ella, when the girl will listen to him, and that is far too
often; and hold secret confabs with that treacherous-looking
wretch, his servant, whose pate I fear I am doomed to break
if he stays much longer. Why he claims our hospitality, I
know not. On that point I must refer you to my respected
father, if you chose to question him."

"But why do you speak so strongly," continued I, "if you
know so little about him ?"

"Cousin William," was the answer, "you probe me, but I
have said all I can say. *You* detest this Count Vautrey—I
know you do. I see it in your manner; I saw it last evening. It seems you have met—casually met—and you can
not bear the sight of him. Can you give a reason for this ?
Neither can I give any," he added, seeing I remained silent,

" for my own determined dislike. But here we are at the glen; and now for the sport!"

We returned to the castle to a rather late breakfast, but with the zest and spirits of successful sportsmen. The delightful change of situation, and the bracing exercise of highland life, told at the outset upon my mind. Hope was again in the ascendant.

XIII.

As we returned from our excursion, we encountered my cousin Ella, a little way from the castle, standing alone, as if waiting for our approach. I at once dismounted and bade her good morning.

"Upon my word, Hubert," she exclaimed, addressing her brother, "this is a new kind of civility; to drag a visiter from his repose before daylight, the first morning after his arrival, to follow yourself and Christie wherever you choose to lead."

"Our cousin Saint Leger a visiter! Shame on you, Ella!" retorted Hubert; "he is no more a visiter at Glencoe than I am; and as to my leading him a ramble, on my word, we have hard work to keep up with him, either in the ride or the hunt. 'Visiter' forsooth! A lad that will do what Saint Leger has done since daybreak, kinsman or no kinsman, is at home at Glencoe."

"How you delight to turn everything to my disadvantage," replied Ella, good-humoredly; "I but desired to show that I was mindful of our cousin's comfort, and you at once torture what I say into an appearance of inhospitality, or something worse."

"Because, because, Ella," said her brother, "what you said was not heartfelt; you knew that Saint Leger enjoyed such excursions. You knew that he would enjoy this; and yet, with the petty affectation of the day, which by the way is my especial abhorrence, you accuse me of dragging him out against his will."

"Hubert!" exclaimed Ella, half reproachfully; as she spoke, her brother at once dismounted, and running up to her exclaimed:

"Now do not be serious, Nell, for if you get into that strain I am done; but," he added quickly, "who did I see in the distance as we rode up?"

I had now an opportunity of coming to the rescue; and not waiting for Ella's reply, who was looking indignantly at the question, I turned to her, and said:

"Let me advise you to answer nothing which is so unreasonably put. As for Hubert, I believe hunger has made him arbitrary. I prescribe a hearty breakfast for him instanter."

"That will I have," said Hubert; "and what is more, my physician is invited to partake of the meal. Good-by. It shall be ready by the time you arrive; that is, if you come with Ella, for she has the art of making gentlemen walk very slowly in her company." So saying, he mounted his horse and galloped rapidly on.

"Ella," said I, when Hubert had left, "let us become better acquainted forthwith; if your madcap brother is in the habit of teazing you, it is quite necessary that you have an astute champion."

"I do not know what is the matter with Hubert of late," said Ella; "but since—that is, within a few days, he takes occasion to criticise every word I say, and to inveigh against French foppery, as if I were better pleased with it than anything else: then he accuses me of being affected, and I do not know what else."

"And know you of any reason for your brother's conduct?" I asked. "Hubert is a noble fellow, fond of fun, to be sure, but not so thoughtless as to hurt his sister's feelings by his nonsense. Really, Ella, something must be at the bottom of

this; that is, if you are serious in what you say of him."
"I am not mistaken, I assure you," replied my cousin;
"and what vexes me more than all is, that instead of receiving his speeches with good humor, and so disarming him, I
lose my temper at once. Surely I am changing too; but
Hubert looks at me so sternly when he speaks, that I can not
help it." And as she said this the eyes of the laughing, light-
hearted girl filled with tears. I saw that her feelings were
touched; but I felt convinced that she could account for
Hubert's conduct if she chose to do so. There was then
something which she wished to keep back. My heart beat
quickly but with steadiness as I mused upon what she said
and I felt that I was taking my first practical lesson in the
knowledge of woman's nature. Eager was I to learn it, for
my long and lonely studies had sharpened the desire. I
paused a moment. I saw Ella would not speak again, and
that she was desirous to change the conversation. Looking
at her with earnestness, I said:

"If you are serious in what you relate of Hubert, let me warn
you to do him no injustice. Are you not conscious of giving
him some occasion for his conduct? In other words," I added
more playfully, "do you not teaze him as much as he teazes
you? Confess, confess, cousin, before I ask further particulars."

Ella burst into one of her merry laughs, which almost dis-
armed me of my suspicions.

"Behold," cried she, "my new champion! A moment
since, ready to set lance in rest against all the disturbers of
my peace, and now that he has the field to himself, coercing
his 'ladye faire' into a humiliating confession."

"The reason, then," continued I, with mock gravity, and
without noticing this last sally, "why Hubert teazes Ella is
—because Ella, with all proper perverseness, will laugh and
talk, and walk, and look sentimental whenever she pleases,
and as much as she chooses, with——"

"Count Vautrey!" you were about to say, interrupted my cousin, half angrily, and with a slight sparkle of her fine eyes; "and if I do, is Master Hubert, a mere boy, to dictate to me on such a subject?" And the little beauty beat her foot upon the ground in all the consciousness of offended dignity.

"Count Vautrey!" returned I, with affected surprise; "indeed you mistake me; I was going to name—the young laird of Glenross. But if you insist that it *is* Count Vautrey, I must not gainsay it."

An impatient "Pshaw!" rose to the lips of my cousin as I made my last response; but her good nature prevailed, and she replied with an excellent humor:

"Since, Cousin William, you have discovered the cause of our bickering, I will frankly tell you all about it. About a fortnight since, a foreign-looking personage made his appearance at Glencoe, bringing letters to the earl, my father, which, whatever their contents may be (and concerning this I have never presumed to inquire), were sufficient to insure for him the hospitality of our house. He was presented to the family, my father announcing him as distantly related to us. More of him I know not; although Margaret, who knows everything, can tell all about him, I believe: but I always tire listening to her genealogical stories; and about our present guest she has seemed to be particularly mysterious, so I have purposely avoided making any inquiries. Well, Count Vautrey remained. My father and mother treated him from the first with politeness. Frank has done the same, although he seems to force it altogether. Maggie has been very reserved and very dignified whenever the count approached; and as for Hubert, he took a dislike to him the first day of his arrival, for no other reason, I believe, than because Vautrey's servant lamed one of Hubert's dogs by throwing a stone at the poor creature, out of pure mischief. Hubert was terribly angry, and the servant would have received a severe punishment had not Vautrey appeared and interceded for him. But he did it so haughtily, treating Hubert so like a child, that it only turned his resentment from the servant upon Vautrey himself. Of course there were no words between them, for the count was our guest. Well, well; as the count had apparently fallen into disfavor with all the family, and as I was blessed with a fair share of benevolence and good feel ing, and quite a lone maiden beside, without a gallant to flat ter or offend me, I could not help commiserating his unpleas ant situation, and so concluded to be civil to him. He, on the other hand, seemed determined to make up in attention to me for his lack of general courtesy. So affairs have con tinued. Hubert grows daily more incensed against Vautrey; wherefore, he admits he can not tell; and at the same time more out of humor with me. If the count's visit results in spoiling Hubert's temper, and my own along with his, we shall certainly have occasion to remember it."

"And do you like the count? Is he then so agreeable," I inquired seriously, "that you prefer vexing your brother to giving up his society, or rather foregoing this intimacy?"

"What would you have me do?" said Ella; "shall I yield to the foolish humor of a boy, and act discourteously to a guest who claims our hospitality, and is entitled to it besides? Hubert shall not teach me what I am to say, and what not, when I am to walk and when to sit."

"Pray, Ella, which is the elder, Hubert or yourself?" was my answer; "and tell me truly, who besides yourself calls him a boy?"

The young girl blushed to her temples at my last question; I perceived that I had touched a sensitive point; but she an swered with dignity:

"I hope you do not consider me on trial for any grievous offence; if so, I shall insist upon the privilege of the ac cused, and refuse to answer questions. It is but natural," she continued, "that Count Vautrey should feel Hubert's daily conduct toward him, and if he alludes to it when talking with me, it certainly can not influence a sister in her feelings toward a dear brother."

"Are you sure of it?" replied I.

"Sure of it, Sir Englishman."

" Then am I content.   But where is Vautrey, and why did he leave you so suddenly?"

Again the face of my cousin crimsoned; again her eye flashed; again I knew that all was not told.

"William Saint Leger, between Hubert and yourself, I shall be demented.   Pray what have I done to excite your suspicions!   What if Count Vautrey had been walking with me, and did leave me when you approached, or if you please, because you approached?   Why should it excite your wonder or alarm, and why should you catechise me so closely? Is it courteous?   Is it fair?"

" Neither the one nor the other, my dear coz, if you speak in *that* tone.   Not a word more shall you hear from me; but I love Hubert as a brother; I could, nay I do, love you as a sister.   I am young, younger than Hubert, whom you call a boy; but here throbs a heart whose restless pulsations beat with a manly force.   Accuse me of no conceit for speaking as I do.   It is a word I care not for.   I did but think that happiness was at stake between you two; and ——"

A loud shout from Hubert, bidding me hasten to breakfast, as he would positively wait no longer, prevented the conclusion of my sentence.   I was glad to be interrupted; I felt that farther intercourse would be awkward and unpleasant; so leaving unfinished what I was about to say, I replied to Hubert that he should not have to wait a moment, and hurried into the hall.   As we separated, Ella repeated in a low but distinct tone :

"You do not know me, Cousin William."

XIV.

I BEG the reader, who has followed me thus far in my narrative, not to be impatient at this record of minute and apparently unimportant incidents which throw around it more of the air of romance than of fact. I have before intimated the course I should pursue; namely, to put down everything which operated upon me as determining influences; and who that has studied his own heart, and the several changes which come over the spirit, as one period succeeds another, but must acknowledge how trivial are the circumstances which from time to time control our destiny. Again; if the mention of the fearful apprehensions which oppressed me, of the impending doom which seemed to overhang me, and of my severe religious struggles, should appear inconsistent with the enjoyment of the stirring sports of the field, with the relish for youthful pastimes, and at variance with those feelings which had taken strong hold upon me, which youth ever produces and reproduces, and which have *sentiment* for their source—and by sentiment, I mean that peculiar appreciation of the sex in man which nature has implanted, and which society with its refinements changes into almost every phase and shade of feeling—if, I say, there seems to be an inconsistency in all this, I can only reply, " The record is true."

It is true—true to the life—to myself. And I appeal to the experience of every thoughtful man, to say that I recount no peculiar history. Bare your own bosom; have courage to tell the truth of yourself; confess every hypocrisy and every deceit; every secret sin and every error; publish the inconsistency of a lifetime; out with the whole "damning record ;" and then say, if you can, that I have drawn a fancy sketch.

I have commenced the work. I will go on; I speak of vague fears; of religious superstition; of thoughts of God; of serious ·brain-tasking study, of relish for hardy exercises and the chase, of love of the sex, and of society and of the world; nay, of everything that tortured and perplexed my soul and made me what I was, and what I am, and what I shall for ever be. Ha!—pause one moment ere we go on together: didst thou ever think that what thou art now, perchance thou mayst be always? Stop! catch thy shadow upon the wall and mark its outline; will that content thee for an eternal portraiture? And when with a strong brain, a healthful heart, with veins full of the best blood of youth, thou biddest defiance to the arch destroyer, and dost welcome every enjoyment of sense, every gratification which the world can bring—Death grins a more ghastly smile at thy delusion! Satan himself smiles complacently on thy fancied strength, and fain would spare thee a few more years of life, for more certain would be thy endless destiny.

X V.

"You do not know me, Cousin William!" The words rung in my ear. They were delicious sounds to me; they intimated a growing confidence, and they told of *heart*. I was thrown into the society of two beautiful females; one, just my own age, and the attractive graces of the girl just ripening into womanhood. While I, a boy in years, felt a spirit and intellect beyond those years. I had no thought for my cousin which a relative might not confess. I only sought her confidence and sympathy; the sympathy of a softer, gentler being than man; yet a sympathy different from a mother's feelings. I thought again of Vautrey. There was something in him that excited almost my detestation; something which made my blood turn, as it might, from sudden contact with a serpent. And the idea that he should so far insinuate himself into favor with Ella, as to be privileged to walk by her side and whisper confidentially in her ear, was to me horrible. I believed there was danger in such intimacy. I felt that I knew my man. An instinctive aversion could not deceive me, for it never had. I determined to warn my cousin, but what reason could I give for my prejudices, as they would be called; beside I had said enough to put her on her guard, and anything further might be misconstrued. Moreover, I did not believe that her own good sense could be entirely overcome, although I knew that Vautrey employed the most resistless of all weapons with which woman is assailed—flattery. I resolved, therefore, to watch and wait; I resolved, besides, that nothing should induce me to quarrel with Vautrey, so long as I could possibly avoid it.

XVI.

The time passed delightfully at Glencoe. Week succeeded week until midsummer had come. We rode and hunted, shot at target, and played at the sword exercise; made excursions of two or three days into the highlands; lodged out among the forests, and drank of the pure breath of heaven from the summits of the everlasting hills. In the more arduous excursions, Hubert and myself went alone. At times, Frank and Margaret joined us. Ella but rarely, and Vautrey never. His countenance wore the same ironical, heartless smile whenever we met, or exchanged the courtesies of the day; he had some excuse for declining every invitation; he occupied himself with an occasional stroll into the woods, where his servant accompanied him, or he would sit with Ella in the drawing-room, telling her tales of foreign tiavel, and discoursing of the pleasures of a life spent under an Italian sun. Since the conversation between us, on the day succeeding my arrival, she had carefully avoided any recurrence to the topic. This was singular, after what had passed. I felt chagrined; I accused her of fickleness, but I had too much pride to say anything to her. We continued the best of friends; but there was no confidence between us; and while she seemed frank and open, I felt that she was not so. Still, what I had said was not lost upon her. She had a strong mind, as I have remarked, although vulnerable at certain points. I knew the part that Vautrey was playing. I knew that he reported us as engaged in juvenile occupations, worthy of children only; that he attempted to act the man and the admirer, throwing around his character that appearance of mystery which always charms the sex. He spoke French and Italian fluently, which he offered to teach to Ella. How I began to hate him, that Vautrey! Hubert had managed very well to restrain his impatient temper, but daily he had to encounter new trials.

The earl of Venachoir was obliged to leave for Edinburgh, and his absence removed the natural restraint his presence produced. Public business of urgency took him to the capital. He had a confidential conversation with his eldest son before he left, and giving us all a good-humored charge to demean ourselves properly in his absence, he departed.

The departure of the earl was an evident relief to Vautrey. In his presence only the latter could not maintain his sardonic character. Although the countess remained behind, and none knew better than she how to maintain the dignity of her station, yet she could not from her position, exert the same restraining influence for which her lord was remarkable. Before this, intercourse had come nearly to an end between Vautrey and Hubert, and the feelings of both were much embittered; the more so, because there had been thus far no vent allowed to them. Vautrey in everything treated Hubert as a child. He would show him marked respect, or disregard him, or, on occasion, yield to him as one would to an inferior, carefully abstaining from direct offence, which made such a course the more unbearable. Toward me, Vautrey pursued a similar plan, at times treating me with an air of pretended deference, when he thought nothing else would carry him out. I had learned to look upon him as something beneath me; and I resolved to bear myself toward him with calmness and dignity: my chief care was to avoid intercourse with him. Hubert, though one year my senior, was much the younger in those feelings which the man alone acquires, and could not curb his impatient spirit. Several times he resolved to quarrel with the count, when Frank and myself restrained him. Ella's conduct toward her brother had not improved, and she continued to walk and talk with Vautrey, although I believed that my conversation had not been forgotten. Young, impetuous, gay, and full of spirits, and full, too, of that deep romance of which poets love so much to write, I felt, because something instinctively whispered it to me — for where had I gained experience ? — that if she ever loved, she would stake her existence, her happiness here, and her hope of happiness hereafter, upon her love. I did not believe that Vautrey could compass this, but I feared. I gave him credit for more than he chose to exhibit. His education was highly accomplished; his mind well stored with the lighter literature; he had an ear for music, a fine voice, and the power of seeming to feel when his feelings should be touched. He was insinuating and designing; a flatterer, who knew well when and how to act his part. I gathered thus much of Vautrey's

character from close observation of him when in Ella's society.   Indeed, no one seemed to know him.   Was I not right
then, in believing him to be a most dangerous person to as-
sociate with an innocent and unsuspecting girl ?   He was heartless, crafty, without feeling, subtle, and remorseless; one who
could smile on the desolation which he had himself produced :
to whom the world was nothing, save as a minister to his ends.
And yet I could not perceive that he had any ends in view, or
that he acted from any motive.   He would have made a perfect
hater, but his was rather the character of the mocker and de-
spiser; one who sneered at everything, at goodness and at
vice, at the pure enjoyments of the innocent, and the unhallowed pleasures of the vile.   He affected to be beyond the
reach of accident and of circumstance, of misfortune or of
favor, and cared not for censure or praise.   I say he affected
all this; for I could not bring myself to believe him quite a
devil.   I gave him credit for assuming the peculiar attributes of
the fiend, reserving my opinion as to any characteristics he
might claim, savoring of the human.

Not content with studying Vautrey's character, I applied to Margaret for information regarding him.   With her
I had become more and more pleased, as our daily intercourse
elicited the higher traits of her character.   Her native dignity
of manner was so beautifully adorned with a genuine benevolence, that I both respected and loved her.   What wonder
then that she had won much upon my confidence, especially
as she sympathized in all my purposes and plans, and seemed
interested in my future.   Yet in my intercourse with Margaret, there was none of that super-sentiment which invests
woman with unreal attributes.   She was agreeable, particularly so, she could appreciate the finer feelings, and understood every truthful emotion of the soul; nevertheless she was matter-
of-fact, and dealt with these feelings and emotions as one

would deal with a truth in natural philosophy, or a fact in history. They were analyzed and examined, and commented upon, until the gossamer texture in which they were woven was entirely dissolved, and nothing remained of the fanciful drapery but a few practical remnants. My cousin was unconscious of the ruin she caused. She did not understand that she could express sympathy and yet give pain while she sympathized. I observed this almost daily in her intercourse with Ella; and almost daily would poor Ella exclaim, "Margaret can not understand me." Yet Margaret did understand her sister, but each attached importance to different objects. To me, the former was a delightful companion: but I was careful, when I did soar in fancy to a wild world of my own creation, to remain its sole occupant. There can be no participation in the deep romantic, even with a kindred spirit. Into these high and inscrutable paths the soul must enter alone — as it must alone pass through the valley of the shadow of death. They admit of no companion — no confidant. As our appreciation of the sublime is lessened by the presence of another — for the soul to be greatly impressed must be solitary — so the enjoyment of the deep romantic must be a solitary enjoyment, for the presence even of a loved one distracts and divides the feelings, and prevents the highest concentration. I hope I may not be misunderstood. I who speak, could love; and not a thought, not a feeling, would I keep from my chosen one. But when I should summon the deep emotions which well up from the hidden springs — when I should survey my never-ending destiny, and thank my God that it was linked with hers, and pause and dwell upon the mysterious relation which unites two hearts, and calculate its effect upon all time and all eternity — in those solemn moments, I would be alone. How would I delight afterward to recount all that I had felt to her, and bless her as the inspiring cause of all!

XVII.

As I have remarked, I took occasion at a fitting opportunity to speak to Margaret of Vautrey. "Cousin William," she said, "I dislike the theme you have chosen, but that is no reason why your question should not be answered. You must have patience with me if I go back a century. Your grandfather, Hugh Saint Leger, had a younger brother, Wilfred; he was a wild and headstrong youth, impatient of wholesome restraint, refusing all control. He did not possess a bad heart, but his violent and ungovernable temper always led him into difficulty. In consequence of disagreement with his father, he left his home when he was twenty, and fled to Scotland. He there became acquainted with Julian Moncrieff, cousin to my grandfather, the old Earl of Venachoir, who had been brought up at Glencoe, and passed most of his time there. This Julian was no fit companion for Saint Leger. He was three years his senior, was most tyrannical in disposition, yet subservient in his manner where he desired to make an impression. In person he was elegant. His features were regular and handsome, and were it not for the dark smile which played around them, a stranger would have discovered nothing in his appearance to indicate his true character, which in a word comprised all that was fiend-like and malignant. Dissatisfied with his own position, jealous of his cousin's rank and title, yet too crafty to quarrel with him, he remained at the castle as a near ally to the house, professing faithful adherence to the earl. His intrigues the while were remarkable. He was the cause of many a bloody feud between the highland clans, who were then open to the least occasion for a rupture. To the earl he was the source of constant uneasiness. The former would gladly have found a pretext for getting rid of so troublesome an adherent, but nothing could ever be proved against him. Only satisfied when causing all the mischief in his power, he took good care not to appear himself as its author. Before he reached five-and-twenty, he became extensively known, dreaded, and hated.

"Just at this time, Wilfred Saint Leger appeared at Inverary, and Julian Moncrieff made his acquaintance. Strange to say, an intimacy sprang up between them. I can not account for such a connection. It is probable that Julian saw, in the hasty and uncontrollable spirit of the Saint Leger, fit matter to serve his own plans and intrigues, and in the youth himself a ready (though unwitting) instrument of their accomplishment. Wilfred was brought to Glencoe, where he was made welcome, without question or ceremony. The two young men at length grew dissatisfied with the narrow range of the highlands, and planned to leave the country together; but before this, Wilfred Saint Leger had made an indelible impression upon the heart of the beautiful Isabella Seward, a young ward and relative of the Earl of Venachoir, an innocent, confiding girl, to whom the young Englishman confessed a powerful passion. I pass over particulars. Moncrieff and Saint Leger left Glencoe together. A few days after their departure, Isabella not appearing at the breakfast table, a servant was despatched to her apartment, and found it vacant. She had fled to join her youthful lover, and soon the seas separated her from her home. The earl, as may be supposed, was deeply incensed at this gross violation of the privileges of hospitality; but the fugitives were beyond his reach, and his anger was unavailing. Arrived in Paris, the friends of Saint Leger's family, who were among the nobles of France, came forward and received Wilfred and his bride into their society. This was done no doubt through the influence of his father, who, although he refused all communication with his undutiful son, felt a parental anxiety in his career, and had, without his knowledge, bespoke for him the favor of his friends abroad. For a season, everything passed off happily, and it seemed as if the young Saint Leger was about to redeem his character, and become worthy of his race. Julian Moncrieff, in the meantime, had been absent from Paris, and he was left free from his pernicious influence. After the lapse of nearly a twelve-month, Julian returned, bringing with him a young and beautiful bride. She was an Italian, and possessed all the warmth of feeling, all the passion, all the imaginative fancy, which the soft sun of Italy gives to those who dwell under its influence. The return of Julian was an unhappy circumstance for Wilfred Saint Leger. The effect was at once perceptible and most lamentable. He began to neglect his wife, and report whispered that he was seen too often in company with the wife of Moncrieff. If this was the case, it was passed unnoticed by Julian. Time rolled away. The story is a long one; it is the record of unfaithfulness on the part of man toward woman, who clings to and loves him; of infidelity on the part of a passionate woman toward a husband who loved her not; of bitter jealousy and of broken hearts; of quarrels between friends; of strife unto blood; of a too late repentance; and of death. I will not go over the history; some other time you may learn it all.

"Julian Moncrieff had one child, a daughter. That daughter lived, grew up to womanhood, and married Henri Laurent de Vautrey, the father of the individual of whom you question me. At present I can tell you nothing more; you have heard enough, I am sure, for one sitting, and Hubert has been inquiring after you half a dozen times since I commenced. Let us go and find him."

XVIII.

My cousin arose; while I was half stupified at her rapid narration, which although entirely new to me, did not appear unfamiliar. But there was no room for farther remark, and as Hubert was not within call, I left Margaret and proceeded toward the old tower, a spot where the young men staying at the castle usually congregated when nothing more agreeable called them elsewhere. Here they were accustomed to jump, leap, pitch the bar, wrestle, fence, and go through every spe cies of gymnastic exercise. On the present occasion there were assembled several young men, friends of the Moncrieffs, and the sport went on with great spirit. A young highland laird seemed about to carry the day with the bar, which at the last throw had fallen full a foot beyond Hubert's cast, though the latter was not willing to yield without another trial. At this moment, Vautrey was observed emerging from a thick copse, and coming toward the old tower on his way to the castle followed by his servant. As he passed the spot, he cast toward us one of his most contemptuous looks. In so doing, his eyes rested a moment on Hubert, who, nettled perhaps at his late failure, was more ready to take offence than usual: "You are particularly gracious this morning, count," cried Hubert; "I feel flattered by such a mark of, I may say, royal favor, that you should deign to pass so near us. Perhaps you will condescend still further, and consent to take your turn at the bar."

"When I try my strength, I prefer to select the place and opportunity; and then my antagonists must be *men*," replied Vautrey, slowly.

"Now by the best blood that ever ran in your veins, or in any of your race, I will not bear such insolence!" said Hubert. "Count Vautrey, what mean you by saying that your antagonists must be men?"

Simply, that in age, in temper, and in character, you are a boy, if you must know," retorted the other, coolly.

No more of this to me, count!" said Hubert, in a changed tone, and with a great deal of dignity. "I have borne with you too long already, and were you twenty times the guest of my father, I would not hesitate to call you to an account."

"Well, what do you wish?" asked Vautrey, in an affected tone.

"Wish!" sternly demanded Hubert. "Wish? I wish for satisfaction for repeated insults; and after that is afforded, I desire that you would rid my father's house of your detestable presence."

"To the former, I suppose, there may be no objections," said Vautrey; "the latter may be more difficult of accomplishment."

Frank now came forward, and taking his brother by the arm, endeavored to appease him.

"Do not," he said, "forget the count's position with us. Bear with him, therefore, for that reason, if for no other. Count Vautrey, I appeal to you," continued Frank, "not to put my brother in a situation where his feelings as a man conflict with the conduct due to a guest under our roof. In the absence of my father, I control; and there must be no strife between you."

"Who was the aggressor?" replied Vautrey, sneeringly. 'I do not meddle with the young man, but he must keep clear of my path, that's all." So saying, he turned and went his way.

"Brother," said Frank, "you have been over-hasty in this matter. I regret it. Do, I beg of you, make amends by a considerate forbearance. Let us have no brawls while the earl is absent."

"Be it so," answered Hubert, deliberately. "You are in the right. But we must not meet. My friends," he continued, addressing the young men near him, "which of you will call me your guest for a few days, and thus relieve me from this dilemma ?"

There was a most hearty response to this appeal from the lips of every one present; but the young Highland laird, who had come off conqueror in the last trial of strength, insisted on his right to a preference.

"Moncrieff," said he, "it is no weary way to Kilchurn Castle, and 't is mony a day sin' the banks of Loch Awe ha' seen us in company; and—and——my bluid is up, and I canna say more. I ken your position, my lad, but ye shall na be bearded in your ain castle, your hands tied the while, and your true friends ganging their ain gait as if nothing had happened. By the tartan I wear, na'ne shall control me, and I'll question nabody of what I'll do; so you will gang with me ?"

"This instant, Glen !" cried Hubert; "here is my hand on it; only let it suffice that I become your guest; forget the cause, together with the prime mover in this matter," added he, fearing from what the young laird said that he intended to take up his quarrel: "come, let us mount directly."

"Stay but a moment," answered Glenfinglas, for that was his name, (called familiarly by his companions "Glen"), "I have a little business at the castle, but I'll soon join ye."

"Follow him, Hubert," said Frank, "and prevent farthor scandal in the absence of our father."

"It is of no use, Frank," said his brother. "You may try your hand if you like; but Glen, with a generous, honest heart, is as obstinate as a goat. You can do nothing with him. I would rather undertake the count."

"That will I never do!" said Frank, sternly, and in a tone which surprised us. "It is enough that I have interfered as my father's representative, when interference was a duty. I would still preserve peace, but not by asking a favor from him."

"That may I, nevertheless," said I, "and without dishonor." For I felt alarmed at the turn affairs were taking, not that I cared for Vautrey, but I apprehended danger in some way to the honest-hearted fellow who had so promptly stepped forward to cover a friend's insult. So leaving the group — Glenfinglas had previously departed — I directed my steps toward the quarter where Vautrey was last seen, thinking that he might not have entered the castle, in which case I should meet him before the former would arrive.

I was not mistaken. Among a clump of trees, in the rear of the castle, I discovered the count in close conference with his servant. The conversation was carried on in a low tone, but was rather animated, at least on the part of the latter. Disliking to appear as having stolen upon them unawares, I put myself in view as soon as possble. As I came up, the servant disappeared. Vautrey regarded me for a moment with surprise, but quickly regaining his ordinary sardonic manner, bowed stiflly, and looked as if he would ask, " Well, what is coming now?" I spoke at once:

"Count Vautrey," said I, " we do not profess to be friends; indeed, we are not; but I have taken almost a friend's liberty in saying to you in a word, that a young laird, by name Glenfinglas, angered at what he considers an insult from you to Hubert Moncrieff, is determined to seek you and make it a cause of quarrel. I have come, unrequested by any person, to desire that, while you remain at Glencoe, you will avoid any encounter with him. This is all I would say to Count Vautrey."

While I was speaking, I could not discover that Vautrey's countenance changed a muscle. One of his habitual sneers played over his face, as I concluded, and then he asked:

"May I inquire the reason of Mr. Saint Leger's solicitude in such an affair?"

"Because," I replied, "under the circumstances, it would prove particularly disagreeable to the Earl of Venachoir, now absent, as well as to every member of his family."

"And is that all?" said Vautrey.

"Plainly, no," continued I, deliberately. "In the event of an encounter, I fear, for the honest-hearted Glenfinglas, your superior skill and experience in the use of deadly weapons."

A grim smile played across Vautrey's features, showing that he acknowledged this doubtful compliment, while my avowed anxiety for the young laird carried with it such an indifference toward himself that it filled his bosom with rage.

"Boy!" he exclaimed, "you have come on a simple errand; simple every way. I am no brawler. I seek not to quarrel on slight occasion, much less would I bicker with children. But let them beware how they put themselves in my way. I shall not turn aside; they must—or be gored. And, William Henry Saint Leger," added Vautrey, coming close up to me, and speaking between his teeth, "you who assume to be more than the child you are, know that henceforth I will take you for what you wish to be considered—a man. You said that we were not friends. I say more than that. I tell you something you will have cause to remember your whole lifetime; therefore forget it not: WE ARE ENEMIES!"

"Fool!" replied I, indignantly; "you forget that you are not practising a part to overawe some thick-skulled clown, or to astonish a young girl, grown romantic but not sensible. Bring your wares to a market where they will serve you."

At this instant, and before Vautrey had an opportunity to

reply, Glenfinglas came up, and in considerable haste, exclaimed :

"Now, Saint Leger, if you anticipate me, it will na be the handsome thing. Count Vautrey, I ha' the honor to wish your lordship gude morning, and to say, sin' my young friend Hubert Moncrieff, is not at liberty to answer you as he would, I claim the privilege of standing in his place."

" You may stand where it pleases you, sir," retorted Vautrey, sneeringly, " so long as you stand not in my light."

" Na, na, count ; you canna misunderstand me, and you shall na. I ask satisfaction of ye for the insult which ye ha' given to Hubert, I ask it, and ye shall grant it."

" Children, all of you !" said Vautrey, impatiently, using his favorite term of opprobrium ; " I have no cause for deadly quarrel with Hubert Moncrieff, and you I know not except as a stranger ; therefore beware how you put me at bay."

Thus spoke Vautrey, evidently vexed at the serious complexion matters were taking. He was doubtless astonished at Hubert's sudden outbreak. Knowing that he had borne so much, he had mistaken his character, and treated him really like a child. He gave Hubert no credit for the consideration which he really possessed, and he was consequently the more vexed by the incident at the old tower, which certainly took him by surprise ; although his imperturbable indifference of manner had brought him thus far out of the difficulty. But here was a new obstacle, in the shape of the honest and determined, not to say obstinate Glenfinglas. Although too scornful to admit it, Vautrey was nevertheless desirous to get off without further quarrel with the laird. The latter, on the other hand, began to mistake the character of Vautrey. Incensed at his insulting manner, he was ready to charge his desire to avoid a rencontre to a lack of courage. He changed his tone somewhat, as Vautrey concluded his last sentence, and said :

"I dinna understand such excuses, count. In the highlands they do not pass for ready siller. In a word, will ye
gi'e me the honorable satisfaction I demand, standing in the
place and stead of Hubert Moncrieff, or will ye not?"

"I recognise no right which you claim to represent young
Moncrieff, and it will be time enough to answer you further
when I am satisfied of it. I shall not say more at present:"
and with this, Vautrey turned to depart.

Glenfinglas, doubly incensed by this response, stepped
toward him, and laying his hand lightly upon his shoulder,
said, in a low tone:

"I did na think Count Vautrey was a coward!"

Rapid as lightning, Vautrey drew his dagger, which was
concealed under the folds of his vest; rapid as lightning, and
almost before Glenfinglas had uttered the last word, did the
blade descend into his breast, and he fell at full length, carried down by the force of the blow.

Astounded as I was by the suddenness of the action, I
sprang forward, and bent down over the prostrate youth. At
the same moment Vautrey coolly drew his weapon from the
wound.

"An escape, after all!" he muttered; "my hand is out.
Six months ago my weapon would not have served me thus."
Turning to me, he added: "Remember, young man, that I
was not the assailant;" and disappeared among the trees.

Glenfinglas had fainted. I immediately gave the alarm, and
he was carried to the castle. On examination, it was found
that the blow was planted so as to penetrate the lungs, but
was turned aside by a large buckle which the young laird
wore, and which served him for various uses when sporting.
It had served him now. The weapon of Vautrey had glanced
from the outer edge of this buckle, making a deep though
not dangerous wound in the breast and shoulder.

The whole house was in commotion. I related the occurrence calmly and minutely, The youth present were for instant vengeance, but Frank and Hubert both interfered :

" He shall leave the castle," said they, " instantly ; but he
must leave it unharmed, and without danger of harm, while
in this vicinity."

This was finally agreed to, and Frank went to carry the
resolution into effect. It was unnecessary ; Vautrey had left ;
his servant remaining behind only long enough to announce
his departure and secure his luggage.

XIX.

THE day closed. It had been an eventful one to me. I
had witnessed the strife of human passion ; I had myself participated in it ; I beheld upon how slight a cause
blood could flow ; and I trembled when I considered what
my own thoughts had been, and how envenomed my own
feelings had for the moment become ; and I murmured, " Oh, my Father, are we made for this !" I could
not control myself. I hastened to my chamber, and there
in its solitude I prayed once more. It seemed as if I
was launched upon life ; breakers were before and around
me ; I could not recede ; on, on I must go ; and again I prayed—and was comforted.

Had I found abiding peace, or was it only the first recoil
of the heart's emotion upon itself, before the untried world
of strife on which it had entered ? Had Faith led me to
prayer, or did Conscience, tremblingly alive to tne realities
of existence, flutter like a scared bird, and seek to return its
trust to God ?

XX.

TIME went on.   The young laird recovered slowly from the wound received from Vautrey, but a deeper wound rankled in his heart.   The disgrace of being struck to the earth by an antagonist, without the power of resistance, was the all-absorbing idea which filled his mind.   For myself, I was not versed in the code of honor, and could judge of an insult or an affront only by its natural effect upon my feelings.   A cowardly and assassin-like attack upon my person I should have resisted as I would the assault of some dangerous brute; but to suppose that such an attack could bring with it insult or disgrace, seemed preposterous.   Not so reasoned Glenfinglas.   A true Highlander, he possessed the faults as well as the virtues of his race; one of the former was, never to forgive an injury: a supposed insult was remembered even to the third and fourth generation.   What a strange attribute!   Whence did man derive it?   Of a certainty not from GOD his CREATOR.   Here was matter then for deadly feud for a century to come, should the instruments survive to carry it on.

The moment he was sufficiently recovered, Glenfinglas was conveyed to his home.   The laird had a servant who usually attended him, a young, shy, wild-looking highland carle, named Donacha Mac Ian.   He belonged to a roving robber clan which had for years infested the vicinity of Glencoe, and became, by their numerous depredations, a constant source of terror to both highland and lowland, until the Duke of Argyle, under commission from the crown, undertook their extirpation.   This was carried out almost to the letter.   The clan was surprised while reposing in fancied security in one

of their most secluded fastnesses. This retreat had been discovered by the capture of one of their women, who by threats
of instant destruction if she did not disclose the place where
her people were secreted, and by the promise that her own
life and that of her child should be spared if she would point
it out, was prevailed upon to betray it. Glenfinglas, then not
much more than a boy, had accompanied his father on the
expedition, and was present when the woman bargained for
the life of her child. The assault was made and the surprise
most successful. The devoted clan, cut off from all means
of escape, their weapons having been first secured, were
massacred without the power of resistance. Three or four
of the assailants accompanied Jean Mac Ian (for that was her
name) to protect her boy from the general slaughter. They
did not find the lad in the spot where his mother had left
him, and almost frantic with apprehension, she flew from place
to place, urging the men to follow her. Young Glenfinglas,
who had joined the party, was the only one who felt sufficiently interested in her fate, or that of the child, to keep pace
with her. Of a nature somewhat sluggish, he was energetic
and daring when roused into action. At length, Jean Mac
Ian discovered her son at a distance, surrounded by several
of Argyle's men, who having driven the lad from one retreat
to another, were amusing themselves, before putting him to
death, with aiming at him rapid blows and thrusts with knife
and broadsword, in order to witness his singular dexterity in
avoiding them. The poor boy was unarmed, and almost
naked; he had retreated to the angle of a rock, where he
stood penned up by his assailants, now turning adroitly to one
side, now bending dexterously to the other, as successive
thrusts were made, while his eyes flashed that peculiar fire
which is produced only by the feeling of intense and deadly
hate, coupled with mortal despair and desperation. Tired
of the sport, the soldiers were about to despatch their victim,

when the frantic mother burst through them, and casting her arms around the boy, sunk senseless at his side. Glenfinglas came up a moment after, and just in time to save both mother and son. Turning aside their weapons, he exclaimed in a fierce tone: "Ye fause cullions! is this the way to keep faith and obey orders? Ye cowardly knaves, to be torturing ane of your ain kin as if he were a wild beast, just in a word like the bluidy thieving karnes ye come out against! The lad is safe by MacCallum More's order, an' he were not, ye suld ha' pit him to death like braw men, and not torture him like brute beasts."

It is most probable that the remonstrance of the stripling would have been wasted on the fierce highlanders, now become excited by strife and bloodshed, had not Argyle's name been mentioned; as it was, they desisted sullenly from further prosecuting their cruel sport, and left the ground, after remarking that "it wadna be mickle gude to keep the skeen fra the hause of siccan a skellum." It would have been inhuman to have left the poor wretches to the chances of further violence; so the youth resolved to continue his protection; he took them under his charge, and finally brought them to Kilchurn Castle. Here the woman died in about a twelvemonth; enjoining upon her son, who had not in the least changed from the wild untamed savage he at first appeared; to be always devoted and leal to the house of Glenfinglas, and especially to the cause of the young laird, who had saved his own and his mother's life. The boy listened with heedful attention to all that she said, and never left her until her eyes were closed in death. Not a tear did he shed, not a sigh escaped him; but that same night Donacha Mac Ian left the castle and was not seen again for more than a week. When he did return, he was emaciated and haggard, and in the last state of destitution; his clothes were nearly torn off from his body; and his hair, always in frightful disorder, looked more

frightful than ever.   On being questioned about his absence,
he only exclaimed "the worriecow!—the wraith!" and
avoided all farther explanation.

The fact doubtless was, that Donacha, overcome by his
passionate grief at the loss of his only surviving relative, and
not wishing to give vent to it in the presence of others, had
fled into the wilderness, where for a time he was in a state of
frenzy akin to madness.   No further notice was ever taken
of this strange incident, and the lad soon recovered from the
effects of it.   He now attached himself to his young master,
after the most devoted manner.   Fierce and vindictive in his
passions, the latter could always curb and control him at will;
but to every one else he was the same wild savage as at first.
As the young laird grew up, he began to have a pride in the
relation which subsisted between Donacha and himself.   He
had beside a real affection for the lad, for never had he swerved
in his devotion, or proved recreant in moments of peril.   More
than once had he saved the life of his master by freely periling
his own.   He would endure fatigue, hunger, privation of every kind, in his service, while he continued wild and intracta-
ble in every other respect.   The above account I obtained
from Hubert Moncrieff, who narrated it to me as I have now
written it.

On the day when Glenfinglas was struck down by Vautrey,
Donacha had accompanied his master to Glencoe.   I remember to have seen him near the old tower while the sport
was going on, and he must have heard what passed between
Vautrey and the Moncrieffs.   He left the ground at the same
time that Glenfinglas started to find the count, and no one saw
him afterward.   He came not to render his master any assistance, neither did he return to Kilchurn Castle.   The sup
·posed defection of this strange but faithful adherent was a
source of deep mortification to the young man, and preyed
strongly on his mind during his illness.   Suspicion would at

times whisper that Donacha was after all a traitor, and in some way leagued with Vautrey or his servant; but as there was nothing reasonable in so idle a supposition, it was not long entertained. Again the thought would occur that Donacha might have fallen in attempting to revenge the supposed death of his laird, but this seemed hardly possible, considering his extraordinary strength and agility; besides, no one could tell whether Donacha knew of his master's hurt, as he was not seen near him at the time. The matter remained in mystery, and some time after, upon inquiring if anything had been heard about the fugitive, I was told, that although search had been made, and the most diligent inquiry instituted, no trace could be found of him, and no clue to explain his absence could be discovered.

XXI.

Ella Moncrieff—Thou wert indeed a bright and beautiful creation! Looking back, as I do now, over eight years of existence; years, some of which seem to have been ages; for duration of life is measured by events, and not by minutes and hours, as some suppose—looking back, I say, over all these, I call thee still as I have written it, "bright and beautiful!" Thou hadst more of soul than to an ordinary observer would be apparent; thou hadst somewhat less than should satisfy a deep, fond, manly heart. Yet that thou hadst less, proved perchance thy safety.

I hardly know why I have paused to con over these hidden memories. It was a natural outburst, and I did not restrain it

XXII

A few more weeks elapsed: my stay at Glencoe could not be much further prolonged. After Vautrey's disappearance,

everything went on delightfully. The earl returned, and
seemed greatly relieved both that Vautrey had taken his departure, and that Glenfinglas was convalescent. Ella and
myself became more intimate; for a few days, to be sure, she
was quite distant, but I soon succeeded in restoring her to
good humor. Now that the count was gone, and not likely
to come back, I took the liberty of telling Ella my opinion of
him with great frankness.

"Cousin William," said Ella, when I had finished, "I
agree with you in all that you say. I believe you are among
the few who know Count Vautrey, so far as he can be known.
You were angry with me—nay do not deny it—because I
seemed not to heed your warning; but I told you (have you
forgotten it, and how abruptly you ran away from me just as
I was about to confess all?) yes, I told you, cousin, that you
did not know me."

"And surely," interrupted I, "you have afforded me very
little opportunity to improve the acquaintance during my stay
at Glencoe!"

"Not so fast, Mr. William," retorted my cousin; "suppose
I should now make you acquainted, in one grand lesson, with
more than you could have learned by constant intercourse
for the past six weeks, would not that be making an honorable amend?"

"Alas! not quite," I answered; "who can restore to me
the loss of that same intercourse you speak of? Not Count
Vautrey, of a certainty."

"A truce to farther jesting," said Ella; "let me try to be
serious. Of late it has not been so difficult a task as formerly.
You were kind, very kind, to speak to me as you did, and I
was wayward, very wayward, to receive what you said so
unhandsomely; not that I doubted the goodness of your motives; not that I believed Count Vautrey to be a true man;
no, no; how can I express what I wish to say? how can I

explain to you why I should, knowing him to be false and hollow-hearted, permit him to be so much in my society, and allow his assiduous attentions? William Saint Leger, have you never read, in descriptions of the wonders of the East, of a serpent with glossy satin coat, strange lustrous eyes, with double tongue, curiously forked, that shot out ever and anon like lambent flame; a serpent, cold and glassy, deceitful and treacherous, which, in very wantonness—caring not for food—seeks the place where the singing birds rear their young; and first lying quiet and motionless, then gently rearing its head till its presence is perceived, then swaying from side to side its bright shining crest, as the poor bird flies round and round, in giddy circles, now uttering faint cries, now apparently attempting to dart off in another direction, but forced still round, and round, and round, nearer and nearer, to the fatal centre, until at last the poor creature falls fluttering into the very fangs of her tormentor? You have read of this?" exclaimed Ella, with nervous emotion; "how to the very life, how exact the similarity between this Vautrey and that same serpent? I can compare him to nothing else. Do not interrupt me," she added, as I was about to speak, "till I have said all I was going to say, and then we will have done with the subject. You saw, I am sure, that I was not ingenuous with you; you saw that, with an air of candor, I was not really candid. When Vautrey first came to Glencoe, he seemed to select me as an object of his attentions. From the very first—what word can I use? not hate, nor dread, nor fear, nor loathing; none of these; but I felt, as it were, an instinctive, inner *shuddering* at his presence, as if he were some lost malignant spirit, going to and fro upon the earth to mock and sneer at poor humanity. And yet he was always so courteous, so polite and civil, so interesting, nay fascinating, when he strove to engage the attention, that it was impossible to resist his influence. But, while I labored under the charm,

I was not deceived. Like the wretch who, oppressed with horrible visions in the night, has yet a dreamy consciousness that he does but dream, and that when he wakes, all will be well again : so I, though I was charmed, yet still abhorred, and felt a consciousness that I should one day be freed from the baleful influence. Surely, surely, some evil spirit has possession of that man ; for it was not what he said to me, it was not his manner, it was not he himself that produced this fearful impression, for in his conversation there was nothing directly exceptionable ; his manner was always decorous, and so was his speech. It was the atmosphere of his presence that disturbed and poisoned all. Do you understand me, William ?" continued the young girl. " I know you understand me ; for you have read this man aright. I feel freer and happier now that I have told you this. Thank God ! he has left us ; and yet if he should return, it seems to me that I should again be charmed—again become a victim."

" Fear it not, dear Ella !" said I, with earnestness ; " you are safe. Believe me, I had little fear for you ; yet I could not refrain from a word of caution ; and while I admit that Vautrey is still a mystery to me, I am sure that so far as I have spoken, I have not mistaken him. In this you corroborate me. Now I feel that we are indeed better acquainted."

"And now *I* feel," said Ella, " that you are beginning to know me."

How buoyant were my spirits when I left my cousin, after the foregoing interview ! How did my young heart throb with renewed joy ! And wherefore ? Why did my pulse quicken ; why did my mind become animated by a thousand cheering thoughts, as I left her presence ? We had only an explanation—nothing more. And although I have put down but little of what was said, still it went simply to the better understanding of each other. There is something in the

lovely graces of early womanhood, that partakes of all that
is desirable on this earth. I mean not the influence of a direct passion: to the lover I know that everything wears a
charmed aspect. But I was no lover. Ella, in this way,
cared not for me. Yet there was confidence between us;
two youthful souls, believing in each other. What were ages
of plodding, calculating, dusty existence, compared with the
golden moments, which I then enjoyed! Just, too, before I
expected to leave Glencoe, my real happiness was commencing. Is it not always so? Just when blind Man im-
agines that he has secured some certain lease of joy—the
curse, alas, "not causeless"—cometh, and he is miserable.
Would this be so, were God his Friend?

XXIII.

I HEARD frequently from England during my stay in the
highlands; each succeeding letter was read with increased
pleasure. I began to value the privileges and enjoyments of
home, in consequence of my temporary absence from them.
Everything about Bertold Castle was regarded with a new
interest, and the slightest occurrence was charged with unusual
importance. From my brother I did not hear directly, but
the accounts of him received through my mother, awoke in
my breast something like a spirit of emulation. I felt that I
was little else than an idle dreamer; but what could a youth
of sixteen *do?* This question I asked myself over and over
again. Too young for action, certainly, and for that matter,
not sufficiently educated for practical effort; the preparation
itself seemed but drivelling work. "Preparation for what?"
I would ask; and then Destiny, with her pale face, seemed to
whisper: "Thy labor shall come to naught!"
Besides, I could not think of entering upon any of the customary pursuits of the world. Political life had no charms

for me, for I dreaded to bring its unhallowed intrigues into
collision with my moral sense. The law, as a profession, I
abhorred, because I perceived that while it sharpened men's
minds to a wonderful acuteness, it narrowed their intellects
after a peculiar manner, until no universality remained. I
was too conscientious to quarter myself on the church. so long
as I could lay no claim to a religious character. A military
life I detested more than all. Yet I was a younger son; and
although my fortune, in right of my mother, would ultimately
be ample, and while I knew my father to be just toward his
children, still I must resolve on some course. I always struggled against the doctrine of fatality. Early in life I took for
my motto :—

"SED mihi res, non me rebus submittere conor."

But I felt that without some direct purpose in view, circumstances would control me instead of being controlled by me.
Again I pondered over the business of humanity, inquiring
what man was made for? Was it for political intrigue and
chicanery—for intricate, acute but belittling special pleading—for dishonest peculation from the church—for war
and bloodshed? For none of these, assuredly. Then was
he made for seclusion; to sit and think and wonder and be
still, or to labor and delve and toil like beasts of burthen?
And if either, *cui bono?* One generation succeeds another,
each teaching its successor the tricks and the devices current
in the world, while everything is managed badly enough.

Such were my reveries, as I anxiously stole away from observation, and seated myself in my chamber, in view of the
lofty peaks which frowned down upon the castle. The solemn
presence of the old hills, so still, so awful, in their repose,
must have had no small influence upon my sensitive spirit.
Yet while I felt a determined repugnance to enter upon any
course which did not commend itself to my conscience, I was

fast coming to the conclusion that there was no work for man upon earth suited to his true desires and his true capacities. Desiring to pursue a right course, I was insensibly losing all native benevolence of feeling, and giving way to a morbid spirit of fault-finding with the affairs of the world. This made me intellectually selfish, and cut me off from a happy communion with my fellows.

I am now chronicling my feelings as they were when I was about to leave Glencoe. Bear with me patiently as I put down these apparently unimportant changes in my inner life. I trust that before I close I shall be able to furnish an instructive lesson. And let me now say to those who may have followed me thus far, in hopes that my dry detail might lead ultimately into the flowery land of romantic fiction, that they are sure to be disappointed; and unless they can find matter of interest in this very detail, having in view my ultimate object, we had better part company here, instead of voyaging on together, with the certain prospect of disappointment in the end.

XXIV.

I HAD concluded my visit, and was busy packing my portmanteau for my return to England. Having emptied its contents, I was proceeding to assort them, when my eye lighted upon a small package, which till now had been overlooked. I took it up. It was the parcel handed me by Aunt Alice when I left Bertold Castle, and which had entirely escaped my recollection. Upon the outside my name was written, as follows:

"WILLIAM HENRY,
Youngest Son y' Saint Leger."

I opened the package: I came to envelope after envelope,

but discovered nothing save blank paper. At length I found an enclosure, which read:

" My child, deliver these as directed."

I rapidly unrolled the parcel, till a small but massive ring of gold, curiously wrought, dropped out. I found that the cover which enclosed it was addressed:

"To the Wœdallah of St. Kilda,

"These!"

This was the last enclosure, and was unsealed. I took the liberty of seeing its contents, for the exterior certainly gave no clue by which I could ascertain the object of the writer, or the destination of the parcel with which I was intrusted. So I opened the last envelope and read these words:

"To dweller on the Ocean Rock
Where the storm-sprite rages but harms he not
The Wœdallah!

"His heart is lone, his mind is free,
Patient, he sits and waits his destiny;
The Wœdallah!"

On the other side I read:

"This too is a Saint Leger; receive him,
But poison not his soul, for it may not be."

I stood contemplating these singular and apparently incoherent sentences in utter astonishment. Although I was ready to expect from Aunt Alice something strange and uncommon, I could not fathom this to me inexplicable jargon. "Aunt Alice is certainly crazed:" I exclaimed; "and yet there is something in these lines which puts my brain upon the whirl. St. Kilda—The Hebrides! I have it! Here have I been nearly three months in their very neighborhood, without giving them a thought! England sees not me till I have seen those storm-isles of the ocean!"

Without farther reflection, I ran down to the court-yard, where I had left Hubert shortly before, half angry because, as he said, I insisted on leaving Glencoe so soon. "Ho! Hubert!" I shouted, "what say you to the grand tour of the Hebrides? I have made up my mind. I set off to-morrow morning. Go with me you must, and we shall want Christie for helmsman."

Hubert looked at me for an instant, as if he was not quite positive whether I was jesting or beside myself. He soon discovered that I was neither, and believing that a sudden enthusiasm possessed me for a wild and romantic excursion, he whirled himself round three times, clapped his hands, struck me heartily on the shoulder, and, when he could find breath, exclaimed: "Glorious! We are off on the instant! Grand idea! capital thought! How did it come into your head? We will get ready at once. But my father?" said Hubert, stopping short; "I fear he will not consent to it."

"I will answer that he will," said I; "pray go and ask him directly."

In a few minutes he returned with a joyful countenance, saying that the earl, so far from making any objection to the proposed excursion, expressed his approbation of it, as evincing a love of hardy adventure, which he did not like to see altogether laid aside, in the happy change of the times from disturbed to peaceful. The freedom of Scotland had often depended, the earl remarked, upon her wild mountain fastnesses and the rude islands which formed a part of her territory. In his day, the youth boasted of their skill in navigating the perilous channels between these islands: he had himself twice narrowly escaped with his life, in passing the dangerous strait of Corryvrekan; "and doubtless thought it proper," added Hubert, "that his younger son should be exposed to a similar ordeal. But," continued he, "I am no novice at channel-sailing, to say nothing of my dexterity in a whirlpool; for what with frequent passages between Mull and Skye, with an occasional visit to Coll and Muck island, together with a pretty intimate acquaintance with the storms that are always howling about Islay and Jura, I count myself (Christie being present to aid and abet), something more than a mere fresh-water sailor."

What a bustle did we create during the day in our preparations! Old Christie was summoned to a confidential conference. I have already spoken of this veteran. In age he was nearly fifty, though his hardy frame, his alert step, and the quick glance of his eye, told of one in the very prime of physical existence. His beard was, however, somewhat grizzled, the only revenge Time seemed to have taken upon him. In person he was tall, bony, and muscular, with not an ounce of superfluous flesh to encumber him. He was a sort of major-domo at the castle, in consequence of his long experience, well-tried fidelity, and great good nature. He was born at Glencoe, and was, if I mistake not, foster-brother of the earl. He had always been near his person, had accompanied him abroad, and had served him in cases of extremity. As the young men grew up, Christie seemed to renew his youth, and entered into all their sports with as genuine a zest as if he was of their own age; they, by the way, always deferring to him, in matters of practical expediency. In this way Christie would often make excursions with them to the neighboring islands to hunt, fish, or explore, "it being very necessary," as he would remark, "that the education of the puir lads suldna be quite negleckit; for wha could tell what mightna just happen ony time yet?" The earl, it would seem, tacitly approved of Christie's reasoning; he certainly made no objection to it; so that the young men were initiated into all the hardy exercises of their race.

The summons for Christie was shortly followed by the appearance of the old fellow himself, who had no sooner entered the room than he was seized by Hubert, who, after ineffectually endeavoring to give him a whirl round (a familiiarty exercised toward no other servant), shouted merrily: "Rouse yourself, my old lad! Did you know that you are getting so rusty that the earl has ordered you banished from Glencoe, and I am commissioned to see the order put into execution? You have till day-break to-morrow morning to make ready. So lose no time; off we must go, I am to be along, for fear you will be stealing back before your time is up!"

During this edifying discourse, the old man stood regarding the youth very much as an old, sagacious, and well-trained mastiff watches the pranks of a favorite young dog who is cutting gambols around him, and although well pleased with the capers, is hardly willing that his own dignity should be entrenched upon by them. When Hubert therefore paused for breath, Christie very coolly turned up his gray eyes, exclaiming:

"What's in the wind noo?" "Pshaw, Christie! don't affect so much indifference, when you know you are crazy for a scamper of some kind;" and thereupon Hubert proceeded to give the detail of the proposed excursion, which comprised a visit to some of the adjacent islands, and afterward a bold stretch out as far as St. Kilda, the most remote of the Hebrides. "And now, Christie, you know all about it; keep our plans secret. We have the earl's permission, remember; we shall leave everything to you. We can expect nothing fit to eat after leaving Skye, so see that you lay in a good stock of small stores, and—

"But, master Hubert," interrupted Christie. ' I dinna ken
an' I can be spared just noo at the castle, and ye ken weel I
am getting just ower auld for the like o' this. I wadna mind
to ferry ye over to Skye, but when ye talk about St. Kilda,
it is quite anither thing, ye suld mind; for I wadna care to
catch a blast o' the hurricane outside o' Lewis."

Christie's countenance, during this harangue, would have
been a model for a painter. From the first, I perceived that
he was only practising upon Hubert in return for his speech;
and to see the old fellow's endeavor to assume an expression
which was so unnatural, was ludicrous enough. Hubert, on
the contrary, at first mistook it, and was about to express his
impatience and astonishment at such an extraordinary dis-
closure, when a humorous twinkle of Christie's eye explained
matters in an instant, and Hubert was himself again. "Ah,
Christie," said he, "you are the true metal, after all, but—"
Christie here cut off all further superfluous discourse by insisting that we should proceed to business. First, a plan
must be drawn up, to be followed explicitly; then a consul-
tation about the craft we should go in, and who to select
for the crew. The first was soon settled; about the second
there was more difficulty. Donald MacCae's fishing smack
(belonging to the earl) was not quite the thing, in Christie's
opinion; "she was ower wet in a gale of wind," though that
was not to be minded, but she was withal a lubberly sailer.
The earl's new yacht would do for a trip to Mull in fair
weather, and poorly enough at that; (it had been ordered
without taking Christie's opinion on the subject). Finally,
Donald Lairg's craft was selected as best qualified to perform
all the offices required; but Christie feared that Donald was
not yet home from the herring cruise; he would send down
to the loch and see.

After long hesitation, and after discussing with himself the

merits of the various retainers about the castle, for the purposes of our enterprise, Christie finally made choice of two
brothers, Hugh and Aleck MacDonald, as most competent to
do duty in it. These two he insisted would be quite sufficient, and more would only be in the way. We ascertained
that Donald Lairg had fortunately returned; whereupon
Christie took leave, to see that the craft was well provided,
and her ballast properly stowed. Next, fowling-pieces, pistols, bows-and-arrows, and fishing-gear of every description,
were put in order, and an abundant supply of everything that
was deemed needful, made ready. We kept the house quite
in an uproar. Both Margaret and Ella entered most actively
into our preparations, and did much to aid them. Frank was
not at the castle; he was spending a few days with Glenfinglas, who had quite recovered from the effects of his late
wound.

XXV.

THE morning was fair. I was first up. For it was scarcely daybreak when I threw open the window looking toward
the mountain, and let the cool air breathe through the room.
A heavy fog covered the summit, which was now slowly dis-
persing before the light just dawning in the east. Presently
I heard the noise of some one in the court-yard; and going
down, I saw Christie busy in getting together what we were
to take on our voyage. He was alone, and I watched
him a few moments unperceived. He was whistling a stirring
highland air, while he worked away with all the glee of a
lad of fourteen, who had broken from school. "A plague on
the lazy loons!" muttered he, after awhile; "I'll just gie
them another call." So saying, he ran past where I was
standing, almost overturning me in his hurry, and I soon
heard him shouting: "Hugh! Aleck—Aleck! Hugh!" ac-

companied with various expletives which should have aroused
the Seven Sleepers themselves, had they been so forcibly addressed. Hubert soon made his appearance, and everything
was got ready. We sat down to an early breakfast, where
we met the young ladies only, and having received their kind-
est wishes for a pleasant excursion, we left the castle.

Proceeding to the loch, at no great distance, we found the
men ready to get under way. We had a pleasant breeze
from the north, and sailed rapidly down the frith, till we
made the coast of Mull; then changing our course, we stood
to the northward and westward, intending to land at Skye.
This was my first experience at sea, and everything was new
and strange to me; but the effect was salutary; a world
seemed opening before me, of a new but not unwelcome
creation. Shut out from the pleasures, the enjoyments, the
occupations of earth, the mind undergoes a distinct change.
It discovers that its former classes of ideas were not absolutely essential, for new images crowd upon it, new thoughts
take possession of it, while new feelings characterize the
heart. I felt that I was still in a transition state. But for
the first time, almost in my whole life, I felt my soul enlarge.

My curiosity was also active. I had not betrayed my secret to Hubert; for some reason I felt disinclined to do it.
So impatient was I to reach St. Kilda, that I would willingly
have foregone a visit to the intermediate islands, but I did not
care to urge this; so I could only revolve in my mind the curious incident of the package intrusted to me by Aunt Alice,
and the more curious character of its contents. Something I
was sure awaited me in that island. The impression was too
strong to be shaken off. So I nursed it the more carefully.

"Wœdallah! Wœdallah! Hubert," said I, rousing myself from the revery, "what is the meaning of Wœdallah?"

"Wœdallah? I am sure I can not tell. I never heard

the word before. Pray where did you pick it up, and what possesses you to be mumbling it over now?" answered my cousin. "Up with the helm, Christie, and let us speak that fisherman. I will wager, that we overhaul him in half an hour. Now we have her in a line—keep her so. Come, Saint Leger, no more moping. Wait till we reach St. Kilda, and then ask the old Norsewoman, if she is still alive, about that unintelligible word. She can tell you, I doubt not.

" I hope so," replied I, musingly.

XXVI.

Our voyage was full of those incidents which youth most love; exciting incidents, quickly succeeding each other, of novel character, quite out of the common course : healthful, heart-stirring incidents; serving to break up old associations, causing the mind to form new estimates of everything; in short, effecting such an essential change in all the feelings, that it seemed an entire change of being. The strange appearance of things in the different islands at which we touched; the singular manners and customs of the inhabitants; their isolated position with respect to all the world, and our own isolated position with respect to them, gave additional interest to our voyage. Then came the storm and the hurricane (for it rarely only stormed there), around those bleak, wild, surf-beaten landmarks, where tempests prevail continually.

But as I am not writing a book of travels, or a geographical history, or a tour of any sort, I shall not depart from the plan I have adopted, although I might devote many pages to a description of all that we saw and heard in the Hebrides. Possessing in my eyes, as I have before mentioned, so much of interest, it is with the more difficulty that I repress the desire to copy from my journal a full account of this excursion

But I will repress it; for if I allow myself to deviate from my course at this stage of the narrative, I shall find more abundant excuse for a like deviation at every succeeding stage.

After a short stay at Skye, we steered for the range of coast called the Long Island, and touched at Harris, in order to see the "steward," a name given to the proprietor of St. Kilda, or rather to the lessee of the proprietor, who is always his near relative. Mr. Alexander MacLeod was at that time the steward. We found in him a strange mixture of many excellent qualities with many whimsical peculiarities. He was a highland gentleman, naturally of agreeable manners, exceedingly polite and honest-hearted; but from being almost always surrounded by inferiors, he had become somewhat arbitrary, somewhat impatient, and not a little conceited. His pride of birth was excessive, and equalled only by his pride of territory, which consisted of a bleak unfruitful island, some five or six miles in circumference, and several large rocks contiguous thereto. This feeling of territorial aggrandizement had made Mr. Alexander MacLeod an antiquary; he gave abundant proof of this whenever he could find a listener. Shut out from the world, excepting always an annual visit to his cousin the "proprietor" at Edinburgh, it was little wonder that he had acquired habits unavoidable to his manner of life; but these could not abridge a particle of his overflowing hospitality. Coming as we did from the household of the Earl of Venachoir, to whom the "steward" was well-known, there was an additional incentive on his part to receive us with a cordial welcome. When, however, we told him that the object of our present voyage included a visit to St. Kilda, Mr. Alexander MacLeod look serious; then he shook his head; but at last he smiled, and after that he spoke:—

"Are you resolved on this, young gentlemen?—for if ye are, it will be useless to attempt to discourage you by telling

the dangers of such a trip at this season. It will be only adding fuel to the flame, for I know the stuff such lads are made
of. Just one look at ye tells the story. But I am sorry you
had not come six weeks earlier, so that we could have taken
you in the large boat. I make but one visit to the island during the year, and that is in the summer: indeed, we consider
St. Kilda inaccessible at any other season. You are, I trust,
still in time, but the September hurricanes are brewing; and
believe me," he added, seriously, "no craft fashioned by
man can encounter them and live."

Seeing that we were determined, the steward did not attempt further to discourage us; but insisted that as the weather
was unpropitious, we should become his guests for two or
three days, when the moon would change, and in all proba-
bility we should have a more favorable time to put to sea.
We accepted the kind invitation, and took up our quarters at
Mr. Alexander MacLeod's house. We spent the time prin-
cipally in listening to the account given by that gentleman of
the islands adjacent, and the character of their various inhabitants. The steward's conversation, although savoring of the
peculiarities of his character, was in the main exceedingly
interesting. I must except, however, his long and wearisome
genealogical disquisitions, and his never-ending discussions
(with himself) about the original peopling of the islands;
although the steward sometimes, fearing he was carrying his
assumption of royalty a little too far, would be pleased to
say, with a sort of affected candor, that, "to be sure his kingdom of St. Kilda and its dependencies afforded him but a
barren sceptre, still the inhabitants looked to him for protection, and he was bound to afford it, even as his fathers had
done for centuries." I did not exactly understand the nature
of the protection alluded to by the steward, who never, as I
could learn, visited his dominions except to collect his rents.
Still I did not venture to ask an explanation, but chose rather

to lead him on to topics about which I had more curiosity to
hear. To my inquiries about St. Kilda, or as the steward
usually called it, Hirta, his replies were full and sensible.

"You will find," he observed, "that island to be one of
the greatest curiosities in the known world; ay, or in the unknown. Its situation, the situation of its inhabitants, and their
peculiar customs, should make it an object of attention to
civilized man. Notwithstanding," continued Mr. Alexander
MacLeod, waxing warm, "I do not believe there is one person in a thousand in Great Britain who knows of its existence. Two hundred years have our family been in possession
of Hirta; and those two centuries, which have marked their
history so impressively upon all the world besides, have left
untouched the rocks and islands of the Deucaledonian."

Perceiving that the steward's heart was in the matter, I
ventured one question after another, hoping at last to get a
satisfactory solution of the mysterious inscription upon the
package with which I was intrusted. "Of late years," continued the steward, "'The Society for Propagating Christian
Knowledge" had with his consent and assistance annually
sent a missionary to Hirta, for the purpose of giving the
people general instruction, and especially to afford them the
privilege of listening from week to week to the living preach-
er. The present missionary, Mr. David Cantyre, was now
on the island, a good and zealous man, laboring with
great earnestness, and as he believed, with excellent success.
The entire population of the island was only about ninety!
—a little community of honest, simple-hearted creatures, obtaining a bare subsistence by the most hazardous exposure;
encountering danger with a fearless intrepidity; exhibiting
in their fortitude, their perseverance, and their contempt of
danger, all that is manly and heroic in character." After the
steward had exhausted the topic upon which he was descant-

ing with so much enthusiasm, I ventured to inquire if there was any local government in the island.

"Certainly not," said Mr. Alexander MacLeod, slightly drawing himself up, "I have delegated no authority to any one. The islanders form one community; they have one religion; are devout, observe the sabbath, live harmoniously together, have very few wants, and such only as they are themselves capable of supplying."

I gained nothing by this last response; but I was determined to persevere; so, after speaking on various topics, I gradually reached the subject of ancient names and titles; putting myself, by way of encouragement, in the attitude of an attentive listener. But I had not calculated upon so desperate an attack upon my patience. I was compelled to undergo an infliction which lasted, it seemed to me, the best part of the day; in which the antiquities of the island were descanted upon with the temper of a man who had his heart in the work. I did not attempt to follow the thread of the steward's discourse; my ears were only open to catch a word which might throw some light upon the before-mentioned inscription. Going back to the time of Julius Cæsar, Mr. MacLeod proceeded to give an account of the antiquities of Hirta, and in so doing made plentiful quotations from Virgil, Suetonius, Tacitus, and other ancient authors; while, as he advanced, he dived into the historical records of the Volscæ, Cymbri, Sacæ, Allemanni, Picti, Scotti, Brigantes, Pæones, Cyclopes, and Bagandæ, until my head ached. I bore the infliction, however, with exemplary patience, until at last, I seized upon the opportunity to ask a direct question, as the steward paused in the middle of a disquisition about the word "Bholg," which was, he said, by generally received opinion considered pure Hibernian, but which he insisted was derived from the Russian "Wolga," the name of a river, and which carried him at once back to the ancient Rutulians, when, as I have remarked, Mr. Alexander MacLeod paused; whether for the purpose of taking breath, or because he was getting involved in the mazes of his own discussion, I do not presume to say. Wishing to gain something to repay me for listening so long, I asked my host abruptly, " Pray, Mr. MacLeod, can you tell me the meaning of " Wœdallah?"

" Wœdallah!" said the steward, peevishly, looking at the same time not a little disconcerted; " Wœdallah! It is a word never used as a compound. ' Wœd' is simple enough: ' allah' is well understood; but they are never put together. Unless you use it as a corruption of the good old Norwegian. ' Udaller,' signifying the original chief or possessor of the soil."

" Then you never have heard the word before?" said I, inquiringly.

" It is not used as a compound, my young gentleman," retorted the steward, quickly, and without answering my question; " but I have puzzled your brain enough for once, I see plainly. And now," continued he, looking at me significantly, " pray let me ask, since you are so determined on a visit to Hirta, what it is that takes you there?"

" Curiosity," replied I, slightly piqued by the manner of the questioner; " curiosity, now still more active to witness the wonders you have described to me." Mr. Alexander MacLeod slowly placed the fore-finger of his right hand upon the side of his nose, giving the latter member a slight deflection to the left, nodded knowingly, as much as to say " I understand it; never mind an explanation;" then took his finger down and remained silent. It was now my turn to ask a solution of such conduct, which in this connection excited my interest to the highest pitch; but just then the steward was summoned to attend to something requiring his immediate presence, and much to my disappointment, our conversation was not again resumed. I felt satisfied, however, from what had passed, that the steward knew more about the mysterious word than he was willing to admit. But I had no opportunity for explanation, for the next day we took leave of our hospitable host, who gave us a letter to the minister, Mr. David Cantyre, commending us to his especial care. As we were departing, Mr. MacLeod came close up to me, and taking my hand, whispered : " Have a canny care of yourself, my young friend; you will not find the coast so clear as you imagine perhaps; take care —*take care !*" And not waiting for an answer, the steward, with a hearty " God bless you !" turned hastily away.

XXVII.

We now set sail, and after touching at North Uist, stood out for the stormy Hirta.

During the voyage we had constant occasion to admire the promptitude, the coolness, the ready wit and able seamanship of old Christie. I could not but reflect how little we can judge of an individual, until he is placed in a position to call forth his real powers. It occurred to me more than once, during moments of peril, when our lives depended upon the self-possession and presence of mind of one person, how little the wisdom of the statesman, the devices of the political intriguer, the subtlety of the lawyer, or the craft of the scholar, could avail to save life and limb, as we were situated, with the sea lashed into fury, and the winds howling around us. How rapidly men's relations to each other change under circumstances of danger. I learned many lessons of practical utility, which I shall never forget, from old Christie in that voyage.

At length the wished-for point was made. We had experienced a terrible "blow" which had shortly subsided, and about three o'clock in the afternoon the sun came out; when suddenly Hubert exclaimed, "Land ho! Huzza! huzza! huzza! See, see, Saint Leger! There is old Hirta herself."

I looked in the direction indicated by Hubert, when 1 beheld what appeared to be the point of a high rock, rising abruptly from the ocean.

"Why do n't you look, Christie!" continued Hubert; "there is St. Kilda. She bears by compass just as our friend MacLeod told us 'northwest by west half-north.' Do n't be in ill-humor because you did not see it first. Look! look!"

A smothered exclamation of contempt, escaped from Christie, at the mention of the name of Mr. Alexander MacLeod: but he simply replied: "Not quite so fast, Master Hubert: I see nothing of St. Kilda, though I *do* see, and have seen for half an hour, the great rock of Boreray. We have two leagues of southing from there, at any rate, compass or no compass; and after that, we must double Livinish (another large rock) before we make St. Kilda."

Christie was right, as usual; but the gale had abated and the wind was happily in our favor. We rapidly passed both of these stupendous land-marks, when St. Kilda itself actually came in view. I can not describe my emotions on beholding the towering cliffs of this storm-beaten isle. My ideas were indistinct; my thoughts were confused; so I tried not to think at all, but turned my attention to the localities of the spot which were becoming more and more visible. We passed near an immense battlement of fearful rocks, and laid our course to the landing-place, which was no more nor less than a solid rock sloping down into the sea, and called by the natives "The Saddle." We were espied by the inhabitants long before we were ready to land. A large party of men, women, and children, had assembled to receive us, the arrival of a "boat" being a remarkable event. Among the number was the worthy missionary, Mr. David Cantyre, who hastened down, on learning that a strange boat was approaching, in order to render all necessary assistance. By the exertions of the men on shore, we effected a landing, though with considerable difficulty, not unattended by danger, as the sea still ran high, and the "saddle" was covered with a species of Lichen Marinus, called in Scotland, slawk, which was so slippery that it was almost impossible to take a step upon it without falling.

Our arrival was a matter of considerable surprise to the natives, when they perceived that we had not put in in distress, or come upon any business of the steward. The first thought which struck me, on observing these people, was, that they were warm-hearted and hospitable. The habitation of each was freely offered to us so long as we chose to stay; and we should have been puzzled where to have made choice, had it not been for the missionary, whom we soon discovered, and to whom we presented the letter of Mr. Alexander MacLeod, which served at once to procure for us the warmest reception. Proceeding a short distance from where we landed, we came to what might be termed "the village," where all the inhabitants of the island dwelt. It consisted of a double row of square stone huts, not over nine feet in height, with flat roofs, and which certainly gave no very striking indications of good cheer within.

Hubert cast a rueful glance at the prospect before us, for it was near night-fall, and we were much fatigued and needed repose; but the good missionary, guessing what was passing in his mind, remarked: "We have few inducements here to tempt visiters; but I have an abundance of room in yon habitation to accommodate you all, and plenty of homely fare to stay your appetites, if you will consent to become my guests.

The invitation was thankfully accepted for ourselves; but Christie, with his usual tact and good sense, said that he had already made arrangements, for himself and his two followers, with a Harris man, with whom he had once sailed on a herring cruise, and who had taken up his abode at St. Kilda. Leaving Christie, therefore, to take care of himself and his men, we followed the minister to his residence. Passing through the first apartment, which was unfurnished, we came to the next and only habitable room in the dwelling. Here, it seemed, we were to eat, drink, and sleep; although I could discover no accommodations for performing the last-named function, unless upon bare floors. A smoking supper soon put the apprehension to flight, by appealing to my present wants. It consisted of a roasted solan-goose, stuffed with gibain; eggs, cooked and raw, in several varieties, but all of wild fowl; tulmers, fried in their own oil, and hot cakes of oatmeal. Our sharp appetites were a sufficient incentive, and we did ample justice to the minister's board.

Drowsiness succeeded the repast; whereupon our host threw down a little door in one side of the apartment, and discovered to us a wide bed, inserted as it were in the very heart of the wall. This was so much better than I had anticipated, that I did not stop to scrutinize; but telling Hubert to follow me, I crept through the narrow door-way, and throwing myself upon what proved a delightful down-bed, was soon in a sound slumber.

XXVIII.

I awoke early in the morning, notwithstanding the fatigue of the previous day. I lay for some time in a dreamy revery, revolving every incident which had occurred to me since I entered the highlands. Then my thoughts strayed back to

Warwickshire, to my home in "merrie England;" and a chill came over my spirits when I thought how far I had wandered, and where I was. I asked myself what had brought me hither; a youth little acquainted with the world, making a tour of pleasure to this wild and almost inaccessible region; how strange the conceit—how singular the motive! And then that same pale-faced Destiny which so often haunted me, whispered that something should come to pass in this island which would tell upon my future : what it was, I dared not surmise. Was I then at the wished-for spot? Was the hour so soon at hand? My mind rallied under these exciting thoughts, and not caring for longer repose, I rose, leaving Hubert still sleeping, repeating as I arranged my dress the words of Prospero :

> "Now does my project gather to a head :
> My charms crack not; my spirits obey; and time
> Goes upright with his carriage. How's the day?"

As I had no "dainty Ariel" to answer the question, I stepped boldly out to see for myself. The morning had just dawned, and the rays of light emerging from the east were fast extending over the horizon. None of the inhabitants of the village were as yet visible; so I stood upon the lofty Hirta solitary and alone! I walked at first toward the sea, keeping to the southward of where we had landed. Here I had a good view of the whole northeastern part of St. Kilda How grand, how terribly impressive, was the scene! On all sides, so far as my view extended, the island was girt about with an immense perpendicular breastwork of solid rock, to look down whose toppling height the head swam, and the brain grew dizzy. Defying storm and wind and ocean, ages upon ages it had remained a representative of earth; an outer sentinel, successfully resisting the enemy; casting back triumphantly the waves which sought to overwhelm it, and do-

fying the utmost fury of the tempest.   During every change
of season, by day and by night, while its inhabitants slumbered,
and while they were awake, the towering cliffs of Hirta stood
unshaken and immoveable.

After surveying for a time this impressive scene, I turned
back to the village.   My first impulse was to call Hubert,
and propose to him an immediate exploration of the whole
island; on second thoughts I determined to go by myself.   I
had got from the steward a general idea of the different localities, and as the island was but some three miles long, and
only two broad, I had little fear of losing myself.   Ascertain-
ing, therefore, as near as I could, the points of compass, I
took a course nearly west, as the prospect was more inviting
in that direction, and appeared less obstructed by hills, which
in some parts of St. Kilda rise to an immense height.

Proceeding about a mile, I encountered one of these eleva-
tions, which by dint of extra exertion I soon passed, and de-
scending from the other side into a most delightful valley,
found myself within half a mile of the ocean.   I followed a
small, winding rivulet which flowed through the valley until
it emptied itself into the sea.   Here the soil was exuberant; the ground was covered with an almost infinite variety of the richest plants, including the white and red clover,
the daisy, crowfoot, and dandelion, and plantains of every sort.
I was surprised to find a spot of so much beauty where I had
expected to see only wild and uncultivated hills, or bleak
rocks and waste ground.   I stood near the edge of the shore;
for where the stream fell into the sea there was some appearance of a landing-place; indeed the steward had told me that
on the northwest part of the island there was a spot where
the inhabitants, when forced to so dangerous an experiment,
made shift to put in, and I believed from his description that
this was the place.   So much, however, was I enchanted by

the exquisite beauty of the little valley through which I had strayed, that I turned away from the bold and magnificent view of rock and ocean to gaze upon it; and so abstracted did I become in the contemplation, that I did not notice a boat which had in the meantime approached the shore, and was attempting to land. Not wishing to be seen by those on board, I stepped aside and took a position where I could have a fair view of them, without being observed. There were but three persons in the boat, two of whom managed the craft, while the third steered. From the distance at which I stood, they did not appear to be inhabitants of St. Kilda, and apparently they were not fishermen.

As the boat approached the shore, it was hid from sight by some rocks which were brought between me and it. I still kept my position, and awaited the issue of what now looked likely to turn out an adventure. After several minutes I perceived two of the party clambering up a steep ledge, some distance below me; and on reaching the top, proceed in an opposite direction from where I was standing, and consequently not in a way to gain the village. My curiosity was aroused; so I followed slowly after, carefully keeping out of sight, yet endeavoring not to lose track of my men. I went on in this way for some five minutes, when they disappeared behind the cleft of a huge rock, and I saw them no more. I walked cautiously forward till I passed the rock in question, but found no one; I still persevered, but without making any discovery, and was on the point of giving up the search, when I noticed a small grotto, partially in ruins, the walls and part of the roof of which were still standing, so as to afford sufficient protection from storm and bad weather. Through an aperture on the side toward me, I beheld the figures of two or more persons, but could not decide whether they were those I had previously seen. I stole cautiously up till I reached the grotto, and looked in. I saw two persons; the one whose face was toward me was a beautiful girl, apparently about nineteen; she was engaged in earnest conversation with a man, whose countenance was turned from me. The girl was considerably above the medium height; she wore a Spanish mantilla, richly ornamented, which was thrown entirely back, displaying a face of great beauty; deep, dark, passionate eyes; regular features, and a mouth the most expressive I ever saw. Her hair, which was black, and parted plain across her forehead, was exquisitely braided and secured behind by a ring and arrow of gold. The man—but I need not describe him, for as he turned partially round I saw his side-face, and perceived that it was—Vautrey!

I stood petrified with astonishment. I could not believe the evidence of my own senses. I began to think I was dreaming, and that I might presently awake and find myself upon the bed in the minister's dwelling. But no; this was no illusion. I could not mistake; the scene before me was real; and at the risk of being discovered, I leaned forward to get a better view of the parties; as I did so, these words met my ear:

"Remember, count, this is the last time."

"Unless, signora, you can be persuaded to change your mind," was the reply of Vautrey, in a tone so soft and so insinuating that I scarcely recognised it.

"Never, so help me Heaven!" exclaimed the girl, impetuously; "I can not, do not, will not love you; and you shall no longer persecute me. What if my father knew of these meetings? What if he knew that you had come hither after what he has so fearfully sworn?"

"What if he did?" interrupted Vautrey, in his natural, sneering tone: "what if he *did?* Is the Wœdallah my keeper?"

"Enough,' returned the girl, with dignity; "enough:

such a tone and such an answer best become you. We part," she added, as she turned to leave the grotto, "never to meet again in this way."

"Not thus, not thus," replied Vautrey, in a gentle tone; "you must not, you can not leave me thus. Remember what we have been to each other. Have you forgotten the season spent in Genoa? Do you never think of Naples?"

"Never without a shudder, Vautrey," replied the girl, for the first time calling the count by name; "and it is despicable in you now to allude to the past. Away! I despise you."

A bitter exclamation escaped the count. He raised his finger in a menacing attitude: "Leila," said he, "though a woman, you may provoke my vengeance. Beware!"

"A woman derides your vengeance, count, even while you threaten it," said the maiden, scornfully; so saying, she turned again to depart. I stepped hastily back in order to escape observation; as I did so, I met a pair of wild, sharp-looking, piercing black eyes glaring intently upon me from behind a thick clump of low bushes, with a gaze so fixed, that it seemed to belong to some spirit of darkness. As may be supposed, at the first sight of this unlooked-for apparition, my blood ran cold; but I was not daunted, although surprised and shocked. It was evident that I had been noticed; yet I endeavored to be cool. Keeping my eye, therefore, boldly on this strange being, I slowly made good my retreat. The savage, as I took him to be, moved not, stirred not, till I was about disappearing, when he made a significant gesture toward the grotto, nodded his head, and waved his hand impatiently, as if to hasten me away. I did not need such a hint, but making what speed I could, I turned back the way I came, nor did I slacken my pace until I was in sight of the village.

At the door of the minister's dwelling I met Hubert, who exclaimed, "Thank God, Saint Leger, you are safe. Pray tell me where you have been, and what has happened to you.

I missed you when I first woke; we have inquired at every house, or rather hovel; have searched at the landing-place, and everywhere else, and I had begun to be seriously alarmed. This was unfair to steal away from me, and take the first survey alone. But, tell me; something *has* happened, I know What have you seen? Come, out with it."

"I have seen Vautrey," said I; and thereupon I related to Hubert minutely all that I had witnessed that morning, although I was first tempted to keep the matter to myself; but I thought it was not treating my cousin with the ingenuousness he deserved. Hubert looked very serious for a moment; then his boyish love of adventure got the better of every other feeling, and he clapped his hands with delight:

"Now for something that is worth the chase," cried he; "now, Count Vautrey, have a care. We are no longer at Glencoe. Three in the boat? we will match them: Christie is a host, of himself, and the two MacDonalds are no cowards. Yes, I was right; Vautrey is—yes, he *is*—the devil! No embodiment, but very Satan! Come, Saint Leger, here is a compact for you: the girl is yours, by right of discovery; besides, you have got a clue to that ever-to-be-remembered Wœdallah, which strengthens your title. But Vautrey, mark me, is mine, and you are not to interfere with me there."

"You meditate no violence, Hubert!" I replied, alarmed by his emphatic tone.

"I am a Moncrieff;" replied my cousin, proudly.

"Enough;" was my response; "there shall be, as there ever has been, confidence between us."

"We have said it," cried Hubert, "and now let us break our fast, for I have waited for you, and am hungry enough to devour a solan-goose alive. First, let us satisfy our hunger, and then, come Vautrey, Wœdallah, Circe, Syren, Caliban, and the foul fiend!"

XXIX.

I MUST go back a little, to resume the history of my inner life. Bear with me, though you may have become more or less interested in the incidents of the last few chapters. Recollect our compact when, declining to part company with me, as I advised you many pages back, you ran the risk of suffering the penalty of a dull companionship, if you should not be able to sympathize in my feelings. Once more I give you an opportunity to bid "Adieu!"—once more I say; expect nothing but facts.

When Glenfinglas was struck down by Vautrey, my whole moral nature was strongly affected. Fearfully impressed by the malignant passions manifested by the latter, my soul instinctively sought refuge in GOD its CREATOR. Like an inexperienced child which has strayed for the first time out of sight of the parent, enjoying from the novelty, everything within its observation ; till, frightened by some untoward occurrence, it runs hurrying back, oppressed and terrified, desiring only to be secure in those loved arms, never again to wander away ; so it was with me : I poured out my heart unto GOD afresh ; I prayed and was comforted. How happy was I in forming new resolutions for the conduct of my future. Earnestly did I pray to be guided aright; earnestly did I supplicate not to be abandoned to temptation. For a few days I enjoyed a serene peace of mind ; then something like ennui began to take the place of it ; then my old heart-pangs slowly returned, leaving their leaden load in the very centre of my young heart. Then I sought relief in my Bible and in prayer in vain ; and then again I ceased to pray, seeking to cheer my spirits in a thousand exciting ways. The voyage to St. Kilda had broken in so completely upon my former habits, both physical and mental, that good appeared likely to grow out of it. Yet I had no opportunity in such a voyage for reflection. But I did think sometimes. There were occasional texts of Scripture which would for weeks be ever present to my mind, and which, in spite of me, I could not help almost constantly repeating. I distinctly remember the following to have been among the number:

> "O EPHRAIM, what shall I do unto thee?
> O JUDAH, what shall I do unto thee?
> For your goodness is as a morning cloud,
> And as the early dew it goeth away."
>
> .   .   .   .
>
> "And the last state of that man is worse than the first."

These solemn passages of scripture were at that time continually in my mind. They stood out in my imagination like the handwriting upon the wall. I felt condemned; my former terrors revived; my soul was in darkness. I found myself suddenly thrown back to my old ground. I had travelled through so many mental changes only to find myself at the starting-place. In the meantime, I began to understand the world something better. I saw pleasure and enjoyment in it. Sin, to be sure as did Satan, came also; but there was gratification nevertheless. I now felt the seductive influence of the god of this world creeping slowly upon me. It was as yet only the foretaste of what I was to experience, but the poison had begun to work. The fiend Vautrey had roused strange feelings in my bosom. I hated him and despised him; but with all that, I envied him. Yes, I envied him his knowledge of the world, of life, and for all that he had seen and experienced. Besides, my soul longed for gratification, and I envied him for what he had enjoyed. So strictly had I dealt with myself that it seemed as if sinning with a high hand would act upon my nature as a moral alterative, and prove of healthful influence. Like the convalescent who has been confined for weeks to a low diet, and who hankers for high-seasoned and rich-flavored food, even so I yearned after the flesh-pots of Egypt, longing " to roll sin as a pleasant morsel under my tongue." Alas ; what had become of all my good resolutions; my enlarged plans for benevolent action ; my earnest desires to benefit my kind ; my rules for self-improvement ? How strangely vanished. How suddenly forgotten.

> " How is the gold become dim !
> How is the most fine gold changed !"

was the lamentation of the prophet, and bitterly did I afterward take it up. Bear in mind that I am inditing this story several years subsequent to these events. I do not wish it to be understood that I came to an open avowed resolution to commit or to live in sin ; such nevertheless was my private secret conclusion, kept secret even from myself; for the arch enemy, when he would most successfully enslave the soul, inculcates the Christian rule :

> " Let not thy left hand know what thy right hand doeth."

Now that all has come to pass, I can speak understandingly. As I have before said, I write for the young; for those whose sympathies are not yet destroyed. Hearken, then, to my appeal. Read and reflect upon my history, and pray GOD it may prove to thee an instructive lesson ; and may that lesson not have come too late.

Thus much at present of my inner life. It may appear inconsistent with what I write of my external. But again I repeat. the record is true.

XXX.

AFTER we had breakfasted, Hubert and myself sat down to a protracted conference, rendered necessary, as we thought, by my report of the extraordinary occurrence of the morning. In this conference we discussed matters of high importance. We certainly had many difficult questions to pass upon. In the first place, who *could* that beautiful girl be? What had sent her to this remote spot? Who was her protector? Then, what had she to do with Vautrey; what was Vautrey doing here; and who and how many were in his company? Such were the points canvassed over and over by us, but about which we could come to no satisfactory conclusion. I now told Hubert why I had been so inquisitive about the word " Wœdallah," and we both agreed that the package of Aunt Alice might prove of much assistance to us. In the meantime, we undertook to get all possible information from the missionary and the inhabitants of the island. Christie also was to be put on the scent, and his two followers if necessary; and thus the campaign commenced.

We spent part of the day in the company of the worthy, Mr. David Cantyre, whose hospitality had been so freely tendered, and who did all in his power to render our visit agreeable. From him we received a minute account of the island and its inhabitants, which would have afforded me at any other time abundant source of entertainment; but after the exciting events of the morning, I found it difficult to fix my attention upon anything else. I forbore to question the minister about that which I most desired to know, until I had gained further upon his intimacy. To this end I asked him about his own personal history; and, in order to draw him out, ventured to express my wonder that he should have consented to bury himself in such a remote spot, cut off from all communication with the world, and enjoying nothing like refined society, or the pleasant intercourse of friends. To this the minister replied, that no sacrifice was too great which the cause of CHRIST demanded; and that in the performance of his simple duties he derived a lively satisfaction which to him was beyond all price. He recounted much of his past life, gave an account of his first landing at St. Kilda, and of what he had done and hoped to do among the inhabitants. Altogether, the minister was a man to be loved and respected. And the contemplation of such a character might, under other circumstances, have deeply impressed me; but now nothing could divert me from the pursuit in which I was embarked; I do believe that nothing, not even the fear of everlasting perdition, would have forced me to abandon it. Hubert, in the meanwhile, had conferred with Christie, and Christie had promised soon to give us all the information we desired. His opinion was, that Vautrey, had taken possession of some one of the small rocky islands near St. Kilda, perhaps Boreray or Soay. He was told that a strange boat had been seen for two or three weeks past hovering about the island, and it was at first supposed when we landed that it belonged to us. Hubert communicated nothing further to Christie, except his desire for immediate information; and in such a case where, as the faithful old follower believed, the honor of his young master was at stake, to hear was to obey. The next day, Hubert and myself set out on a tour of observation. We visited some of the prominent localities of the island. We climbed together the lofty Conagra, which rises with fearful abruptness from the head of the bay to a height of nearly six thousand feet, commanding from its summit a view of more

than one hundred and fifty miles in extent.　Thence we took
a survey of the entire coast.　There was nothing which could
be called a harbor belonging to the island, and but two places
where it was even possible to land; the first was near the
village, the other was at the spot where I had seen Vautrey
put in.　The island was full of little cells or grottoes, like the
one I have mentioned, which were evidently of great antiquity; at least we could learn nothing of their origin; none of
the inhabitants could give us any information about them;
and Mr. David Cantyre, to his praise be it spoken (in view
of what I suffered from Mr. Alexander MacLeod), was no an-
tiquarian.　In making our circuit, we came to the place of my
previous adventure : we looked about over rock and valley,
and into every secret nook, in hopes to discover something —
we cared but little what — to throw light upon the strange
scene I had witnessed.　But our labors were fruitless.　The
grotto where Vautrey and the maiden had parted, was deserted, and nothing within betrayed that it ever had been the
trysting-place of lovers.　We were both disappointed, and in
consequence began to feel the fatigues of the day more sensibly.　The route to the village would complete the circuit we
desired to make; so we returned home, wearied but not dis-
couraged.　Full of resolution and youthful ardor, we retired
to rest, determined on the morrow to continue the search.

XXXI.

WHAT a wonderful impression had Leila (yes, that was
the name Vautrey had pronounced) made upon me.　Never had I beheld so beautiful a creature ; never before witnessed such grace, such exquisite perfection, such incompara-
ble charms.　I remembered with singular minuteness every
look, and every expression, every feature and every linea-

ment of her face; and the more I thought of her, the more impatient I became to solve the mystery. A young maiden, dressed in a style adapted to the most refined society, alone in St. Kilda? Impossible! Again, she was known to Vautrey, and the count had intimated in what he said to her, that they had formerly been friends; how my heart beat at the thought: but it was evident they were friends no longer. The more my mind dwelt upon this strange enigma, the more excited I became, until I resolved to speculate no further, but await the result of our investigation. Hubert was up betimes the next morning, and roused me. His determination to find Vautrey was after all occasioned, as I believed, more from a natural desire to solve the mystery of his presence at St. Kilda, than from any feeling of revenge for the old affront. Indeed, what to a youth of eighteen could be more exciting than an undertaking of this sort? As Hubert had waived all interest in the beautiful Unknown (not having beheld her, he could do so, as I thought, the more readily), we made an equitable division of our labors, he undertaking, with the aid of his followers, to find Vautrey, "dead or alive," as he expressed it, and I agreeing, by no means unwillingly, to discover the fair maiden of the grotto. Leaving my cousin to his plans, I set out once more to visit the delightful valley, which the minister told me bore the name of the "Female Warrior's Glen," from an amazon very famous in the traditions of the island. I was resolved this time to be thorough in my search, for I was sure that there must be a habitation of some sort near at hand. Nor did the result prove me mistaken; for after traversing the valley in every possible direction, I went around a small ledge of rocks, which were apparently so near the coast that it had not occurred to me there could be any considerable space beyond. I was much surprised to discover there a miniature valley or glen, remarkably beautiful, in the centre of which stood a small stone building.

This picturesque little spot was presented so suddenly to my view, that I stopped short in amazement, and was for a few moments lost in admiration of its beauty. Presently I beheld a man come from the hut, for it was little else, and leisurely advance a few steps, as if to take the air. Whether he saw me or not, I could not tell; at any rate, he took no notice of me whatever. Observing him closely, I perceived that he was a man past the prime of life, perhaps fifty years of age; he was of middling stature, of rather spare habit of body, having a bold, prominent, but narrow forehead, thinly covered with gray hair. What was remarkable, he was dressed with scrupulous exactness, and in every respect after the English style, and his garments were made in the fashion of the then present season. My resolution was taken : I determined to accost the stranger. Walking toward him, I did what I could to attract his notice, but to no purpose ; his eyes were turned in every direction but toward me. It was not till I had come close upon him, that he recognised my presence. Begging pardon for the interruption, I asked him the nearest route to the village.

"On your honor, young man," said the stranger, " have you lost your way, or has an idle curiosity brought you hither ?"

" Neither," returned I, boldly ; " but ———"

" Pass on, then, pass on ! annoy me not with the sight of my kind. It is burthen enough to endure myself. Pass on, pass on, and molest me no further !" exclaimed the stranger, waving his hand as he spoke. ·

" I will not pass on," said I, roused by his tone,　till I have said what I have to say to you."

" What sends you here ?" interrupted he, pettishly.

"Destiny," returned I.

"Destiny," muttered the other; and then continuing, as if to himself: "To hear the world prate of destiny: as if destiny were a god to direct and control: destiny, forsooth: why, destiny is what is." Then turning to me, he added, "You rave, young man."

I now narrowly examined the speaker. His appearance indicated the misanthrope; not the misanthrope by nature, but one who had been soured with the world, perhaps from good cause: one who had endured the "slings and arrows of outrageous fortune" until there was no sensibility left in his bosom. I looked once more at the clear sharp outline of forehead, boldly developed (though narrow), the deep-set, expressive gray eyes, the dignified though slightly petulant air: and in all I saw — shall I say it? — some strange, mysterious resemblance to — myself. I paused — I trembled; I resolved on one more trial: "In the name of all that you hold sacred, tell me," I exclaimed, "are you called the Woedallah?"

"There is nothing I hold sacred, young man," answered the stranger; "you adjure me in vain; but if it will satisfy you to learn the fact, so that you will then leave me and pass on your way, I answer that I *am* called the Woedallah."

"Stay one moment, and I have done," I exclaimed, perceiving that this singular man was returning to his dwelling; "stay but a single moment"—and drawing forth the little package with which Aunt Alice had intrusted me, I handed it to him without speaking, and awaited the effect it might produce. He took the parcel, examined the superscription without emotion, and proceeded to open it. When he beheld the ring, his countenance changed, first to deep red, then to deadly pale; his whole frame was convulsed, his limbs trembled, his lips quivered; he was evidently laboring under agonizing emotion; but he recovered somewhat, and proceeded to read what was written. This done, he turned and looked at me with a gaze so earnest and so penetrating that I almost shrunk from it. As he looked, I thought I discovered tears start in his eyes; his countenance changed to an expression of deep melancholy; and pointing toward the door of his dwelling, he said to me, in a low, indistinct tone, " Enter."

I obeyed the direction, and on going in, found myself in a small, but neatly furnished apartment, in which was, among other articles, a well filled bookcase; over it were suspended a musket and small-arms: a sword and several daggers. There was no one in the room: of this I took care to assure myself when I first entered; and despite the excitement of the moment, I felt disappointed. My host pointed to a chair, and I sat down; he also took a seat beside me, and examined my countenance with searching scrutiny. As there was no appearance of impertinent inquisitiveness in his manner, I remained quiet, resolving that I would not be the first to break the silence.

"It is even so," observed he, at length, as if communing with himself; " it is even so; my eyes again behold a Saint Leger; one of my own flesh and blood is before me; and although I have forsworn all, ay, everything upon the earth, and all above and all below, yet since the race began, has never a Saint Leger met a Saint Leger face to face unacknowledged or uncared for, nor ever shall. But why came you hither?"

As this interrogatory was addressed to me, I replied: " Why I came I know not, nor can I give any satisfactory reason. I was about to spend some time in the highlands, and as I was leaving Warwickshire, Aunt Alice put in my hands the package you now have. I have told you all."

"Warwickshire," exclaimed my kinsman; " beautiful, lovely Warwickshire: its gentle Avon, its enchanting landscapes! Accursed be they," continued he, in a lower tone, "now and for ever. Did you leave all these, and to come *here?*"

"I did leave all these, and to come here,'" was my calm reply. I was about to add something further, when the door of the adjoining apartment opened, and the beautiful Leila stood upon the threshold.

XXXII.

YES—the beautiful Leila stood upon the threshold. There could be no doubt of her identity with the maiden I had seen with Vautrey. She stood motionless, and for a moment seemed lost in astonishment at beholding a stranger. She was about retiring, when her father—for so he proved to be—prevented her retreat. "Leila," he said, "come hither." The latter slowly obeyed the summons, advancing, without, however, in the least noticing me. "My child," said the Wœdallah, as I will now call him, "this is our kinsman, William Henry Saint Leger, from Warwickshire; you will receive him as such."

The maiden drew herself up, made me a distant salutation, which I returned with equal hauteur, and said to her father in Italian:

"I beg you will not force upon me a new acquaintance; pray let me retire." To which I immediately replied, "Unfortunately, mademoiselle, I am sufficiently acquainted with the Italian to comprehend what you say; I am equally unlucky in understanding French, German, Spanish, the dead languages, and my mother-tongue. If you will have the kindness to select any other, I promise you I can not play the caves-dropper."

The girl was fairly taken by surprise at my impudence, and

seemed for a moment at a loss whether or not to receive it in good part. The oddity of the whole scene, I think, turned the scale in my favor. Extending to me her hand, she exclaimed :

"Since our kinsman has so many weapons at command, submission on our part is discretion. Welcome, Mr. Saint Leger, to the rocks of St. Kilda."

"And since," replied I, warmly, "I have at last received a kinsman's reception, I beg to make an apology for my rudeness."

"Enough," interrupted the Wœdallah, much to my chagrin ; "enough for this once, or you will exceed bounds. So it is ever with youth ; one extreme or the other; now all ice, then a burning heat ; ecstasy or despair; frowning like Medusa, or smiling like Helen. Why should it not be so ? What would the world come to, if the young had experience ? To an end, speedily. So, go on—go on; freeze and seethe, bubble and boil, till life has ended, and not even the vapor remains."

I stood regarding the speaker in mute astonishment during this strange harangue. When he had concluded, I turned to witness its effect upon Leila, but discovered that she had taken advantage of it to effect a retreat to her own apartment. Feeling no desire to encourage conversation of this sort, I resolved if possible to put an end to it. "I know not," said I, "to what such remarks tend, nor why they are addressed to me. Indeed, why I thus meet you I can scarce tell. You invited me to enter, and I did so. If you are my kinsman, treat me with the confidence our relationship merits."

"If you are my kinsman !" echoed the Wœdallah, rising and regarding me with a searching, anxious look : "miserable boy, do you doubt it ? Or—is it possible ?—can I have been deceived ?" he continued, again scrutinizing my features.

" No, no—it can not be."   Taking the ring, which I had de-
livered, from its envelope and again reading what was within,
he exclaimed, in a louder tone, "Ay, ay, receive him—receive
him; but—but poison not his soul—for it may not be."

His appearance all this time was so like a madman's, that
I turned away my face in horror.   The Wœdallah paused,
and then addressed me precisely as if not one word had been
uttered by him, and I doubt much if he was conscious of
having spoken.

" The confidence you ask," he said, calmly, " shall be extended to you.   Indeed, you have a right to demand it.   But
first tell me how fare all at—Bertold Castle.   Your father
and your mother ?   You have a brother and a sister also; are
they well ?   And—and Aunt Alice, as you call her—
bears she her years bravely ?   Has time left many marks
upon her frame ?—but her spirit will resist the spoiler
for ever and for ever—tell me, how is she ?   Then she knew
of your coming hither, and gave you these ?"

One question had followed another in such rapid succession that I could not reply to any till the questioner paused.
I then answered particularly as to our family, stating, as I
had previously done, that my visit to St. Kilda was almost
accidental.

" Did she not tell you that I was here?" was the next
question.

" She did not," was my reply.

" It is strange; yet not strange," he continued; " but I
embarrass you.   I am in fault.   And so you struck boldly for
Hirta.   A hardy enterprise : how old are you ?"

I stated my age.   "So young—I pity thee : I supposed
thou hadst fewer years in which to suffer ; but I see thou hast
not begun to experience.   Hast had any misgivings, any
doubts ?"

It seemed while I heard these words from the lips of a kinsman, words which echoed back my own secret distrusts and fears, as if the arch enemy stood before me, luring me to destruction. I shrunk from the tempter. My better nature rallied to resist the insidious attack, and by this I knew how necessary was temptation to a salutary state of mind and heart. I answered calmly and with courage :

"Who trusts his Maker knows neither misgiving nor doubt. His providence protects from both."

"Wait a while," returned the other, sneeringly, "and you will tell a different tale. Does Job fear God for naught ? Have you not youth and health and senses—a full capacity for earthly enjoyment? Does not the blood go beating through your veins in the very heyday rapture of young life ? Confidence in your Maker, forsooth : say rather confidence in your own glowing energy ; but energy will wane by-and-by, and confidence with it."

I was startled at such bold and impious language ; but my heart grew firm under the attack, and I answered, "And why should not man trust his Creator ? Why should he have any misgivings, any doubts, as you call them, when he knows that Creator to be all-wise, all-just, and all-powerful ? And why should not confidence increase with years ?"

".Because—because," returned my kinsman, impatiently, "neither in youth nor in early manhood do we enjoy the fruits of our labors ; because we are put off, put off till old age, before the reward cometh ; until the reward is known to be vanity, and we care not for it ; and therefore do distrust and apprehension creep gloomily over the soul."

"We should carry the reward daily in our bosoms," said I. "He is a supremely selfish being who looks to the reward merely *as* a reward and selfishness itself is very desolation to the heart."

"Ho, ho," shouted the other, scornfully; "a philanthropist, I perceive; and universal benevolence your rule of action. Wait till Sin has turned Virtue out-of-doors, and Folly has sent Benevolence to keep her company; till Ingratitude has soured your mind, and you have found in your bosom-friend a viper; till you have spent life's progress in that utter toil of the human spirit, and you awake, as from a dream, the victim of delusive, presumptuous Hope, and find yourself borne down by a stern, unaccommodating, unyielding Necessity into deep interminable perdition, while the MAKER whom you worshipped—ha, ha—mocks at your distresses, or coldly regards the helpless struggles of his victim, as if he rejoiced at his agonies! Ay, wait—and the time is short—wait till then, and you also will exclaim, even as do I, 'Oh, humanity, humanity, how truly do I pity thee.'"

During this harangue, it seemed to me as if I was encountering Satan in bodily presence. At the same time all the strength of my moral nature rose within me. I came close to the speaker, and boldly met his sarcastic sneer. "Man!" exclaimed I, "tempter! fiend! avaunt—I defy thee. If I choose to do right and be virtuous, it is not in the power of Omnipotence to make me miserable. If I choose to do wrong and be sinful, GOD himself can not make me happy."

As I pronounced these words, the Wœdallah started up and turned upon me a countenance in which a thousand evil spirits seemed struggling for expression. Rage and hate and dark despair were stamped upon it, but he spoke not. Just then the scroll which Aunt Alice had sent by me fell accidentally open upon the floor. I took it up and handed it to him, at the same time placing my finger upon the words he had before repeated, "but poison not his soul." The poor man turned his eye upon the paper. All trace of anger and hatred vanished. Deep melancholy again took possession of his features, and he exclaimed: "True—ha! true; too true! No—I will not—I will not:" and rushed into the adjoining apartment.

I stood in strange perplexity. Curious fantasies flocked through my brain. I began to believe that I was in the abode of some powerful necromancer, who had chosen this storm-beaten island for his habitation, and that the fair Leila was but the sorceress through whose blandishments I had been lured to it. I should not have been much surprised to have seen her step forth a wrinkled, ill-favored, shrivelled hag. In short, I would most gladly have changed localities with old Gonzalo, whose isle, though "full of noises,"

"Of elves, of hills, brooks, standing lakes and groves,"

was also filled with

"Sounds and sweet airs, which give delight and hurt not."

How I wished for something to destroy the horrible illusion which was stealing over me. Had Hubert then made his appearance, or had old Christie thrust his head through the narrow doorway, it would have been an indescribable relief. What was I to do? Should I leave in silence, and if so, was I privileged to return?

At this moment, the beautiful Leila, the influence of whose name had certainly caused the last interrogatory, again opened the door and came into the room.

"Mr. Saint Leger," she said, "my father desires that you will excuse his not seeing you again to-day. He has suddenly been taken ill, and requests that you will visit him to-morrow."

"Ill?" said I; "nothing alarming, I hope. Can I not render some assistance?"

"None, I assure you," replied the maiden, "yet I must

not leave him ;" and with rather a formal salutation, she disappeared.

Nothing was left for me but to make my way back to the village, where I found Hubert impatient to see me.

XXXIII.

It required, I acknowledge, a great effort to turn from the exciting and intensely interesting events of the morning, to give attention to Hubert's vivacious account of his doings and discoveries. At first, I could not bear to have the image of Leila displaced for a moment from my mind, and I listened with so bad a grace for the first few moments, that Hubert began to lose patience. This brought me to my senses; and promising to pay better heed, I soon became interested in his narrative, which I shall condense, leaving out nothing of importance.

He had seen Vautrey. He had discovered his whereabout in the following manner : Christie, having been informed that the " strange boat" was in the habit of putting in at the northwest side of the island, proceeded with Hugh and Aleck to watch its movements. They saw Vautrey and two others leave the shore and steer due north. Christie at once set sail after them, and managed to keep in sight till he saw the adventurers land at Boreray. Returning at once, he informed Hubert of his success, and the whole party embarked again, taking in three natives of the island, with whom Christie had become well acquainted, through his friend the old herring cruiser. It being but some two leagues to Boreray, and the day fine, the latter place was quickly made, when all hands landed except one, who strayed with the boat. According to Hubert's account, the isle was "full of wonders;" a little more than a mile in circumference, and girt about with rocks piled upon each other to a prodigious height. A considerable number of sheep and an innumerable quantity of sea-fowl were its sole occupants. The St. Kilda men informed Christie that there was a large stone dwelling in the island, which Vautrey had undoubtedly converted to his use. Thither Hubert and his company repaired. As was anticipated, they found the place inhabited; and on seeking admission, Hubert and Count Vautrey met. The latter was completely surprised, and for the first time almost in his life lost his self-possession. He evidently supposed—for when does guilt ever rest undisturbed in the human bosom—that Glenfinglas had not survived his wound, and that highland retribution had followed him thither. He scarcely recognised the presence of the intruders, but waited for Hubert to speak first. The latter, forgetting for the moment their late quarrel, at once relieved Vautrey from his embarrassment.

"Count," said he, "we have met strangely enough. My voyage to St. Kilda was made without the slightest suspicion of meeting you here; and we have to-day visited Boreray from curiosity, understanding, I admit, that a strange boat had landed in the island."

"Hubert Moncrieff," returned Vautrey, "as I have said before, I have no cause for mortal quarrel with you. I have felt no hatred toward you, neither had I any enmity against that dull fool, Glenfinglas. He bearded me; if he perished, he provoked his fate."

"Not so fast, count," said Hubert, a little piqued; "the life of yon highland laird is not so easily struck from his body, although I admit your skill, and doubt not that you did your best; but believe me, Glenfinglas is as good as new; ready to wage his feud with you for ever and a day; so take heed how you go near Kilchurn Castle."

"I am glad," said Vautrey, "it is no worse. As for his

enmity, why, if he provokes me, I shall strike surer next time. And as for you, Moncrieff, if you choose it so, here is my hand, in token that the past goes for nothing."

It was with no little surprise that Hubert perceived the count adopt a tone so different from his character; but as he had no time to consider the subject, he received his hand and assented, with what readiness he could, to his friendly over- ture. During this conversation, Vautrey's followers had en- tered the apartment. One of them proved to be the same sinister-looking fellow that attended him at Glencoe; the other was, as Hubert expressed it, "the most perfect speci- men of goblin-ugliness" he ever beheld; "the very imper- sonation of all that was wild, savage, and malicious." "It was amusing," said Hubert, "to witness Christie's demeanor during the interview. He was doubtless anticipating violence of some sort; and when Vautrey's men entered, you might have seen the old fellow take a firmer position; his eyes di- lated, his muscles seemed braced up for duty, and his whole person was evidently on guard; while Hugh and Aleck closely watched his motions, prepared, if need be, for instant service. The two St. Kilda men stood directly behind ready for anything that should be required." Without doubt, Vautrey's consciousness of guilt, and the presence of superior numbers, caused him to pursue a course which he knew would not fail to be successful with one of Hubert's manly and gen- erous character.

"As you say," remarked the count, quietly, "it is strange that we should meet here, and by mere accident. Pray, when do you return to Glencoe?"

"Oh," replied Hubert, "we shall be off in a few days; in- deed, I am ready now, for I have had enough of climbing rocks and tasting salt water; but I wait Saint Leger's move- ments. He planned the voyage, so I defer to him."

"Saint Leger," exclaimed Vautrey, starting as if a serpent had stung him; "Saint Leger, is he with you?" Hubert nodded assent. "Saint Leger! Death and damnation! Hell and furies! am I to be doubly thwarted? A pretty story you have trumped up, to deceive me as to the object of your voyage. You think to circumvent me, and you would accomplish this by a low deception. 'Met by accident'—ha, ha. This, then, is the boasted faith of a Moncrieff. A petty subterfuge, and a lie with a circumstance."

"Vautrey," said Hubert, pallid with suppressed passion, but at the same time very calm; "Vautrey, I repeat what I have said; and I add besides, that neither Saint Leger nor myself had the slightest suspicion that you were in St. Kilda when we landed here. And now, unless you retract upon the spot the opprobrious words you have dared to utter against my honor and my name, mark me, Vautrey, you die—ay, you *die* like a dog; for I will not contaminate myself; but you shall be ignominiously put to death by my followers; overpowered by numbers, if you choose so to call it, as a noxious animal is hunted down, and his carrion carcass thrown out to feed the vultures."

While Hubert was speaking, Vautrey stood like some malignant fiend, whose plans of wickedness have suddenly been discovered and frustrated. He even ground his teeth with rage, but did not change his position, except to glance toward his men, only one of whom remained near him. The savage had just before retreated into the next apartment.

Quick as thought Vautrey's whole demeanor changed. Again he assumed a frank and open, though calm manner: "Moncrieff," said he, "you were right—I was wrong. In this case, I was the first to provoke you by unreasonable and improper accusation; still, as you may perhaps know, this same Saint Leger and myself are no friends; and, excuse me, there **was a** particular reason why the mention of his name just then should annoy, nay, very much disturb me. Let it pass. You were excited, and threatened me. You were in the right; so let that pass. I believe you will not deny to me personal courage; and that, fearing as I do, neither man nor devil, you will credit the concessions I make to the right motive. If this does not satisfy you, come on; the stag is at bay: Laurent de Vautrey will die as he has lived, defying his enemies."

"There was something about this speech," said Hubert, "there was something about Vautrey's manner, which almost convinced me that he spoke as he felt, although I remember-ed your explanation of his character : that he had no feeling, and spoke only as he ought to feel. Still, I could not appear otherwise than satisfied with his retraction. I therefore told him I was glad to hear him take back so foul a slander, and that what had passed between us I was willing should be for-gotten. So, after a little unimportant conversation, carried on with restraint, we took leave of this forty-fifth cousin of ours, who was all the time, I know, secretly cursing me from the bottom of his heart. Depend upon it, we shall have trou-ble with that fellow. But he need not think to deceive me by this hypocritical reconciliation. His eyes were full of the venom of the damned, while he was pretending a great desire for peace and amity. He came near his end, I assure you. Christie had advanced half a pace in front, and was longing to begin. But it is best ended as it is—if we have indeed seen the end. Now, Saint Leger, what word from you? What of our beautiful storm-nymph, and the old surly storm-king, her father? See if you can surpass me in the recital of the marvellous."

I was particularly disinclined to give to any one an ac-count of the scene between my kinsman and myself, so I

treated Hubert to a general outline, concluding by informing him that I was to have another interview on the morrow.

"Well," said Hubert, "for my part, I have had enough of
St. Kilda. Our adventures appear pretty well over, unless
you are yet to make something out of yon dark-eyed damsel,
or the old——pshaw, I never can remember that word.
Who knows, by the way, but he keeps the young girl pent up
in this desolate place against her will? What say you to effecting her deliverance, and then 'up stick' and away? Seri
ously, though, when shall we be off? I want to witness a
hunt for birds'-eggs, which I am told is a wonderful affair;
and we shall have one, Christie says, in two or three days;
after that, what say you for Glencoe?"

I mechanically gave my assent to whatever Hubert suggested, for my mind was so full of the events of the day that
I could do little else.

XXXIV.

In my perplexity I resolved to apply to the excellent Mr.
David Cantyre. I readily entered into conversation with the
worthy man, which very naturally turned upon what I had
seen new and interesting during the day's ramble. I mentioned without hesitation my meeting with a "most singular
personage," detailing however nothing of what had passed,
except that I spent some time in his company. I concluded
by asking Mr. Cantyre to tell me the motive which caused
such a person to sojourn here, apparently without occupation
or inducement.

"My young friend," said the minister, "I do not wonder
at your curiosity; but I very much wonder how you could
have prevailed upon this strange man to converse with you,
especially at this time, when he is not alone."

"You refer to his daughter," said I.

"Yes," replied the minister; "you certainly did not see her?"

"She came into the room," I replied, "without being aware of my presence there. But, excuse me, I am eager to hear all you know about them."

"It is a long story," said my host, "but I will make it as brief as possible. Some six years ago, a boat put into the landing-place, containing, besides the crew, a man, a little girl, and an old female servant. After remaining here but a day, the boat again put to sea. Our people are hospitable, and food and shelter were at once offered to the new comers. The man was somewhat past the prime of life, and had evidently experienced that wear and tear of spirit which never fails to bring on premature old age. He seemed to carry within him a restless, unquiet soul, which had long sought for tranquillity, and found it not. Yet there was no shrinking from intercourse with his fellow men, no expressed desire to live apart from them, or in privacy; on the contrary, giving as a reason for selecting St. Kilda for his abode, the advantages of an exclusive sea-atmosphere, he interested himself in the various matters of the island, and appeared desirous to do what good he could. At this time our present worthy and most excellent steward was not the incumbent of St. Kilda; neither was I then in charge of its spiritualities, nor was there, indeed, any minister here. The former steward had the name of being a hard-fisted, griping, tyrannical person. He employed a deputy of the same nature as himself to collect his rents. Not content with putting an additional tax upon sheep, this creature insisted upon receiving, as a special perquisite, every seventh fleece and every seventh lamb, a certain number of eggs and a certain quantity of oil. Upon persons of so small means as the poor Hirta people, this extortion had

a most cruel effect.   In the meantime the stranger began to
feel quite at home in his new abode.   He had been furnished
with a comfortable dwelling, for which, however, he paid
most bountifully in gold, an article the St. Kildans had very
little acquaintance with, but of which they nevertheless knew
the use.   His little girl was a dark-eyed, sprightly, beautiful
child; and altogether, a deep interest was felt by these sim-
ple-minded people for both parent and child.   The cause of
their coming hither remained a profound mystery, nor do I
know if it has been solved to this day.   Although the stranger
evidently carried at his heart some heavy weight, which saddened and depressed his spirit, he manifested no misanthropic
feelings, but availed himself of every means to be useful
to the inhabitants.

"In a short time he was looked upon as a superior being;
his advice was asked and taken, he was called upon in sickness, and his remedies were almost always efficacious.   As
the stranger never had betrayed his name to any one, and as
there was no way to discover it, he was called by the islanders 'The Staller;' literally, 'The Man of the Rocks;' a name,
in a St. Kildan's estimation, conveying a compliment of the
highest kind.   As he gradually became more esteemed among
them, especially for his skill in the healing art, he received
the superior title of Wœdaller, or as some write it, Wœdallah
—literally, 'The God of the Rocks;' and by that name he is
now universally known.   As the autumn approached, the
same boat which had brought this strange being hither, made
its appearance, freighted with necessaries for its owner, received his child on board, and departed.   Meanwhile, the
tyranny of the old steward became nearly insupportable.   He
even objected to the stranger's remaining in the island, and
continued to levy tax upon tax upon the poor St. Kildans,
with increasing rapacity.   In their distress they applied to

the Wœdallah, and begged him to afford them some relief.
He undertook to remonstrate with the deputy, but the only
consequence was, an order for him to leave the island.
This produced a general feeling of indignation, but the inhabitants were so completely dependent upon the steward,
that resistance appeared hopeless. Not so thought the
stranger. He called the men together, advised them to sub-
mit to such tyranny no longer, and offered himself to effect
their deliverance. The St. Kildans were, as you see them,
a hardy but simple race, bold and courageous; nay, performing the most daring feats in their ordinary avocations; yet
the idea of rebellion against what they considered the constituted authority, to which they and their fathers before them
had implicitly submitted, struck their hearts with fear. Although they regarded the Wœdallah as almost superhuman,
and felt that he had done them great service, yet the prestige
of ancient dominion, no matter how unjust and oppressive,
had so strong an influence over their minds, that they trembled
to break through it. The utter helplessness of their situation
no doubt lent a strong argument to this conclusion. The
Wœdallah heard their decision with mortification and anger;
pronounced them craven, faint-hearted poltroons, and declared that he himself would resist in person any encroach-
ment upon his rights.

" In this resolution he was joined by some ten or twelve
hardy young men, who were devoted to him body and soul,
and who now entered into the struggle for liberty with all
the determination and ardor of young and stout hearts. The
next time the steward's deputy approached the island, he was
told very significantly that it would be dangerous for him to
land; and on his attempting it, he was repulsed without
ceremony, and he himself narrowly escaped being drowned
from an over-ducking. The Wœdallah took no active part

in this affair, but it was believed that he directed the entire movement. Soon after, his own boat, which came regularly to the island twice a year, arrived, bringing many necessaries now absolutely required by the inhabitants. These were distributed impartially among them without compensation, and the poor St. Kilda men began to feel all the privileges of freemen. But the steward was too influential a personage to allow the affair to rest in this way. He made a second attempt to land in person, but with no better success. Incensed by such open contempt for his authority, he applied to his cousin the Duke of Buccleugh, by whose influence a company of his majesty's troops were ordered to land in Hirta, and enforce submission among the refractory tenants. Even then, had the whole strength of the island united to resist the assailants, the latter might have been defeated; but the appearance of a military force struck these ignorant people with awe and terror. Indeed, there was scarcely anything like resistance. But before the active participators in ‘ the rebellion,’ as it was termed, could be discovered, they had safely effected their escape from the northwest point of the island, accompanied by the Wœdallah, in a small boat belonging to him. The party, consisting of twelve men in all, took possession of Soay, a small island but a little distance southwest of Hirta, belonging also to the steward, which was uninhabited, except by large flocks of sheep and bevys of sea-fowl. Here the fugitives built a strange kind of residence. We will sail across and take a look at it to-morrow if you like. It is some ten or twenty feet high, the top being level with the earth, by which it is surrounded; thence it extends downward in a circular form, gradually enlarging and enlarging, until the bottom is reached; while at the top it narrows off in the form of a cone, so that a single large stone covers it. By removing the stone, the habitation is ventilated. There is a arge stone seat built around the pavel floor on which some sixteen can conveniently sit, and four beds are built skilfully into the wall, each capable of holding four persons. To each of these is a separate entrance, the whole being most sagaciously arranged to prevent discovery and to resist attack. I believe there were but two attempts made to dispossess the occupants of the curious home they had chosen. Each time the elements seemed to rise in their favor, for a storm sprung up before it was possible to effect a landing, and so carefully was the place guarded, that at any time it would have proved a dangerous experiment.

"For more than a year the Wœdallah and his men maintained this position, without any communication with the main island. He had sent his small boat off with two or three men, on first going to Soay, and in due time another boat landed there, freighted with necessaries. The inhabitants of Hirta began to miss the favors which they formerly received, and fain would have visited the Wœdallah in his retreat, but this the latter would not permit. Meanwhile the steward of St. Kilda and its dependencies having gone, as was his custom at certain seasons, to Edinburgh, where he partook most freely of dinners, of suppers, of whiskey punches and brandy toddy, went home, and—died; some said of a surfeit; others denied this, from the fact that he was in the habit of indulging in this way at least twice every year. So the matter never was settled; except indeed that he did die and was admitted to Christian burial. With his successor everything was changed. The rents were reduced; a minister (my worthy predecessor), was again sent to the island; for no minister would consent to remain under the old steward; and the wants of the people kindly regarded. The change produced by this new state of things was instantaneous. Cheerfulness and prosperity again reigned in St. Kilda, and happiness and contentment univer-</p>

sally prevailed. The men who had taken up their abode in Soay now returned; but not the Wœdallah. He had left that island as soon as his followers had landed in Hirta, and had sailed no one knew whither. At the end of another year he came back. It was the same season I myself came hither. He did not make the usual landing, but put in at the same place which he had left two years before, near the spot where you saw and conversed with him. He had landed and taken possession of his old dwelling (which remained unoccupied) before any one was aware of it. Mystery marked all his movements. Report said that a beautiful female, though past the bloom of womanhood, had been forcibly taken ashore, and was detained a captive in the habitation of the Wœdallah. The boat did not remain, so that no information was elicited from the crew. The only person ever visible about the premises was the same old woman who had before been with the Wœdallah. Shortly after he landed, the old creature brought me a letter from the steward, desiring that the wants of this strange man might be supplied, should he ever require any aid, and requesting that his privacy might *never* (with a particular emphasis on the word) be intruded upon.

"On his arrival, the whole island went to greet him, and welcome him back, for he was looked upon with affectionate regard by every man, woman, and child, in St. Kilda; but the Wœdallah declined communication with any except his fellow sojourners at Soay, whom he received kindly, and conversed with a few moments earnestly. They then took leave of him, and never visited him again. After this, the most singular and absurd reports began to be spread about. The story of the captive lady gained ground daily; but the little glen and landing-place beyond were rarely visited. Regularly twice a year the Wœdallah's boat made its appearance,

freighted with stores and necessaries of every description.
What is remarkable, the Wœdallah became very particular
in his dress: before, it always had a foreign appearance;
now it was plain, entirely English, and was newly replenish-
ed every six months. With him personally I have had no
intercourse; and by thus humoring his wishes, have sometimes been able indirectly to render him desirable assistance;
for there are things in St. Kilda, strange to say, that money
can not command. In return, I have often received from the
old woman a new and valuable book, or some little luxury or
convenience not to be obtained here. I had nearly forgotten
to mention that there was a report about a year ago that the
captive lady had breathed her last. One of the St. Kilda men
affirmed, that passing near the glen one day, he had the courage to steal near the dwelling and peep in, where he saw the
old woman standing by the neatly disposed corpse of the departed female. Another affirmed that when the next boat left, it received on board something very like a coffin. These rumors
it is impossible to place reliance upon; the whole affair is
veiled in mystery; a mystery which I care not to pry into.
All that I know about it you have heard."

I thanked the minister for his narrative, and as the evening
was advanced, I bade him good-night, and turned once more
into my hole in the wall, my brain full of new fancies and new
perplexities. At last I fell asleep.

XXXV.

THE next morning found me up betimes; nor was Hubert
behind me. He had planned an excursion with Christie, in
which I was to be a party if I chose; but my services were
not insisted upon. As I was desirous to make one more visit
to the glen, have one more interview with my strange kins-

man, and take one more last look (was it to be the last?) at the enchanting Leila, I excused myself from joining my cousin. I could scarcely wait for a seasonable hour in which to present myself at the stone grotto. When I did arrive there, I found Leila alone in the apartment before described. She received me almost cordially; and to my inquiries about her father, replied that he had passed a restless night, and was far from well; she then stepped into the adjoining room, and after a few moments returned, saying that if I would have patience for a short time, her father would see me. She turned again to leave the apartment. As the present was the only opportunity I might have for a private interview, I determined to make a desperate effort to realize it. " Patience," said I, " is a virtue I have not of late particularly exercised, and it is especially difficult to practise it alone. Pray, my fair cousin (excuse my calling you so for the first, the last, the *only* time—here too, away behind the world), pray, my fair cousin, have you any very serious objections to gratifying my curiosity upon a subject nearly concerning yourself?"

" What would you know?" said Leila, quietly, yet as I thought, not indifferently; at the same time taking her seat. "At a last interview much certainly may be allowed."

" Lovers at least say so," I replied; " but I have a claim a thousand times stronger than that. A lover may be in despair; but I am bewildered; my brain is turned; I am crazed—positively crazed. I came to St. Kilda through love for adventure merely, but I have been so completely baffled, perplexed, confounded, during my short sojourn, that I shall take advantage of the first fair wind, and—away."

" I certainly regret any incipient symptoms of insanity," said Leila, rather tartly, " at least on your own account, and would recommend an immediate return to some place which can boast of civilization and a lunatic asylum. Still, I do not call some three or four weeks a very short sojourn at St. Kilda."

"Three or four weeks," exclaimed I, in amazement; "three or four weeks? I have scarcely been in St. Kilda as many days."

"Nor in its vicinity?" asked Leila, quickly.

"Certainly not," I replied. "I have not made a single landing at any of the contiguous islands."

"Then you did not come——" Leila suddenly checked herself, and left the sentence unfinished.

"No, I did not," replied I, coolly.

"Nay," said Leila, "you know not what I was about to ask. It was really of no importance, and did not at all concern me."

"You were about to ask," continued I, speaking very slowly, "if I did not come with one Vautrey, and I reply, No: I did not."

"Hush—hush! not so loud," exclaimed the maiden, in a low but excited tone; "breathe not that name here. Yet tell me; did you not really come in his company? Do you not know him? Are you not his friend?"

"Leila," I said, "I will answer your question seriously. I do know Count Vautrey, but I came not hither with him. I have no fellowship nor communion with him. I believe that he is a designing, selfish, cold-hearted villain; a fiend in human shape. I in *his* company! Nay, I had rather go to the bottomless pit in company with the foul fiend. And now let me be questioner. Why do you avoid me, as if I were some repulsive object, to loathe and to shrink from? What have you to do with this Vautrey? Why do you start and become agitated at the mention of his name, and bid me 'hush,' as if it were guilt to mention it? Nay, nay: interrupt me not, but tell me—may I not ask this—tell me why you are here in this strange spot?—when do you leave it, and where do you go? There is some mystery connected with all this. Will you not explain it?"

"When I better understand your right to demand such explanation," said Leila, haughtily. "The private history of every one has its peculiarities, yet that is no warrant for the curious to pry into it."

"None whatever," returned I, in the same tone; "and I am not at all surprised at being refused that confidence as a kinsman which you would doubtless have granted to me as the friend of Count Vautrey."

"What mean you?" said Leila.

"And," continued I, without noticing the interruption, "I beg to state explicitly that I claim no right to ask you a single question, nor to allude to a single event of your life. Surely I can have nothing to do with the affairs of yourself and Count Vautrey. Excuse the presumptuous boldness of detaining you for a moment."

As I concluded, Leila turned upon me a look so desolate, . so full of sadness, that my conscience smote me for what I had uttered.

"And you *hate* this Vautrey," said Leila, slowly.

"If ever man can honestly hate his fellow-man, I do," was my reply.

"Then I love you," exclaimed the girl, passionately, starting up and advancing near me. "And, oh," continued she, bursting into a flood of tears, "if you knew me, if you knew my history—all that I have suffered and endured—what my fate has been, and what my destiny surely, too surely, will be—but why do I speak thus to a stranger? Yet you are my kinsman. Alas, my kinsmen have ever proved my worst enemies. When shall I have peace? and whither shall I fly? Even in this remote spot I am persecuted by the importunities of that wretch. And not one friend have I in the wide world. Tell me, what shall I do? In this moment of agony, when a sense of utter desolation overshadows my soul--alone, alone—it is fearful to live always alone—even at this moment, I come to you, to you whom I have beheld but once before — to you whose heart is young, and not like mine, burnt up within my bosom — to you I come; I *must*, I WILL have one friend; and may Heaven help me, if this last hope shall fail."

The maiden abandoned herself so completely to her grief that it was impossible either to soothe or arrest it. Tears rolled down her face; her dark hair, breaking loose from its fastening, fell dishevelled upon her shoulders; her hands were clasped together, and her arms, partly upraised, were extended toward me. Never have I beheld so beautiful and so affecting a spectacle. My astonishment and the novelty of my situation for a while kept me speechless; my cold English temper could not immediately sympathize with the passionate exhibitions of a nature warmed and fostered under the influence of a more genial clime, and to which circumstances had undoubtedly given additional cause for such violent emotions. But I soon found myself yielding wholly to the influence of so exciting a scene. A sympathizing chord in my own heart was struck, and it responded. For all that, my manner was cold; I felt that it was cold; and it seemed almost unfriendly when contrasted with the ardent temperament of Leila. I took advantage of the pause in her pathetic appeal to re-assure her. "Leila," said I, 'judge me not from this cold habit that I wear about me; it belongs to my race; but judge me by the heart that beats under it. And by its strong pulsations, by my faith, and by my hopes, I swear to you that I will be your friend henceforth. For your own sake compose yourself. Nay, you must be calm and tell me how my friendship can best serve you. Surely you forgot your father when you declared yourself friendless."

"My father!" said Leila, mournfully, resuming her seat as she spoke, and burying her face in her hands: "Alas, I am doubly wretched, doubly sinful, in having a parent whom I can not love, and who loves not me."

I shrunk at such an avowal from one so young and so beautiful. The words of scripture, "without natural affection," rose to my lips, but I repressed them. Leila perceived that I was shocked, and said:

"Do not in your mind accuse me unjustly. When I speak thus of my father, I am unburthening the load that weighs heaviest at my heart. To him I owe everything that can minister to my personal comfort. I know not what it is to have a want ungratified. To him honor and obedience are due; but if you knew my history—and you shall know it ere long—you would not judge me harshly for not adding, love."

"I will not judge at all, till I do know," said I; "but your mother—is she not living?"

"May Heaven forgive you for mentioning the name," exclaimed Leila, relapsing into her former emotion; "mother, mother—I know not if I had a mother. Strange surmises crowd upon me; dreadful illusions pass before me; horrible suspicions force themselves upon me, at that word—mother! Never have I beheld a mother's face, never experienced a mother's love; and now I would barter for a mother's smile all that I hold dear in life, even though the lips that smiled upon me were guilty and polluted."

I saw that I had innocently touched upon a delicate topic, and, fearing the effects of further excitement, I attempted to calm her by assurances of sympathy and friendship. Expecting an interruption every moment from the father, I asked Leila when we should meet again. "I fear we shall not meet here again," said she; "my father is strange, very strange; it is owing solely to his illness that we are now so long together. No, not here. Yet, remember, we *shall* meet. I leave this gloomy island ere the moon wanes. Then you shall hear from me: only let me feel that there is one solitary being in the wide world who will sympathize with me, and I will be grateful. I ask no more."

An old female at this moment made her appearance at a side door, and beckoned hurriedly to Leila, who quickly obeyed the summons without bidding me adieu, and the door closed upon both.

XXXVI.

At the same instant, another door opened from the adjoining room, and the Wœdallah entered the apartment.

His aspect was so completely changed that I scarcely recognised him. His countenance bore marks of extreme physical as well as mental suffering. He looked ten years older than on the preceding day. Advancing slowly toward me, he took my hand, and in a kind but saddened tone asked me how I was. I was touched by his manner, and in turn inquired as to his indisposition. It was nothing, he replied, but the effect of heavy heart-pains which occasionally afflicted him, and which were past cure. As he said this, he sighed deeply, and inquired if I would take a turn with him into the fresh air. He put his arm within mine, and we left the dwelling.

Passing out, we walked some distance along the coast, until it began to rise to a precipitous height. Here my kinsman stopped. The swell from the sea, under the influence of a strong west wind, was tremendous. The waves mounting on high dashed furiously against the cliffs, and then retreating, as if to renew their strength, returned again, and were again thrown back into their ocean-bed. We stood for some moments contemplating the grandeur of the scene. At length, my companion spoke:

"My son, look around you and behold this isolated spot.
Who should have thought that busy man would come hither
to make it his own? Yet here Virtue may dwell secure and
uncontaminated, for here is no place for the pomp and circumstance of this world to triumph. But look away, yonder,
far—far away: nay, you see it not, save with the mind's eye:
behold, crowded together the habitations of the children of
men. See the buildings, closely joined, as if all lived under
a single roof. Must not peace, and brotherly love, and happiness, dwell there? Surely there can be no discords, no dis-
sensions, no conflicting interests. Is it possible that those
strong walls between each dwelling separate the bitterest
enemies, divide the good man from the assassin, the innocent
from the vile, the honest from the knave? Men herd together for mutual concealment, and not for good. Those cities
of the plain, mark me, shall be destroyed, and fire from the
Lord out of heaven shall fall upon them, as it fell upon Sod-
om and Gomorrah. But let us turn from the contemplation
of so revolting a picture. Let me speak something of myself
and you. Canst tell the relation we bear to each other?"

I replied that I could not.

"Then know," continued my kinsman, "that I am the son
of Wilfred Saint Leger—of Wilfred the rash, Wilfred the
unfortunate; a younger brother, as you doubtless have heard,
of Hugh Saint Leger, the lion-hearted, your father's father.
William Henry, I am calm now," continued he, for the first
time calling me by name. "I fear the unhappy effect of our
last interview upon your mind, and I would do what I may
to counteract it. As I said before, I have dreadful heart-
pains which unman me. For what I say when suffering under this terrible affliction, I am not, I can not be, accountable.
You carry truth within your bosom; your sentiments I honor;
I bow to them; would that I could make them mine. But it

is too late. Do not speak to me on this head. I will not hear you."

"But will you not," said I, deeply interested, "tell me why you are here, and explain to me the strange selection you have made for a home?"

"Home," said the other; "home: my home is *there*," pointing into the abyss of waters which foamed beneath us; "for no mortal shall ever tread upon my grave, nor shall any monument stand up to say, 'This man once lived upon the earth.' But you shall be satisfied. Sit we down upon these rough stones; turn your face away from mine, and I will briefly sketch my life."

I did as directed.

XXXVII.

"You doubtless have heard how Wilfred Saint Leger, my father, in company with Julian Moncrieff of Glencoe, made their way to Paris with the fair Isabella Seward, a rich heiress, and a ward of the Earl of Venachoir; how Wilfred Saint Leger wedded the young girl, and how they lived happily together; how in some three years the lovely lady grew pale, saddened, and died, leaving one child, a boy—myself. I have no recollection of my mother; sometimes I fancy I can recall her sweet, pale face, as she pressed me to her bosom, and, weeping, commended her infant to God. It was a sin to leave a guardian's roof and elope as she did; but how sorely was she punished, and how surely. Thank God, she died. Yes, died, instead of carrying the crushing weight of a broken heart and an agonized spirit through a long lifetime. My father was always a slave to the gayeties of Paris. From my boyhood, on the contrary, I detested them. I longed to get upon English ground. I determined never to adopt any oth-

er country for my own.   At the age of ten, my father, more
to avoid the restraint which a boy's observation would naturally cause upon such a parent, sent me to England to his
brother, Hugh Saint Leger, your grandfather, having previously got the consent of my uncle that he would take charge
of me.   I spent in England the only happy days of my life.
Your noble father was about my own age : we rode, we hunted, we read, and we studied, together.   How I loved him then,
and if my heart were not stone, how I should love him now !
For seven long (to children all years are long) happy years
was England my home.   Of these, three were spent at Eton,
and one at Oxford.   Previously to that time, we were attended by private masters at Bertold Castle.   Through the whole
your father was my constant playmate and companion ; and
never were there any serious differences between us.   I considered myself permanently located in England.   From my
father I heard three or four times a year; his letters generally contained some half-dozen lines, expressing his approbation of the course I was pursuing under my uncle's direction,
with some commonplace remarks about duty, and the like.
His remittances were always made punctually, and I soon regarded one epistle but as the *fac-simile* of another

"I had been at Oxford a year.   I was ambitious as a student, without being a book-worm, and I began to feel that I
had laid a foundation which should lead to an honorable distinction among my fellows.   My habits were good, and much did I
owe to your father's influence that they were so.   Still, there
was that about me of which I trembled thoughtfully to consider.
There was a latent desire to enjoy the pleasures of life, and to
taste its follies.   The Untried was constantly before me with
its temptations, but I resisted them all ; yet I felt how necessary it was for me to keep as far as possible from their reach.
Just then — mark me, for the devil's hand was in it — just then

1 received a letter from my father, written in haste, commanding me to come immediately to Paris. I can not describe my feelings at this unexpected summons. For a time I was completely beside myself. I raved, swore, and cursed my destiny; nay, I fear I cursed my parent. At length I became calm. I sat down and wrote him a long letter, stating my situation, what I had accomplished, what I hoped to accomplish; and begged him to allow me to remain in England. I received in return a short, decisive note. He said the most urgent reasons had influenced his decision; that it was unalterable, and that he was already suffering through my delay. I left Oxford at once for Bertold Castle, and asked my uncle's advice. His view of the relation of parent and child was severe. He regretted my father's decision, but advised me to bow to it; perhaps it might be in my power speedily to return. Much more he said, which I need not repeat; and at length I was persuaded.

"I left for Paris. Arrived there, I drove to my father's hotel in the rue Montmartre, and found it closed. A sickening apprehension came over me as I leaned against the ponderous gate which commanded the entrance to the courtyard. Not even the *portier*, who remains a fixture on the premises, was in his accustomed place to answer questions, and the door of the *conciergerie* was shut and fastened. I knew not what to do. My mind was sorely perplexed. As I looked up at the high walls of the gloomy building, rendered more gloomy by being tenantless, I felt that I was indeed a stranger in a strange land.

"I had nothing to do but to drive to some proper place for lodgings, and find my father as I best might. I was about giving the necessary directions, when an old fellow with a patch on his eye hobbled up to me, and prayed that I would, for the love of GOD, read a dirty paper which he thrust into my hands. I opened it and read as follows :

"*'This evening, at eight o'clock, Rue Copeau, No. 4, unaccompanied.*   W. St. L.'

"'There is a franc for you, my poor fellow,' said I, and without stopping longer, I drove to the rue Vivienne to find lodgings. Surmises were useless. I waited patiently until after seven, when I set out on foot, to elude observation, for the rue Copeau. This is a short street far off on the other side of the Seine, leading into the Garden of Plants. I passed slowly into the rue St. Honoré, and followed it through its whole extent into the rue St. Denis; down that to the Seine, thence along the Quai till I reached the Isle St. Louis, where I crossed; thence along the Quai again to the rue de Seine, and up that to the rue Copeau. Do you wonder at this minuteness of detail? I tell you that every step of that walk is as fresh to me now as on the day it was taken. I remember the faces of hundreds who passed me; I see them now before me. There was a little old man with a long cue extending half-way down his back, whom I thoughtlessly jostled as I passed, and who at once turned and begged my pardon. There were pretty grisettes, who stared at me with naïve wonder as I pushed unheedingly on; there were old women on the Quai; there were soldiers about the gardens; there, there are they all—and hark : just as I reached the appointed number in the appointed street, the chimes from the nunnery of the Sisters of Universal Concord, situated just in the rear, pealed merrily the hour of eight.''

Here my relative paused for several minutes. I turned partly round, alarmed at his silence. Large drops of sweat were standing on his forehead; his whole appearance was that of one in mortal agony. Shortly, however, he resumed.

XXXVIII.

"Ding-dong!—one, two; ding-dong!—three, four; ding-dong!—five, six; ding-dong!—seven, *eight*. Yes, eight was the hour. And there I stood before a massive, gloomy old building, which presented a most forbidding aspect. There was not the slightest sign of its being inhabited. Not a solitary light gleamed from any one of the numerous apartments. It bore the appearance of desertion and decay. The entrance to the court-yard was open, but no porter was in attendance in the lodge; though I could read by the uncertain glimmering of a lamp suspended across the street the half-effaced words *Parlez au concierge*. I had stood but a moment, anxiously scrutinizing everything within my observation, when a figure, muffled in a large cloak, approached from the court, came hastily up and exclaimed:

"'You are punctual—come with me.'

"I followed my conductor across the court, up two flights of stairs and through several narrow passages and corridors, first turning one way, then another, till I was bewildered. The house was unfurnished so far as I could perceive, and the air was close and noisome. My companion at last stopped before a door, which he opened, and ushered me into a room of moderate size, but exquisitely furnished. It was also brilliantly lighted. A small table of beautiful workmanship stood in the centre, upon which was laid a choice supper, flanked by wines of every variety and flavor. A cheerful fire of large logs blazed in the fireplace, for the evening was cool, and everything gave taken of good taste in the occupant and abundant means to improve it.

"'Welcome, welcome, my son;' exclaimed my father,

throwing off his disguise and warmly embracing me; 'and may God bless you for obeying the summons, though I feared it was too late. Why, Wilfred, you have grown up to be a man almost. Yet I should have known my child among a thousand.'

"I was struck with the affectionate and subdued tone of my parent. The seven years which had made so great an alteration in me had scarcely changed him, as he was in the prime of manhood, and had not begun the melancholy descent upon the other side of the scale of life. Yet there was a seriousness in his aspect, a something terribly calm in his countenance, quite unlike my father, which filled with me apprehension.

"'Come, come,' continued he, 'you must be faint and weary; sit down. You see I have been expecting you. We have much to do to-night; so fortify yourself with a hearty supper.'

"We sat down together. My father made a show of joining me, but only, as I believe, to persuade me to eat freely. It must be a serious matter which shall prevent a youth of seventeen, after a day's exercise and abstinence, from doing justice to an alluring table. The healthful calls of hunger are rarely disregarded by the young. God forgive me the satisfaction I took that evening at that table. As soon as I had finished, my father bade me sit near him.

"'Wilfred,' said he, 'would that I might now bid you to seek repose; but time presses, and the case is urgent. Can you listen to me?'

"I trembled, I know not why, but I answered unhesitatingly that I could.

"'It is well,' he continued; 'you are in time. Had you delayed another day, you might have found no one to call father.'

"I begged an explanation. 'Listen then,' was the reply, 'and mark my words. You remember, or at least you have heard of, Julian Moncrieff?' I assented. 'Julian Moncrieff, whose fate has been linked with mine for the last twenty years. To-morrow morning, when the sun shall redden the towers of Notre-Dame, it will shine insensibly to one of us!'

"'For Heaven's sake, what mean you?' I exclaimed.

"'Silence!' continued my parent, 'and do not interrupt me. Twenty years ago this night, Julian Moncrieff, with your father and his young and beautiful bride—thy mother, thy injured mother, boy—arrived here in this accursed city; came here to this very mansion; entered here into this very room. See you that couch? On it she reclined—the lovely, the confiding, the virtuous. There she sat, and smiled, and loved, and smiled again. Wilfred, my boy, if I could control everything which is held enviable and precious on this round earth and in heaven above, and could add to it the price of my soul's salvation, I would give all, *all*, ALL, to recall that scene once more, and see my Isabella for one brief moment, as I saw her then, and hear once, but *once* again, the sound of her sweet, dear voice. But she is gone—lost to me for ever. Have not years passed me since then? No; else I had not this fresh grief. When have I grieved before? Do not people lose their wives? Is it then so dreadful? Tell me, Wilfred, that there is yet hope!'

"I saw that my father's brain was wandering, but I knew not what to reply.

"'Wretch that I am,' he went on without waiting for an answer; 'the bitterness of this moment is more than I can bear.' He continued more calmly: 'This now gloomy mansion we selected because there belonged to it a large and delightful garden, and because it was quiet and secluded. A brief year we made this our home. With my young wife's fortune added to my own, we were rich—for Paris, very rich. We took another hotel in the rue Montmartre, where we entertained our visiters and gave fêtes and parties. But here were we most happy, because we lived most within ourselves. I have not time, I have not resolution, to tell my history. You will find whatever I have thought necessary to reveal among my papers. Search for nothing which you find not there,' pointing to a small box; 'everything else has been destroyed. You know that your mother sickened, and then she—yes, she—died. True she died, Wilfred! but not here. No, no; not—here. She was happy here—she was happy here! Well, I was a lost being, and I gave myself up to sin. —utterly gave myself to it.

"'This same Julian Moncrieff—he, my companion in iniquity, my sworn confederate and ally, between whom and myself there is an oath which neither dare break—this same Julian Moncrieff has cause for deadly quarrel with me; long has had cause. Ask no more. Everything is arranged; to-morrow morning at break of day we meet in yonder garden, near my Isabella's bower. The place I selected, for there I will yield myself up a sacrifice. After so many years of criminal neglect, her memory shall be honored. We meet to-morrow—our weapons the rapier—the combat to cease only with the death of one of us—and *I* am that one.'

"'Never,' exclaimed I, starting up, 'never shall so barbarous a conflict take place. I have heard enough; I am a boy no longer. If I have not the power to stop it, I will apply to the authorities; I will go to the police. Father, father, I implore you recall your senses. Speak to me rationally, and not with such portentous calmness.'

"'Wilfred,' said my parent, 'sit down and be calm yourself. You can not prevent this meeting, for I have determined that it SHALL take place. You are too young to understand me. God grant that you may never do so by experience. I am not a lunatic, nor have I lost my senses. But one thing I say—and think not, my boy, that I am lost to parental feeling. No, my son; had it been so, I should not have sent for you that I might once more behold my own flesh and blood—once more look upon her child. But this I say, that I will not live longer on the earth; and I prefer rather to fall by the hand of an antagonist than by my own; and most of all would I choose to fall by the hand of Julian Moncrieff.'

"What could I say; what could I do ? Was I unmanly or pusillanimous in yielding to my father ? Ought I to have resisted at all hazards ? You would think so, doubtless; yet it seemed as if the avenging angel stood before me, frowning, as he uttered the word 'Forbear!' I was silent.

"'Now, my son, to business,' continued my father, calmly, at the same time opening a large case of papers. 'I must give you such information as will enable you to act understandingly.'

"He proceeded to give me a detail of all his estate, with the most minute particulars; directing me whose advice to take in Paris, what to do under this and that state of things, and so forth. The bulk of his and of my mother's fortune, was in England and Scotland; but a very considerable sum had been invested in French securities, in the name of his friend and solicitor, Monsieur Coulanges. I was informed that every precaution had been taken, so that the cause of his decease should not be known, and that the funeral was arranged to take place on the second day after the combat. My father made me promise sacredly that I would not attempt to revenge his death, or harbor malice against his foe.

"It seemed my father's desire to prolong the interview till daybreak. This was a relief to me. I should not have dared to retire to rest. I might have been overpowered by fatigue and slumbered. My father would not have called me, and I should have waked and not found him. I sat the whole night giving a horribly calm attention to all that was said to me. At length gray streaks began to light up the sky, until it was apparent day. Presently the step of some one in the passage-way was heard.

" 'It is time :' said my father, quickly. 'Wilfred, my son, remember what I have told you. And now, farewell.'

" He took me in his arms and kissed me many times with great fondness. I was unmanned; I wept like a child. My father stood calm.

" ' This is not right, my son. This is not like a Saint Leger.'

"As soon as I could speak, I entreated my father to allow me to accompany him. He hesitated a moment.

" 'Will you promise to be composed ?' said he.

" I bowed my head.

" 'It is best so,' he added; 'the sacrifice should be in your presence. Once more, farewell.'

" He then took two rapiers from a side-table, and going to the couch, he knelt before it, and drew a miniature from his bosom.

" 'Here, here,' he murmured, ' my sainted wife, do I expiate my sins against you. At last, ah! at last, I see you as of yore — at last we are reünited.'

" He rose, beckoned me to follow, and left the room. We proceeded from one passage-way to another, down several flights of stairs, to the garden. I had no time to look about me, but followed close after my father into a secluded part of the grounds, until we came to a beautiful bower, the entrance of which was entirely overgrown with vines and evergreens. I could discern the figure of a man pacing impatiently up and down the walk. This figure attracted my whole attention, for I knew it was Julian Moncrieff. As we came up he started on seeing me, made a slight inclination to my father, and hastily exclaimed :

"'How is this?   There were to be no witnesses.'

"'There are none,' said my father; 'this is my son; he understands our arrangement.   He desires to be present, and I have consented.'

"'It shall not be:' said the other, hastily.

"'Nay, but it shall?' replied my father; 'if you wish; go summon your daughter; it will delay us but a moment, and then both will be represented.'

"'Have it as you will,' said Moncrieff; 'we are losing time.'

"I had during this short conversation an opportunity to examine my father's opponent.   I had seen him often when a boy, and I knew his character.   He was tall, well made, and in one way handsome; but there was an evil expression about his countenance which experience and intercourse with the world seemed to have increased rather than diminished. I looked upon him and trembled.   He also brought two rapiers, one of which was laid aside, and the parties, without exchanging another word, advanced toward each other.   You are aware that the Saint Legers were always accomplished swordsmen and masters of fence.   The sword-play is, and ever has been, a favorite pastime of the race.   In point of skill I had not the slightest fear for my father; but his express determination to fall in the encounter struck me with horror.   As the two became engaged in the combat I almost lost sight of the fearful result in admiration of the skill displayed by both combatants.   Do you wonder at this?" said the Wœdallah, turning partly toward me; "you need not, for the mind of man is strangely constituted.   I soon discovered my father's superiority over his antagonist, and hope revived in my heart, and I began to trust that all would yet end well. It did not occur to me that, in case Julian Moncrieff should fall, his young daughter would be left without parent or protector.   Well, the conflict went on.   My father was calm and unruffled; Moncrieff, on the contrary, began to lose temper. This increased my father's advantage, but he evidently avoided availing himself of it. Once or twice, when Moncrieff rashly exposed his points, my father would coolly remind him of it by a slight touch, but nothing more. This added to his impatience, and he used his weapon with a desperate rashness. I could see my father smile calmly as he managed with most admirable skill every stroke of his opponent, entering in spite of himself into the spirit of the combat. Suddenly his countenance changed; it assumed a deadly, fearful, fatal expression. As he turned aside one of Moncrieff's thrusts, he suddenly struck at the left arm of the latter. The stroke told, for the red blood followed swiftly from the wound. Smarting with pain, Moncrieff made a furious lunge at my father's breast. It was a stroke most easily parried, and when parried, would unavoidably expose the party to a fatal charge in return. What was my horror on seeing my father, instead of taking so open an advantage, deliberately throw his arms up and receive his enemy's sword through his body. He fell prostrate to the earth, directly in front of the bower of his ill-fated Isabella. I rushed forward, knelt by his side, and endeavored to stanch the fatal wound. Moncrieff was in a frenzy.

"'Oh, God,' he cried, 'what have I done!'

"He approached to bend over the prostrate body. I repulsed him rudely.

"'Wretch!' I exclaimed, 'dare not to come near him you have so foully murdered; if you attempt it, you will find a Saint Leger, who not only knows his weapon, but has the disposition to use it.'

"'Young man,' said Moncrieff, in a subdued tone, 'I blame not your passionate feelings, but I pray you quiet them. In the name of your dying parent I adjure you to be calm, and allow me to assist you. See,' he continued, eagerly, 'he still lives' (my father groaned); 'let us haste to do something. The wound may not be mortal.'

"I resisted no longer, and with the aid of Moncrieff conveyed my father to the apartment we had left but a few moments previous, and laid him upon the couch at which he knelt before going to the combat. Moncrieff proceeded to examine the wound with the skill of an experienced surgeon, and with all a woman's gentleness; but he soon shook his head despairingly. My father had swooned without uttering a word; still we knew that life was not extinct. After I had administered a stimulant with my own hands, he faintly opened his eyes; and although he looked upon no one, I am confident he knew where he was. He spoke not, save in broken whispers; and as I knelt to catch their meaning, I could only hear faintly articulated: '*My precious wife—my Isabella—receive the sacrifice.*'

"My father survived not quite an hour. All of the time he lay nearly insensible, feebly holding my hand in his, and occasionally giving it a slight pressure. Suddenly he started convulsively—his lips moved; I strained every sense to catch what he said. '*My Isabella, come nearer—I am happy now,*' were the words that died away upon his lips as the spirit parted from the body."

Again the Wœdallah paused. I dared not trust myself to look toward him, but waited until he should proceed.

XXXIX.

"THREE months after, I awoke in a sick-room. At last my brain was clear and sensible. Of nothing was I conscious during that time save that I was in friendly hands. I remember that there was a stillness and a silence that wearied me;

relieved occasionally by noiseless steps and low whispers, but yet dreadfully oppressive. I was reduced to the lowest point, still I lived. My mind, under the strong and conflicting excitements which had been brought to bear upon it, had yielded to their force; fever ensued; then delirium—then convalescence.

"I recovered. Would not my first steps be directed to England, eagerly, rapidly directed thither, to escape from the country which had proved the ruin of my sire? One would naturally suppose so; yet delay succeeded delay. I was still in Paris. I had first to see Monsieur Coulanges. That certainly was necessary; then the friends of my father called to offer their condolences (for all supposed he had died a natural death) and invited me to visit them in proper time. Although you would hardly suppose an Englishman could find much favor at such a time in France, when all Europe was convulsed with wars in which France and England were enemies, still you must remember that intrigue was the great weapon of the day; that I was born in France, and had powerful friends in Scotland, many of whom kept up a constant correspondence with the French court. I was admitted there without suspicion; and—shall I say it—after a short time abandoned myself entirely to its influence. Need I tell you how, when I say it was at the profligate court of Louis XV., with youth and wealth, and the advantage of a fair exterior? So it was that I did evil in the sight of the LORD, even as my father had done. Oh, what abyss so deep that it can overwhelm the ministers of damnation who waited on that court! Yet the fortune of the young Saint Leger was envied, and he was pronounced the most happy of mortals. But what a hell reigned in my bosom. Ten thousand avenging furies were shrieking hourly in my ears, still I went on, went on my journey to the deep perdition of the damned. I had become a wretched voluptuary; and Pleasure, which retired farther and farther in the distance as I wooed her most, began to pall upon the senses.

"I was at a masked ball given by the Duchess of ——. I had no less than six appointments there, and how to manage them, tasked my skill to the utmost. It was in the midst of the revel that a tall female figure in a plain mask approached me, and with a commanding air beckoned me to go with her. As adventures of this sort were by no means uncommon, I followed the retreating form of the lady out of the magnificent *salon*, through one apartment after another, till we arrived at a small door, to which my guide applied a key and we entered.

"I found myself—not, as I anticipated, in an exquisite boudoir, fragrant with flowers and perfumes, to add to the voluptuousness of the scene—but, in a small, gloomy, narrow room, without a single article of furniture, and with only one faint light glimmering on the mantel. I gave a hasty glance over this place of ill-omen. I thought I was betrayed by the intrigue of a rival; but fear is not the foible of the Saint Legers. I was armed, and the struggle for life would be desperate. While these thoughts were passing through my mind, the lady had advanced into the middle of the room, after bolting the door, and stood regarding me in silence.

" 'This is not exactly what you expected,' said the Unknown, addressing me in pure English. 'Not quite so alluring as an interview with the Comptesse ——, to which at this hour you were invited.'

"I made no reply to the announcement of a secret known, as I supposed, only to the two interested; but simply asked, in a quiet nonchalant way:

" 'Pray, what is your wish?'

" 'Nay,' said the mask, in an angry impatient tone, 'ask me

not what is my *wish*, but what is my *will*, for, by Heaven, it shall be obeyed.   I have brought thee hither to hear my commands, thou renegade Englishman—thou shame of a manly house.   *Thou* a Saint Leger!   Go, take the name of one of the strange women who make you their slave; follow on your path even as the ox goeth to the slaughter, or as a fool to the correction of the stocks; go now to their bed which is decked with coverings of tapestry, with carved works and fine linen of Egypt, and perfumed with myrrh, aloes, and cinnamon, and take your fill of love until the morning; but by the Supreme Power above, if you do this, and dare again to call yourself a Saint Leger, I will plunge this dagger into your heart!'

So saying, the mask half unsheathed a small poniard which she wore at her belt, and went on before I had time to speak:

" You have still another course left.   Leave this place of abominations before the iniquity of the Ammonites is yet full. The days of the Jezebels and the Athaliahs and the Delilahs are numbered.   In the portion of Jezreel shall dogs eat their flesh.   Return to England; go where you will; stay here if you have strength to do it; but I warn you, forget not again that you are a Saint Leger.   Sell not your manhood at this debauched and infamous court : if you disobey,' again touching the dagger, 'you know the penalty.'

" The rebuke which these words conveyed, its truth—severe though it was—rendered me for a moment incapable of speaking.   I stood discovered, stripped of the miserable dross and tinsel of unhallowed pleasure, in all the ugly and rude deformity of detected guilt.   Yes, I stood

> "' And felt how awful goodness is ; and saw
> Virtue, in her shape how lovely ! saw, and pined
> His loss.'

I felt piqued, nevertheless, at the threat of the Unknown ;

for man will often listen to persuasion, when he will not be moved by force; and the idea of abandoning even a course of sin, through fear of my life, struck at my pride. I wished from my heart that such an argument had been omitted.

" 'Have you nothing to say?' continued the mask, impatiently, as I was hesitating what to reply.

" 'Nothing,' said I, coldly, 'to one who under a disguise seeks to frighten me into measures which a sense of right alone can make effectual or sincere.'

" 'Spoken like a man, indeed!' said the figure, removing her mask, and disclosing the clear, penetrating gray eyes, the lofty brow and the haughty mien of the Lady Alice Saint Leger. 'Kinsman,' said she, 'I have come to save you from shame and ruin. I did not suppose threats would accomplish this; but I wished to show my determination to preserve our name from further disgrace. Let,' she continued reverently, 'the dead rest in peace; with the living there is hope. I come not to reproach or to direct, but solemnly to warn.'

" 'The warning shall be heeded,' said I, emphatically, ' and ——'

" 'Enough,' said the Lady Alice, with dignity; 'I believe you.' She replaced her mask, and notwithstanding my entreaties that she would remain a few moments, unbolted the door and disappeared. Scarcely sensible whether this was not all a dream, I proceeded to find my way out. The thought of returning to the gay scene I had so lately left, filled me with disgust. I discovered a private entrance into the courtyard, and throwing myself into a carriage, was conveyed to my hotel. I went home a repentant man.

XL.

' The morning after the first commission of a sin, or after
the first resolution to reform, is generally remarkable for severe struggles with one's-self; and I had no small share of
these. I rose as from a fearful dream. I was not certain that
what I remembered of the previous evening was not an illusion. By degrees it all came back to me with distinctness.
I summoned my valet; he brought me a score of perfumed
billets-doux, done up in exquisite taste. The moment had
arrived which should decide my fate : my hand was on the
seal of one which I knew to be from the comptesse. I hesitated : I called for a taper. If I opened the billets, I was
lost—and I knew it. One by one I took them up and deliberately held each over the taper until it was consumed.
Somehow, although that of the comptesse was first in my
hand it still remained there when all the rest were destroyed.
' Surely,' said the Tempter, ' there can be no harm in opening
this one—this last one, as I have resolved not to answer it.
It was too late : by a tremendous effort I brought the doomed
thing across the flame. It turned and twisted into a thousand
contortions as if determined to escape. As the heat caused
the leaves to open, it gave a vividness to the delicately-traced
lines, and I could distinctly read expressions of tender reproach. I turned away my head, by a sort of nightmare effort, but held the billet steadily in the flame, nor did I move,
nor scarcely breathe, till the subtle element, creeping to my
fingers, as if for a further sacrifice, told me it was all over ; I
was saved. I started up and ordered horses for Bloissy.
This is a small and beautiful chateau, about twenty leagues

from Paris, which my father had occupied, though he rarely resorted to it. Once I had been at the chateau since his decease, to find some papers which were deposited there. Report, I knew, had said the place was procured by my father to be a retreat for his young wife, too far from Paris for rumors of his infidelity ever to reach her. It was a pitiable device; as if a husband's dereliction can be long concealed from the trusting heart which has yielded all to him. Well, at night I arrived at this retired spot. How happy I was; the battle had been fought, and a glorious victory obtained over myself. I determined upon a course of self-examination. I took possession of the chamber which had been my mother's; I invoked her presence to enable me to preserve my purpose. I prayed to GOD—I *could* pray then—to give me strength. I have told you that my father destroyed all his private papers. In searching, however, an old bureau, in my mother's room, I found at the end of a drawer one of her letters to him. It was written during the second year of her marriage, and, I presume, on the occasion of their first separation, when my father, representing that his affairs called him to Paris, and would detain him there a considerable time, forgot her and left her alone in that sad solitude. She was still trustful and unsuspicious. Here is the letter," continued the Wœdallah, holding it out to me. I took it from his hands. It was written in a delicate hand, and blurred and blotted, apparently by tears; " Precious signs," the Wœdallah continued, " of my wretched father's repentance." I begged the Wœdallah to allow me to take the letter that I might again peruse it, and as it may lend an interest to the narrative, I give some extracts from it :

"Wednesday Morning.

" DEAR, DEAR WILFRED : I can not realize that you are gone, and to stay from me so long ; but oh ! my heart wants something in your absence; nay, it wants you, my **Wilfred**, at this moment to be at my side; to clasp your arm around me and kiss me, and tell me over and over again that you love me. Do you miss your poor Belle, even now, dear husband, and are you almost tempted to turn back and bring her with you? How dependent upon you I have been since we were married; but I must rely upon myself now; and it is well: I feel that it is for our good that we are parted, and this reconciles me." . . . .

Oh, gentle, loving, trustful wife! Oh, base, perfidious, deceitful husband. But she writes on:

"Do you know, dearest Wilfred, that I feel more like staying here, quietly thinking of you, than mingling in the gayeties of Paris? Somehow, I can not feel that I am a mother in yon strange city; and shall I confess it, dear, dear Wilfred, I have almost thought that you did not love your Isabella so much when surrounded by its attractions. Now, dearest, forgive me, for you know that I do not. believe this; the whole wide world could not make me believe it; only I love to have you reassure me, Wilfred, and then—how confident I grow again!

"*Six o'clock.*— My precious love, I am home-sick to see you. The day has been lovely thus far, but now it rains. All nature is so beautiful about me that I can not but be cheerful; and yet methinks this very loveliness of scenery, which so cheers us in bright daylight, lends a saddening influence in sweet melancholy twilight; sweet when we are together, dearest; melancholy when we are parted.

"My chief solace is our dear babe; all is new to him here, and he looks at everything with great surprised eyes, wondering what it means. He has just gone to his rosy rest. Heaven make his slumbers peaceful; for troubled waters sweep even over the bosom of infancy.

"*Eleven o'clock.*—I am going now, my dear husband, to my solitary bed. I have been talking this evening with old Hannah. She has entertained me by telling me of your childhood. I culled a fresh bouquet of roses for my table this morning, but an instinct of love led me to preserve in my chamber those *we* gathered yesterday. Where is the rose I gave you? And now love, my precious love, with a sweet, sweet kiss—good night!

"*Tuesday*, 3 *o'clock.*—Oh, my Wilfred, I have been so agonized! How have I been tortured! What shall I say or do? To-day Count Davrainville called. He was just from Paris; and do you think the wretch had the audacity to speak of you as—— Oh, no; I will not insult my Wilfred by naming it; but the count spoke of it so as a matter of course, that it seemed as if I should sink, although I knew every word was false. I assure you I left the room without waiting for a repetition of such despicable slander. Oh, Wilfred, Wilfred! what a load is on my heart! If I could only come now and creep into your bosom, and have you soothe me like a poor grieved child. Ah, were it not for my precious babe, how quick would I fly to you."

XLI.

"This letter," continued the Wœdallah, "this letter, written by my sainted mother, completed my reform. I knelt down by the side of the bed where she expired, and made a vow to live a virtuous life. I shuddered at my recent narrow escape, and could hardly believe it was real. Meanwhile my absence from Paris caused a thousand reports to be set in circulation. I abstained as far as possible from listening to them, and finally I was left in peace."

Here the Wœdallah paused again. He was silent so long

that I turned toward him, as before, and again perceived that
he was in extreme agony.　As he did not seem inclined to go
on, I said : " This can not be the end of your narrative ; excuse me, but I am painfully interested to know all."

" I will proceed," said he, hesitatingly ; " and yet I would
pass briefly over the remainder of my life.　We can not well
bear to look back upon opportunities of happiness unim-
proved, nay trifled with, thrown away, and for ever lost ;
especially is it painful when wretchedness and despair
come in their place.　But I wish my history to make you
wiser and better; and this effect might not be gained should
I stop here.　I had sworn to live virtuously, and I kept my
vow ; but let me tell you, my son, that man escapes not easily
the consequences of an evil course, however he may have
reformed.　The remainder of my history conveys this single
moral : ponder it well.　I will say, in brief, how, continuing
in my retirement, I became enamored with the only daughter
of an old French count, whose château was near my own ;
how the loveliness and innocence of the young Leila" (I started) "de Soisson appeared ; for she was lovely and innocent !
how I sought her, wooed and wedded her, and brought her
to Paris in triumph ; how, in consequence of my previous ir-
regularities, I became unreasonably jealous of my wife, who
had all the freedom and gayety of manner that distinguished
her nation ; how I believed that I had proof of her guilt ; and
how, when calling her to my presence, I accused her, I was
met with indignant denial.

"Ah, now my ' pleasant vices' began to be my scourge.　1
was not satisfied, but swore I would forsake a world which
virtue had deserted.　I made ample provision for my wife,
and after warning her that I should provide for strict watch
upon her conduct, took our young daughter, whom I already
began to hate because she resembled her, and placing

her at a nunnery to be educated, sailed for Scotland. Without making myself known to any one, I proceeded to the highlands, and having arranged to keep up a constant communication with the main land, I came hither. Here I resolved to do what good I might. I became interested in this simple-hearted honest people. My heart was not yet turned quite to stone. My daughter I frequently sent for, for I could not bear that she should altogether forget her father, though he could not love his child. You have no doubt heard how I was forced to leave this island, and to take up my abode in a neighboring one. I acted through the whole conscientiously for the good of this poor people. When the new steward took control, instead of returning, myself, I went to Paris, in consequence of what I had heard from my correspondent of my wife's conduct. I went to Paris, but she was not there, but living, as my agent informed me, at my château at Bloissy, in order, as he said, to enjoy still greater freedom. · I determined to stop this dishonor at all hazards. I repaired to the château. I sent for her, without announcing myself. She came, and on seeing me, threw herself into my arms and fainted. I placed her upon a couch until she should recover. Had I found her pale and emaciated, I should have believed her innocent, but although dressed with simplicity, she looked as healthful and beautiful as ever.

"She soon recovered from her swoon. 'Oh, my Wilfred!' said she, faintly 'have you returned to me at last?'

"'Hypocrite!' I said, sternly, 'cease such abominable deception! I know all—nothing is concealed. Your guilt has been discovered to me.'

"Perhaps you have some time in your life," continued the Wœdallah, "unfortunately bruised a young and beautiful flower, and as you turned to view the ruin you had effected, it would seem as if the tender petals, so full of rich and vario-

gated freshness, and life, and beauty, strove to convey, by their
very crushed and shrinking appearance, a reproach for your
wanton carelessness.   So it was with Leila.   Oh, what a look !
—so subdued, so injured, yet so reproachful !   My God ! how
can I bear to think of it !" he exclaimed, starting, stamping
his foot in frenzy, and then reseating himself.   "Yet she said
nothing; she would deny nothing; she would acknowledge
nothing.   So the fiend was busy with me, and I still believed
her guilt.   I bade her prepare to accompany me, and told her
she should never return to France.   The good old count, her
father, was dead years before, and the countess had long pre-
ceded him.   Leila seemed not at all distressed at the thought
of leaving, and the next day we set out for Bordeaux, and
sailed thence to Scotland; and then—we came here.   My
wife had an apartment appropriated to her exclusive use, and
a single female attendant.   She had books, and everything
necessary to her outward comfort.   But I never allowed her
to converse with me.   I never spoke to her.   Sometimes her
pride would give way to her love, and I could hear her address me tenderly : ' Wilfred ! oh, Wilfred ! this is not such
severe punishment, to be ever near you, under the same roof,
and to feel that you are near me, even if you will not speak to
your poor Leila.'   But she never alluded to her crime—never
denied it.   My own heart was wearing away within me.   I
held no communication with the world.   My life, in that terrible isolation, was one of the most exquisite and changeless
pain.   One morning our attendant told me her mistress was
ill.   I hardly knew what to do, but I bade her ascertain the
symptoms.   As she opened the door of Leila's apartment, I
heard my name called, and in tones that evinced extreme
earnestness and agony.   It was her voice.   I hesitated.   At
that moment she saw me, and shrieked.   ' Oh, Wilfred,' she

exclaimed, 'if you do not come, you will be fearfully judged, for ever and for ever! Oh, come, *come*, COME to me!'

"I rushed into the room, threw myself into her arms, and burst into tears.

"'GOD be praised!' she exclaimed, 'for this last mercy. Dearest husband, before my Maker, before him in whose presence I shall so soon appear, I swear I am innocent of any crime toward you. My pride, my sinful, foolish pride, is all I have to repent of. You have been treacherously deceived, my husband. Do you not believe me? Do you not believe your Leila, now that she is dying?'

"'Oh, yes! oh, yes!' I sobbed, 'I do believe you. Forgive me, my injured wife! I ask not GOD's forgiveness, but yours, yours I must have.'

"I can not dwell upon this scene. Her days were numbered; yet we lived a lifetime in those brief hours. And then I first learned how, for fiendish purposes, which he could not accomplish, my correspondent had lied to me; and how a noble pride in my traduced and suffering Leila prevented her from making an explanation. She died praying for blessings on the wretch who had embittered her life almost to its latest moment. She rests gently, beside my mother, under the shade of her own favorite evergreens, at Bloissy. And here am I, the stricken of GOD."

XLII.

The Wœdallah had concluded. I was not disposed to break the silence. The shades of evening began to gather; the waves grew black in the twilight; the roar of the ocean resounded with a more ominous distinctness, until darkness was over all the waters. The elements, the spot itself, the circumstances, combined to produce a thoughtful and exalted solemnity.

And there we sat; the gloomy meditator upon what had been, and the eager expectant upon what was to be—a strange companionship! There we sat; and while we lived upon the Past and Future, both forgot the eternal Present; the everlasting, never-ending Now, for which only man exists; for in it are embraced yesterday, to-day, and for ever. Vain mortal, to feed upon dim recollections, or upon the unsubstantial framework of false hopes, forgetful of that which is!

But must faith, must hope, be banished? Ah, no. "Does not the earnest expectation of the creature wait for the manifestation of the sons of God?" Assuredly. But it must be such faith, such hope, such expectation, as will make the Now important. Tell me of a faith that bids me forget the present, and I will brand it false. Show me a hope that connects not with what is, and I will mark it vain. Summon me an expectation that refers not to what I now am, and I will stamp it futile. And yet man sits, and waits, and hopes, and expects, and waits again, while nothing comes of it; and he murmurs, but still expects, and still the river runs by full flowing, and the current will not diminish: still the wheel goes round, but nothing is accomplished. And what has his faith, or his hope, or his expectation, done for him? Therefore, oh being,

created by the Almighty Father, when, unquiet and dissatisfied, thou busiest thyself with vain imaginings, know that thou
neglectest the present, and if thou neglectest *it*, thou art lost.

XLIII.

The Wœdallah had concluded; but it was evident that he
had given a very brief outline of his history. More I could
not ask. Yet how I longed to question him about the young
Leila. Here was a mystery unexplained. Not love that
beautiful creature! not love the only child of his unfortunate
and so much wronged wife! But the Wœdallah had not
said that he was regardless of his child. True, Leila had
confessed that she could not love him. Perhaps—— But it
was idle to conjecture; and I was consoled with the hope
that time would explain all. I now went back to myself. I
was adrift again. The narrative of my kinsman made me
tremble at the resolution I had taken a little before. Like a
successful ambuscade, it found me at unawares, and put to
flight my fancied security. Pleasure!—what *was* pleasure?
It seemed to me like some accursed fiend, whose end was to
accomplish my destruction. My heart acknowledged to itself
an incipient guilt, which waited only for temptation to be developed. In vain I determined on adherence to my resolution. It had vanished; I could not grasp it:

> " Ter frustra comprensa manus effugit imago,
> Par levibus ventis volucrique simillima somno."

Everything was gone save one absorbing idea, and that was
Leila. I say idea, for I had as yet no conception of the
ideal. Ah, beautiful and holy ideal! thou belongest not in
thy perfection to youth, for youth is attracted too much by
earth, to worship thee. The dross must be first expelled,
the flame of life must burn clear and pure—fed no more by

the exuberance of too young and turbulent blood. How do
the many, led away by mimic Fancy,

> ——" which, misjoining shapes,
> Wild work produces "—

create for themselves a world of ecstatic dreams, nurtured by
unhealthy excitements, consuming the heart by their false
fire, and withering up for ever the well-springs of life; leaving the fountain which should flow with perpetual freshness,
parched, and arid, and desolate.

But who can *realize* the IDEAL! They only upon whom
Imagination waits; who live in the momentous Present; who
yield not to Fancy's airy nothings—they shall enjoy it, for to
such Heaven has already begun.

XLIV.

WHEN at length I parted from the Wœdallah, and proceeded toward the village, my mind was in a whirl of excitement.
I saw in fancy nothing but Leila; I thought of nothing but
Leila; I gave myself up entirely to Leila. Why, to what
end, I did not ask—I did not care—I would not think. If I
could only have one more interview, that was all I would demand; all the happiness I required—one more interview! I
accused myself of rudeness, of heartlessness, of everything
unkind. I thought of every word she said; I remembered
every step; every gesture. How I dreaded to think of anything else: how I loved that night: how I hated the thought
of the morrow, with its dull routine.

My bosom full of these emotions, I reached the habitation
of the worthy minister. I paused upon the threshold. I
turned and looked up at the still heavens, so quiet and awful. The stars which lighted the dark-robed night glittered

with unusual brilliancy. Perhaps Leila too was at that moment gazing at them. I felt that she was. My soul drank in a world of bliss—of rapture—of indescribable ecstasy. Were we not in a perfect sympathy? Were not those stars charged with destiny—revealers of every fate? Could the transport have been greater were we gazing into each other's eyes? Glorious stars, truthful stars! and I repeated from the Orphic Hymns:

> Ἀστέρες οὐράνιοι, Νυκτὸς φίλα τέκνα μελαίνης
> Ἐγκυκλίοις δίνῃσι περιθρόνιοι κυλίοντεσ
> Μοιρίδοιο πάσης μοίρης σημάντορες ὄντες
> Ἐπταφαεῖς ζώνας ἐφορώμενοι, μερόπλαγκτοι
> Αὐγάζοντες ἀεὶ νυκτος ζοφοειδία πέπλον!

Were these feelings true? Did my heart beat with a healthful excitement? Was I experiencing what writers of romance delight to describe as first love? We shall see.

X L V.

THE next day there was to be a hunt for birds and birds'-eggs. As the St. Kildans subsist chiefly on wild fowl, and the eggs of the wild fowl, it follows of course, that enterprise, courage, and alertness, in securing these necessary articles of subsistence, form their highest accomplishments. The bold adventurer who by feats of extraordinary hazard captures the solan goose, as the creature sits upon a shelving rock a thousand feet from the toppling crags above, or secures the eggs of the lavie, deposited midway between the top of some fearful precipice and the foaming sea below, is regarded in the island as a hero, and his praises are chanted by the St. Kildan maidens in songs remarkably descriptive and full of fancy. The heroic actions of the men; their disregard of fatigue and peril; their success in these enterprises, and sometimes their untimely fate, form the main topics of St. Kildan song.

All the rocks in the island, which overhang the sea, are divided among the inhabitants in the same way as the land, and any infringement upon the right of possession is regarded as heinous as theft itself, and punished accordingly. Each family owns a "rope," which is absolutely necessary as a means of subsistence. This rope is made out of cow's-hide and cut into three thongs, which are plaited together, after having been thoroughly salted. This three-fold cord is remarkably strong, and with proper care will last for two generations. It always descends to the eldest son, and is considered equal in value to two good cows.

The St. Kildans seemed desirous to afford us a fair exhibition of their skill. The hunting party consisted of the boldest adventurers of the island; the most dangerous crags were selected, and the sport commenced. Two of the men, having made themselves fast to each other, began the perilous descent. First one would take the lead, throwing himself carelessly from rock to rock, when, darting away from his precarious foothold, he would hang suspended in the air, his partner supporting him by bracing against some sharp angle. It was next the turn of his companion, who, pursuing a similar course, did all he could to surpass his comrade, by exposing himself to the most extraordinary perils. After spending some time in this way, the two returned, each having secured a fine string of birds and a large quantity of eggs. Another couple succeeded these, with exploits still more hazardous, and thus the afternoon passed away; some ten or twelve St. Kildans engaging in the hunt. In the evening it was resolved to invade the territory of the solan goose. These creatures engage so industriously during the day in fishing that they are content to sleep soundly at night. They select some large rock where hundreds of them herd together, and after placing a sentinel to keep guard, abandon themselves to repose. The fowler, having a large white napkin tied across his breast, to deceive the sentinel, approaches cautiously. Too late the un-suspecting bird finds an enemy in the camp. The sentinel is despatched. The hunter lays him among his comrades, who, by this time waking up, gather round the unfortunate creature, bemoaning his death; nor do they think of flight till a large number of their company are killed by the active fowlers, who take this cruel advantage of their ill-timed lamentations.

Much sport was expected the present evening, for it was discovered that an immense number of these birds had set-tled upon a well-known rock on the east side of the island, inaccessible to ordinary pursuit, but presenting no insur-mountable difficulty to a St. Kildan. I had watched the whole proceedings during the day, accompanied by Hubert, who shared fully the excitement. As we were about start-ing for the scene of the new adventure, the latter said to me:

"Saint Leger, have a care; Vautrey is somewhere near us."

"Indeed," said I; "have you seen him?"

"I have been watching him," answered Hubert, "all the afternoon. His body-guard are with him; his foreign ser-vant and that peculiar imp of Satan whom you saw at the glen. They are apparently spectators of the hunt; but let us be watchful during the evening."

We both agreed to this, and proceeded to join the party. But two couples undertook the perilous descent to the spot where the birds were congregated. At one time hanging over dizzy heights, at another resting upon the edge of some slippery rock, so narrow that there seemed no place even for the slightest foothold, the daring adventurers proceeded on their perilous way. Below, at a distance of some thousand feet, the sea raged and foamed and lashed itself into a resistless fury; while the sharp projections seen here and there, from the different cliffs, indicated with a fearful certainty the fate of the wretch who should miss his uncertain foothold.

All eyes were turned toward the intrepid fowlers. Now the heart quailed at their fearful risks; now admiration for their extraordinary daring was paramount. In the midst of the excitement, and when all were watching the adventurers with breathless interest, I perceived a person coming cautiously toward me, along the side of the cliff. I knew the stranger to be Vautrey. He was, as I thought, alone; but on looking more carefully I fancied that I could detect some one following in the distance. The count was apparently getting a position to see the fowlers to the best advantage; at any rate he paused at the place where one of them had descended, and leaned over, as if watching their movements. My own attention was soon directed to the same object; and when I again glanced toward the count, I was surprised to see that the figure, which I had before observed, had approached near him, and that it was his attendant, the wild savage. There was something so treacherous in the manner of this hideous creature, that I at once suspected a plan hostile to myself; but on closer scrutiny it seemed as if he was attempting to come up, unobserved, with Vautrey. He certainly did not seem aware that I was near. So extraordinary did this appear, that I turned my attention entirely toward the count and his attendant. The latter approached nearer and nearer to his master; he would pause and glance hastily around, or skulk behind a rough mass of rock, and then resume his cat-paced course. I rose instinctively to warn Vautrey—I knew not of what; but I felt that there was danger. At the same instant the savage started up, ran swiftly toward the count, and rushing upon him with a sudden, desperate fury, seized him, and by a tremendous effort hurled him over the precipice — clear down into the frightful chasm.

It was so horrible, that I shrieked in spite of myself. In a moment the savage was by my side. I was upon my guard, yet he attempted no violence ; but throwing off a quantity of coarse hair from his head, I recognised the wild highland follower of the young Glenfinglas Donacha MacIan. His eyes gleamed with malignant fire ; his soul seemed completely abandoned to the furies. Pointing with exultation toward the cliff, and then to himself, as if glorying in the act, he turned, uttered a fierce highland cry, and disappeared in the darkness. This was the work almost of a moment. The alarm was given ; the whole party were in confusion.

But Count Laurent de Vautrey was not thus to perish. Strange, nay incredible, as it may appear, although he was cast by the sudden attack of Donacha completely clear of the cliff, still, after falling several feet, he caught the projecting point of a rock, which, although it wounded him severely, served to arrest his fall. But he could not hang by it ; it only gave him an instant longer to think upon his fate. It will be remembered that the count had chosen a place for his observation where one of the fowlers had descended. This choice saved his life ; for only a few feet below, the same fowler was cautiously ensconced upon a narrow shelf of rock, braced up to meet any emergency of his partner, who was linked to him, and was pursuing the way toward his eyry, some hundred feet below. As the miserable Vautrey caught upon the projection, he was seen, and the St. Kildan's energies instantly summoned for his rescue. The next instant Vautrey fell heavily down, but not into the fearful abyss that seemed gaping to receive him. The hunter watched him as his hold loosened on the crag, and by an extraordinary effort caught and held him in his descent. His partner was called

to ; the rope was tied round the count, and he was drawn to
the top of the cliff, lacerated and bleeding, but without any
mortal injury.

He was conveyed to the house of the minister. Hubert
and myself yielded our bed to him, and sought accommodations elsewhere. As I was the only eyewitness of the attack
made by Donacha, I hesitated to state that I recognised in
him the follower of Glenfinglas. I finally concluded to speak
of it to Hubert only, and leave it for him to make further
mention of it, if he chose to do so. My cousin heard me in
silence ; walked up and down a moment with a serious air ;
then stopping, exclaimed : "Saint Leger, mark my words,
Vautrey is a dead man."

"What do you mean ?" said I.

"A dead man," continued Hubert, "Donacha is as sure
of him as if his dirk was now through his heart. I know the
race ; but I did not know that Donacha, being a captive, acknowledged fealty to Glenfinglas. Dead ? yes, if he escaped
seventy times. Never did a MacIan lose sight of his victim,
when revenge sharpened the pursuit. The blood-hound has
not a surer scent ; the fox is not more subtle, nor the tiger
more fierce, nor the cat more stealthy, nor the tortoise more
patient, than a MacIan of the Black Cloud when pursuing his
enemy."

"Nonsense," said I ; "Vautrey will be on the continent
in less than three weeks, beyond the reach of all the thieving
caterans 'twixt this and Ben Nevis."

"You will see," said my cousin ; "and as for telling Vautrey who his enemy is, it will only alarm him without in the
least assisting to prevent the danger. No, no ; let him imagine that the savage undertook this as a revenge for some
supposed affront while in his service, and let it pass. I 'll not
put my finger in a dish of the devil's cooking, at any rate.

If Vautrey does not like the entertainment, he must cater better next time."

I saw that Hubert had a full share of highland prejudice,
which I did not care to interfere with; so I left the matter
with him altogether. I thought much about it, nevertheless.

XLVI.

IT was quite time for us to be away. I went once more
to the glen to make my parting salutations to my kinsman.
He received me with a composure I had not before witnessed
in him. He was evidently calmer and happier. We conversed some time, and I rose to leave. "My son," said he,
"I thank you for this visit. It may result in good. I will
make your adieu to Leila"—I had asked for her—"she is not
well. Perhaps you will see her when she leaves this."—I
started and changed color.—"Speak of me to the Lady Alice.
I remember her token; and, my son, forget not my farewell
admonition: '*At the parting of the ways mistake not; seek
no pleasure which satisfies not; be self-denying and be great.
Adieu.*'"

Much affected, I turned from the Wœdallah. I took my
last look at the stone grotto, at the delightful little valley, and
the scene beyond. I hastened to the village; all was ready
for our departure, and we set sail. Soon the threatening
cliffs of Hirta receded; after a quick passage, we made tho
coast, and sailed up the loch to Glencoe. Then came parting
with my dear friends there and then, "Ho! for England."

XLVII.

WAS the WILLIAM HENRY SAINT LEGER who started in the spring-time upon his tour, the same WILLIAM HENRY SAINT LEGER whom the early autumn had returned in safety to his home?

END OF BOOK FIRST.

BOOK II.

'Αλλ' ἐκδιδάσκει πάνθ' ὁ γηράσκων χρόνος.

ÆSCHYLUS, Prom. Vinct., 1002.

Time, as its age advanceth, teaches all things.

Δειλὸς δ' ὡ σκοτόεσσα θεῶν πέρι δόξα μεμηλεν.

EMPEDOCLES, Frag.

Ah, wretch! whose soul dark thoughts of GOD invade.

BOOK SECOND.

I.

Two years!

Time, that mighty leaven, which leaveneth the great current of events, maturing and evolving each in its appointed order, had worked restlessly through two more years, and these were added to the eternity of the past.

And what were those two years to me? Much, every way, save in actual results. In these, nothing.

The result is slow, and sudden. Slow, to the anxious, who labor wearily, and with an almost omnipresent energy, to bring somewhat to pass. To them, how painful are the steps toward the summit, though from the plain its towering height delights the eye! Sudden, to the wondering many who behold what has come to pass, but who know not, nor think, nor imagine anything of the preparation-work. To them how suddenly does the patient laborer emerge from obscurity, and take his stand upon the pinnacle of fame!

This is also true of that which tends downward to perdition: for men look at the results of evil, not at the causes of it. The result is nothing without exclusion. To attain it, one must exclude all that is foreign to the pursuit. If a man serves his passions, he must exclude the higher enjoyments of the moral and intellectual. Or if he seeks the intellectual, he must exclude those baser things which enervate and enslave the mind. If he determine upon moral and religious culture, he must exclude the influences of time and sense.

13

Self-denial, which is another word for exclusion, is a necessary exercise. No matter what the object sought; without it, all labor is empty effort. For no person can at the same time walk in a given direction and in a direction exactly opposite. Attempt first one and then the other, and no progress is made. Self-denial may be painful, or it may not be. It may be every way agreeable; or it may produce a strong and never-ending struggle with ourselves. The sensualist denies himself the exercise of virtue, to please his passions, excluding all the good influences of his moral nature. The worldling denies himself to gratify an ambition of one kind or another, excluding whatever interferes with his aim. The Christian denies himself, to satisfy his moral sense, excluding the various temptations which surround and beset him. Self-denial, then, is a philosophical exclusion of everything which interferes with a given rule of conduct, adopted with reference to a desired result. And yet we often encounter a certain class of *benevolents*, who tell us that "all things were made for man's enjoyment;" that "every creature of God is good;" that the happiness within our reach is the happiness to secure, and that self-denial, if it implies any constraint, is altogether wrong in itself; in short, is too absurd (because too disagreeable) to be tolerated.

These are dangerous philanthropists. They have no notion of the holy in man. They are earthly, sensual, devilish. They can make no distinction between the sensual and the intellectual, much less between the intellectual and the moral. They seem not to understand that the passions may lead where the intellect refuses to follow, and that the intellect may yield where the moral sense condemns. Not daring to avow their doctrine in all its hideous deformity, they cover it over with the gloss of an apparently improved humanity; and by picturing a perfect state of ideal sensuousness (I say sensuousness, because self is the sole object of contemplation in it), they lead numbers away irreclaimably to perdition. They are blind leaders of the blind.

Once more I utter my warning. Once more I say to those in the forming time (reader, if you have passed that period you are beyond my reach), yield not to the sensual; worship not as a divinity the intellectual; rest only in an object of the highest moral purity; anything less will end in death. For no man can find rest in an object unless that object is larger than his own mind, and no mind can rest in an object which is not illimitable. Therefore no merely earthly object can satisfy it. We must have an object of Good, which expands as the mind expands which contemplates it—and that object is GOD. He must furnish the aliment to sustain our souls. In no other way can the soul be elevated and restored to its original purity. Then, if we may not prevent the temptations which beset us, we can defy their power !

II.

As I pass from one period of my life to another, I pause, hesitating to go on,—like one who, after years of absence and of incident, comes back to scenes of a former day, and while he recalls, with all the vividness of reawakened memory, the thousand circumstances which gave interest then to the localities he revisits, is for a time spell-bound. He sees everything precisely as he saw it years before—the landscape, the mansion, a particular apartment, the books, the furniture, and the little articles of use or fancy which lie scattered around. Other things have been changing; these have remained the same; and they speak to him as if they knew not that *he* had changed. They speak the language of past days; they know no other, and therefore the wanderer lingers, ere he resumes his pilgrimage.

III.

I HAD returned from Glencoe an altered being   I felt that an epocha had taken place in my existence.   Before, I sought eagerly after some explanation of the outward form and manner of this world.   I expected to get at the centre from the surface.   The consequence was, that whatever I learned sufficed only for the occasion; it furnished me with nothing inductive.   I was still under a cloud, and saw everything "as through a glass, darkly."   As the tendencies of manhood began more strongly to be developed, those tendencies which received a tremendous impetus from the strange adventures of the previous summer, I felt that there must be some way to break the charm of mystery that enveloped all around me. So far, nothing had indelibly impressed me.   Perhaps I may except the meeting with the Woedallah and my acquaintance with Leila, which beyond question were the most remarkable incidents that had come to affect me.

From Leila I had heard nothing since leaving St. Kilda, though months had elapsed ; so that even the singular occurrences at that remote island began by degrees to lose their hold upon me.   Perhaps I was a little piqued at the silence of my fair relative, after her promise that she would acquaint me with her movements ; besides, I was in no state to cherish recollections of any kind.   I desired to get upon some system of living which would give me peace of mind.   At the same time I felt dissatisfied with everything I had ever tried. I longed for something new.   Restraint of every kind had become irksome, oppressive, unendurable.   I resolved to throw off the fetters of former influences, and learn afresh. This was a hardy resolution for a youth, but it was taken.

It is fearful indeed thus to unsettle everything which previous education has tended to make firm. But it is still more fearful to find, too late in life, that one is adrift. When 1 came home, I began to commune with myself. The return to familiar scenes had nothing of its usual enlivening effect upon my spirits. After a while I went to the old library. It was dustier and more gloomy and more neglected than ever; but I loved it. I resolved there, in that ancient and deserted chamber, to put my resolution in practice. I declared to myself that I would think with freedom; that what seemed to me to be inconsistent I would call inconsistent, and that whatever did not commend itself to my reason I would reject. Full of these notions of new-fledged independence, I began to study.

It happened about this time that my father employed as a tutor for me a man highly recommended to him by a particular friend, as thoroughly learned and accomplished; and in consequence, FREDERICK DE LISLE was domesticated at Bertold Castle. He was an Englishman by birth, a Frenchman by descent, and a German by education. How my father was induced to break over his prejudices and receive into his house any one with Gallic blood in his veins, I can not tell, except that he was carried away by the persuasions and recommendations of his friend, upon whose opinion he placed great reliance. De Lisle was about five-and-thirty; old enough to have formed settled opinions, and maintain them with powerful arguments; young enough to commend himself to my companionship by a tolerably youthful air and demeanor.

I have said that he was of French descent, but he had nothing of the easy volatility of the Frenchman in his manner or in his character. His parents were Huguenots, who escaped into England to save their lives and enjoy religious freedom. England, to be sure, could not at that time boast of universal tolerance, but the elder De Lisle had friends in the country, and to England he came. His son was born some time after the settlement of the parents in their adopted land. His early training had been carefully looked after, and by the assistance of the friend who had recommended the young man to us, he was sent to Germany to be educated. Naturally contemplative and thoughtful, without possessing a deep-reasoning, cause-discovering mind, the young De Lisle found, in the mazy philosophy of a certain class of German writers, a ready-made system, just fitted to his powers of contemplation, and apparently explanatory of the theory of life which he had been accustomed to consider as entirely beyond his grasp. He yielded, therefore, a blind assent to the new philosophy, and became, really without being aware of it, a very religious Pantheist.

I must not do him injustice. He had far more than ordinary powers of mind. He was a finished scholar, a proficient in the ancient and modern languages, and possessed of a fine critical taste. He had nothing of that malignant sarcasm which the doubter is apt to use with so unsparing a hand, with those who do not give a ready assent to his doctrines. De Lisle, on the contrary, was satisfied with having found a theory in which he could himself rest, and which he was happy to commend to others, without assailing their own. In conclusion, I must add, that he was naturally amiable, and his habits of life unexceptionable in every respect.

Such was the person (nearly twenty years my senior), who at this stage of my mental and moral progress was introduced as my preceptor and guide.

Was I not in danger?

IV.

I continued some time pursuing different studies under the direction of De Lisle, without making him acquainted with the state of my mind, although I was won by his pleasing, I may almost say fascinating deportment. Perceiving how much time I spent by myself, he at last asked me, in a delicate manner, what it was that so constantly occupied my leisure? I was not disposed at first to be communicative, but I finally concluded to give him a full account of myself. I proceeded with considerable trepidation to recount all that I had experienced, showing evidently by my manner that I considered the history of my mental trials very extraordinary. When I had finished, De Lisle, much to my surprise, smiled complacently upon me, and said, with an air half of commiseration, half of superiority:

"My young friend, you are but going through with the experience of every one who escapes from the thraldrom of superstition and bigotry into the clear atmosphere of intellectual freedom. You tell me of fears. Man in his proper element can have no fears. Why should he have them? *What* has he to fear? WHOM has he to fear? Is he not a part and portion of the Almighty Essence? Can you resolve his spirit into aught else? Can Self war with Self? Nay, resolve man into what you will, why should he play the trembler? Saint Leger," continued De Lisle, kindly, "I appreciate your distress; I feel with you. Trust therefore to my experience. The ground over which *you* are passing *I* have passed. I too have been in darkness; have had my apprehensions and my fears; my forebodings, my trials and my doubts. I have escaped from them all, into glorious liberty, and in the path which led to my emancipation I would conduct you."

I was completely astounded by these remarks. I supposed that all my experience was peculiar to myself; and I felt no small degree of mortification to learn that I had been travelling a beaten track, and that an ordinary acquaintance could readily describe the journey. I believe I may say with truth that I had a stronger intellect than De Lisle. But so completely was I surprised at this unlooked-for denouément, and so entirely did my friend seem to understand my position, that almost without knowing it, I yielded to his guidance. This certainly was not extraordinary. It probably would have occurred in ninety-nine cases of a hundred. At all events, it occurred in mine.

In this way did De Lisle come to exercise a great influence over my mind. Still, I made very slow progress in my new course. Although I had thrown all former opinions to the winds, they would steal back upon me unperceived, knock softly at the door, and Conscience (for the first time an unfaithful janitor) would let them in without my consent; true, they were instantly turned out of doors again; but they, nevertheless, gave me much trouble.

I was not without my misgivings. After all, I disliked to be convinced that my life had been one grand error, and that I had just discovered it. Was I then so enslaved ? Was not my reason free ? Had my education been so entirely perverted and misdirected ? These were questions that I asked myself daily, and daily I tried to answer them.

At this time I came across, in the old library, the *Tractatus Theologico Politicus* of BENEDICT SPINOZA. I perused this work with avidity. De Lisle, who seemed to understand my disposition, took care not to alarm my pride by too much dictation. He would assist me in a difficult passage, or throw in a remark to corroborate my author, and afterward leave me to myself. Although the doctrine of Spinoza appeared to be a sort of revival of the doctrines of some of the ancient Grecian philosophers, who held that "all things lie in the great body of GOD :"

Παντα γαρ εν μεγαλω τα δε σωματι κείται;

still, much as had been written on the subject of the Grecian theology, it had never in my own mind jarred with my established notions of the DEITY, or run counter to what I believed to be the truths of revelation. But this work of Spinoza struck at the root of all my former belief; entirely destroyed every previous hope ; swept everything away, and left waste every place in its progress. De Lisle saw my despondency, but bade me take courage. He remarked that Spinoza was not free from error, but that whatever man thought he might utter ; and if the *Tractatus Theologico* partook too much of universality (he did not say Pantheism), still it was a book to be well considered.

Just before this, EMANUEL KANT published his *Critique of Pure Reason*, and De Lisle procured it for my perusal. I found the task difficult, from the vast number of new terms employed, amounting almost to a new nomenclature ; but I did master it, and found some relief from Spinoza. Delighted at this, I sought for and read several other works of Kant. So far as he relieved my mind from the fearful system of Spinoza, I reverenced and loved him. Out of real gratitude I became his pupil. From one step I passed to another, until I was fully imbued with the philosophical tendencies of the new German school.

V.

My thoughts became daily more distracted. I had purchased intellectual freedom, and lost my peace of mind. I looked back to my former state, and felt how happy had been my ignorance. I thought of the GOD of my childhood, and a pang went low down into my heart. I seemed to have lost my humanity, and over the warm life-glowing structure of a hopeful heart had been raised a splendid and magnificent but cold and gloomy mausoleum. True, I was no longer a secondary object; I was a part of the sublime whole; a portion of very GOD; ever-changing, always being. But that which flattered my pride, destroyed my happiness; and I exclaimed in anguish to myself, "Who will give me back my soul?" But of all pangs, the most deeply mournful were those that gathered throbbing, throbbing, close in under my heart, whenever I saw my mother. I could not encounter her soft, kind, inquiring eyes, raised to mine, anxiously but silently asking what it was that disturbed her child. There was that in her gaze which I dared not meet. It was so pure, so peaceful, so heavenly—yet so troubled.

And could my new philosophy be truth-inspired and yet not support me under these fresh trials? In my distress I applied to De Lisle, but received no aid. It was not in his power to sympathize with me, for my feelings were beyond his reach. He could only beg me to have patience, and assure me that this was a last struggle between my former superstitions and my new dawning freedom; that it would soon be over, and all would be well. In short, De Lisle had raised a spirit which he could not lay; if he himself suspected this, he was careful not to alarm me by his suspicions, but maintained his usual calm and complacent manner.

I was truly in a pitiable state, but I did not relax my efforts to become free. I studied, and read, and thought, more assiduously than ever. My soul was consuming within me.

VI.

ONE morning, after the arrival of the post, a letter with my address was placed in my hands. The superscription was in a small, delicate hand, but every character was traced with singular distinctness. I opened it, and read as follows:

"I have not forgotten you; I never shall forget you; never —never! At present, I write few words. My father has conversed with me as a parent with a child. He has given me his confidence, and I love him. I owe this to your visit. I love my father, but do not release you from your promised friendship. Let it be abiding; GOD only knows how soon I may require it. We shall meet by-and-by, but not yet: for I know not now where my destiny will lead me. Wherever I am, my consolation shall be, that in the hour of need I have one real heart-friend. Your promise is pledged—do not forget it. "LEILA SAINT LEGER."

"This is from a Saint Leger to a Saint Leger—you cannot misconstrue it. "L. St. L."

How opportune was this short epistle! I read it over and over. I examined it word by word, syllable by syllable, letter by letter. The postscript, although written for explanation, pleased me less than the rest. I felt a thrill of joy, as the recollection of our last interview came back to me.

And this simple bit of paper, with these small characters traced upon it, had the effect to relieve my spirit, which was

on the verge of madness.　Here was humanity interposed between me and the fiend.　A young, beautiful, and almost unprotected girl claimed something at my hands; at least—
friendship; and whatever was or was not, in heaven above or
in hell below, if hell or heaven there were, yet here, upon the
round earth, something real, delectable (as I thought), holy,
presented itself, not for my contemplation—I had had enough
of that—but for positive thought, and action, and feeling.
Something objective, something real, something true.

Thus I reasoned then.

Of course I knew not when I should hear from Leila again.
It did not much matter, so long as I was assured of the tie
between us.　I could now resume my studies; I could look
more minutely into De Lisle's theory of life.　Strange to say,
I felt less repugnance to it than before.　I began to take a
deeper interest in things about me.　Nature seemed more
joyous; and when De Lisle said, in his tranquil tone, "See
you not GOD stirring through all this?—here, and there?
above, around, everywhere?　All is GOD, and GOD all!"—I
murmured an almost satisfied assent.

Yet I was not happy.

VII.

No, I was not happy.　Though I had achieved much in
serenity of feeling; and notwithstanding my repeated self-as-
surances of independence, I continued to ask myself what it
was I had gained, and where I stood.　The future, with what
seemed its solemn realities, had heretofore pressed heavily
upon me.　My great difficulty had been to connect the present life with a life to come, and to fix the relations between
them.　For faith had never been sufficiently cherished by me;
and without this great connecting link between two worlds,

what wonder that difficulties arose which I could not over-come.

But in my present course I was not to be distressed with doubts or fears. I tried to assume the quiet tone that characterized De Lisle, and with calmness to regard my vicissitudes as necessary results of causes long antecedent.

Unfortunately mine was not the temper for such complacency. Besides, I had a fresh enemy to contend with, one hitherto quite unknown; the idea of Death constantly obtruding before my mind. I had never regarded that consummation with any peculiar dread; but now, I could not indulge in a momentary anticipation but the grim form of the Destroyer would stalk before me and whisper, " I will soon be with you!" To be haunted with a positive coming evil is terrible; but to be tortured with fears of what may be, because we know nothing and will believe nothing of what is to be, is still more dreadful.

One thing I *did* know. Death would close all my earthly relations. The beyond—the beyond! what had *it* to do with me? So long as I kept my hold on life, my philosophy bore me along smoothly enough. I was a monarch; all were monarchs. But when I had to admit that at any moment this framework was liable to be shattered, resolved into the dust that composed it, and my spirit diffused into the elements, to enter into new combinations, or return to what it had been before it was me; when the obtrusive thought came that I should then lose my individuality, my identity—my very *self* —ah, my GOD! what terrific apprehensions would gather in clouds about my heart! It is impossible to describe these tortures. I tried to elude them by looking altogether earthward; but the more I sought satisfaction from the prospect, the greater became the power of these distracting influences. By what spectral horrors was I haunted! Yet I roused myself, and with all my strength determined to oppose and break the spells that were upon me. I found I could not cope with them single-handed; that I must call to my aid a superior energy; for my enemy was beyond any mortal power. Alas! I acknowledged no superior. So, in the moment of my chiefest exaltation I was in the greatest need.

VIII.

I will not enter more minutely into a detail of my mental struggles. They partook mainly of the character heretofore described. After battling with them for nearly three years, I felt convinced that I must seek some new ground or yield to them. To travel had always been my delight. The prospect of a journey was in itself a restorative to my spirits; and I looked to change of scene as my only resource. I cast my eyes toward Germany. There I should find religion, philosophy, and romance. There I could commune with men-students, with busy, active, independent thinkers. There I should behold every beauty of scenery, with wild legends of the past, and a present glowing with wonders; and the rising fame of several German names promising a bright poetic day for their fatherland, served also to impel me thither. I told De Lisle my wish. He at once fell in with it, and promised his influence with my father; for the same reason perhaps that physicians recommend change of scene to an incurable patient, to escape the responsibility of a death. I do believe De Lisle thought me incurable; but I will do him the justice to say that his attention to my education was faithful; and as he was every way competent, I made rapid advancement under his instruction. As was agreed upon, he sought an interview with my father, and obtained permission, with less difficulty than was anticipated, for me to visit the continent. The favorable report he was pleased to make of my studies, with the opinion that it would be advisable for me to continue them abroad, induced my father's consent to my going. As I have before said, he was an indulgent although an exacting parent; and if his children came up to his requirements his favors were not measured with a scanty hand. Of course he knew nothing of my inner life; my trials, my heart-strivings; but he knew the rapid progress I had made in my studies, and was willing and happy to reward me. One restriction was imposed; I was not to spend any time in France nor upon the route toward the place of my destination, which was Leipsic. Should I continue to deserve the praise of a diligent student, I was promised, after a period, the privilege of an entire tour of Europe.

How my heart beat with excitement at the prospect of breaking loose! I forgot every grief, every trouble, in the anticipation of what was before me. Even my grim enemy, Death, seemed willing for a while to make a truce, and was no longer thrusting his icy finger before my eyes. Still all did not go smoothly. My mother strongly opposed my leaving England. She could not endure the thought of my going alone to a foreign country, to be exposed to all the temptations to which youth are subject. She knew nothing of the state of my mind, as I have before hinted, but she saw that something disturbed my peace; and she pictured to herself the thousand evils a foreign life would bring upon me; especially she feared the corruption of my religious sentiments. Alas! she little knew the fearful change which had already taken place. Still it was settled that I should go, and the day fixed for my departure arrived. A little while before I was to leave, my mother desired me to accompany her into the garden, which sloped away from one side of the house. She took my arm and walked with me into a small arbor at the

extremity of a shaded walk. Then she threw her arms
around my neck and burst into tears. As soon as she became
composed, she raised her head, and laid her hand impressively on my shoulder: "William," said she, "dearly,
dearly as I love you, it would grieve me less to see you borne
upon your bier into the tomb than to behold you as I do about
to start upon this unhappy journey. But the decision is
made; you go; but oh, William, do not forget GOD; forget not
your Savior; and may the sweet influences of the Holy
Spirit rest upon you."

She kissed my forehead with fervor, and left me to myself.

I was sensibly affected, and felt ready to abandon every
new speculation, even my journey; but after a few moments,
the thought of what lay before me, should I remain, decided
me. I could not stay. With my father the leave-taking was
peculiar. He called me into his private room and requested me to be seated. His words were few and to the
point. "My son," said he, "in sending you to a strange
land I have not forgotten that you are still liable to the temptations which beset the young. But I have great confidence
in your integrity of character and in your self-respect. You
will travel alone to Leipsic. Here is a small chart, upon
which I have indicated the route I wish you to pursue. You
will perceive that I have not confined you to the direct course.
By following the chart, you will see, in a rapid way, France,
Switzerland, and some of the German provinces. Take this
letter. It is addressed to the learned and good Doctor Jo-
HANN VON HOFRATH. He was my early preceptor. He will
be your friend. He will receive you into his house, and will
direct your studies. I have written him fully. I want no
public teaching, where young men herd together for their
ruin. In parting, my advice is, that you bear in mind the un-
certainty of all things earthly, with reference to your account-

ability to God. Read the Sermon upon the Mount, and the parables of the Savior, the Proverbs of Solomon, and the Ecclesiastes. Make them your study. Do your whole duty, and receive a parent's blessing. May the Father of your fathers go with you, guide you, and bring you again in safety to your home."

IX.

All was ready for my journey. I was to leave at seven in the evening, and the clock had struck the hour. I bade our family farewell, shook De Lisle warmly by the hand, and departed. At last I was thrown fairly upon my own resources. "The world was all before me," and my spirits were as buoyant as if they had never known depression. I had first to go to London. Thence my route was to Dover through Gravesend, Rochester, and Canterbury. Arrived at Dover, I took a small packet for Boulogne, and the wind being favorable, we ran over in about six hours. I was in France. It seemed like stepping out from noon-day into twilight. Everything wore an unreal aspect. I was examined suspiciously, my passport subjected to the minutest scrutiny and myself with it. I spoke French well, and with but a slight accent. This occasioned considerable conjecture; but after some delay I was suffered to proceed to Paris. I took the route by Amiens, and stopped a few hours there to view the cathedral. On the evening of a dusty day in the latter part of May, just as the lamps had begun to be lighted, I entered Paris. I was full of excitement. I thought of the story of the Wœdallah, and every particular of his tale came vividly to mind. Here was the scene of my kinsman's follies; here he met his dreadful fate. But I looked further back. Here reigned Louis the Great; here schemed the mighty cardinal; and here they languished like other men, and languishing, died! Here succeeded the fifteenth Louis, who, as he could not aspire to the greatness of his predecessor, strove to rival him in the dissoluteness of his court. And now here I could witness the weakness of Louis the Sixteenth, and the seeds of revolt and misrule already springing up.

I could not stop in Paris, much as I desired to do so. My instructions were positive, and I went next to Lyons. Previously however to leaving Paris, I took my way to the rue Copeau, full of a feverish curiosity to behold the spot where Wilfred Saint Leger lived and loved, and was faithless, and where at last he fell by the hand of Moncrieff.

I found the house, but it was tenantless. Dust and cobwebs had accumulated over the gateway, and an appearance of desolation and gloom pervaded the building. I could not satisfy my desire to visit the garden. Away over the roof, however, I could discern the turrets of the nunnery, whose chimes told the Wœdallah so impressively the hour of eight. I pictured in my fancy the garden and the bower, and could see the combatants engaging in their fatal strife.

X.

I posted to Lyons. The journey was tedious, and rendered sufficiently disagreeable by the constant inspection and examination to which I was subjected. I was in haste to enter Switzerland ; so without stopping long enough to recover from my fatigue, I set off for Geneva. How great the transition from one country to the other ! In civil polity, in character, in manners and customs, in opinions and sentiments, in natural position and scenery, how unlike were the French and Swiss ! But I will not turn aside from the design of my narrative to picture all I saw and all I enjoyed. There rose the threatening Jura; here was Mont Blanc, and in the distance the snow-capped Alps. I felt grateful to my father for allowing such an agreeable departure from a direct route. From Geneva, I passed to the foot of Mont Blanc, and stopped in the pleasant village of Chamouni. I had admired the grandeur of Scottish scenery, but how did it dwarf before the stupendous Alp! What were even the wonders of St. Kilda, compared with the awful magnificence of the Mer-de-Glace, or the perils of the pass of the Tête Noire. I came next to the valley of the Rhone. Stopping a night at Lausanne, I proceeded through Berne, Luzerne, and Zurich, to Schaffhausen, where I first saw the Rhine. My spirits rose as I went on, and now my heart beat with an almost healthful glow. Passing through Carlsruhe and Mayence, I found myself, after a ride of a few hours from the latter place, at Frankfort-on-the-Maine. Everything about me told emphatically of the German. The steady aspect, the substantial bearing, the ever-present perfume of tobacco-smoke, and the thoughtful, composed, sedate look of the smokers, were indeed significant of my whereabout. I passed a pleasant day in Frankfort, and proceeded on my route.

On the evening of the third day after leaving Frankfort, I arrived in Leipsic. I was agreeably disappointed in the appearance of the town; and as we passed through the well-built suburbs, the sight of the beautiful gardens, which belong to almost every house, produced a cheering impression. I had reached my place of destination, and almost for the first time felt the fatigues of my long journey. I retired soon after I reached my hotel, and slumbered soundly.

XI.

· THE next morning I sat out early to seek the residence of
Johann Von Hofrath.   I learned that it was near the Rosenthal, a short way out of town, by a pleasant road.   As I was
anxious to look about me, I sat out for it on foot.   I had at
last arrived at the wished-for spot.   I was in the very heart
of Germany.   Here was the field where religious freedom
had triumphed, after a conflict which could never be forgotten.   What great names were associated with almost every
locality !   I felt that the ground was sacred.   Passing through
the suburbs, I came into the open country, and after a little
inquiry, stopped before the door of the learned professor.

A stout, hearty-looking servant girl answered my summons,
and requested me to enter.   I did so; and was ushered into
a neat but plain apartment, where I found a young girl, apparently about seventeen, engaged with her needle.   She
looked up as I entered, but did not start or blush, or manifest
any of the usual signs which an English girl would so certainly have exhibited on a like occasion.   With a modest but at
the same time a self-possessed air, she asked me whom I
would see?   I answered, "The professor Johann Von
Hofrath."   My accent, as I said this, in only tolerable German, made the girl hesitate; but she presently replied, "The
professor will be in soon; will you be seated?"   I took a
chair, and she resumed her work.   Of course I had little else
to do but to observe her.   I did not neglect the opportunity;
and as the image of that young girl has never been effaced
from my memory—as I have never forgotten her, and never
shall forget her—I may be excused for pausing to describe
her appearance.

She was of a little more than the ordinary stature. Her figure was slight but exquisite, combining grace with dignity. Her complexion was fair, and some light brown hair, in ringlets, partly shaded a brow which for intellectual beauty I had never seen equalled.

Her face was not altogether faultless, for the features, although singularly expressive, were not regular. Her eyes were blue, not very large, yet full of intelligence and feeling. Beyond all, her unpretending dignity and self-possession were unlike anything I ever beheld. They seemed to be derived entirely from a remarkable innocence and purity of heart, which rendered the possessor perfectly at ease under any circumstances. With what interest did I behold her! How did that interest strengthen and increase, day after day, when I came to know her! But I will not anticipate.

An hour passed, and the professor came not. Once only had the girl spoken, and then but to say that something unusual must have detained her father, who certainly would not be long away; and that if I preferred, I could walk into the library, where I would find books to entertain me, or I could stroll in the garden. As there was no hope in either case of any companion, I declined, upon the ground that I was fatigued by long journeying and my morning's walk, and that I preferred my seat by the window. I hoped this reply might provoke conversation; but she only looked at me a moment, in a half-inquiring manner, and then continued to ply her needle.

Another hour passed (it did not seem very long), and I heard some one approach the house. In a moment an old man entered, with another in his company. I did not doubt that my host was before me. I was at once relieved by the daughter, who announced him as her father. I handed Herr Von Hofrath my letter of introduction. He glanced hastily at it, and then seized me cordially by the hand, exclaiming: "This, then, is my young Wilhelm? I have been expecting you several days. You are welcome. Here is your home."

While he was addressing me, I was hastily surveying his appearance. He was of middle stature, with hair as white as snow, yet the bright expression of his clear gray eye, the ruddy hue upon his cheek, and his almost youthful step, showed him in the full possession of his faculties, mental and physical, and that he was enjoying in an eminent degree a vigorous age. The kind-hearted old man continued to address me words of welcome, which I know came from his heart, and which were peculiarly grateful to my feelings. At length he stopped, turned quickly around, and addressed his companion: "Wolfgang, this is a young stranger who has come to spend a season in our good fatherland. He is from England."

"The country of WILLIAM SHAKSPERE," replied the other, in a deep, rich voice, turning upon me dark, brilliant eyes, the expression of which I shall not forget. It was now for me to regard the last speaker, whom I had before scarcely noticed, so absorbed had I been in Herr Von Hofrath. Directing my attention to him, I perceived a man apparently not much past thirty, of fine stature, and with an air of majestic dignity. His features were symmetrical, but large and open. Rarely could so much beauty be found united with so much manliness. There was something about him which indicated such healthful self-confidence, hopefulness, courage, faith, that I was irresistibly drawn toward him.

"The country of William Shakspere!"—the words seemed spoken more to himself than to any one else, as if England was especially associated in his mind with Shakspere, and as if the name of Shakspere was to him a talisman

"Yes," replied the professor, "and my young friend will rejoice to find that Germans appreciate the great dramatist."

"And I am glad," said the other, recovering from what seemed a revery, "to welcome an Englishman to our German soil."

The stranger bowed courteously as he spoke, and a winning smile illuminated his countenance, making him appear still more attractive. As yet I had not heard his name, and I waited with a great deal of curiosity for the information.

"You have forgotten Theresa, or rather you will not recognise your little plaything in that tall girl," said the professor, "but I see she remembers you."

"Forgotten her!" said the other, good-humoredly, as he advanced toward my new acquaintance, whom he saluted on either cheek, while the latter appeared to find in the visiter an old friend; "forgotten her! I need not deny a thing so impossible. Theresa will not believe such slander of me."

Again I was disappointed. I did not hear the name of the Unknown.

At this moment we were summoned into the next room to dinner. It could not have been later than one o'clock. So much, thought I, for the simple manners of the nation in which I have come to live. I managed to get through with the peculiar varieties of a German dinner with a tolerable zest; but we had a far better entertainment than that upon the table. Our host was full of animation, and conversed with a lively humor, very remarkable in a person of his years. His friend was still more remarkable; for without appearing to do so, he went far beyond the professor. Whatever he said came forth without the slightest apparent effort; spontaneously, as if it was not to be restrained. I was perfectly amazed, at the strange, wild fantasies, at the magnificent thoughts which the stranger poured forth one after another without the least hesitation. What rapid perception, what keen appreciation, what humor, what pathos, what power! I was sure that I was in the presence of a great genius. But who could he be?

Theresa sat quietly, listening with interest to the conversation, and I too sat with open ears, eager to gather all that was said. Questions were frequently put to me by both, which I answered as readily as my knowledge of the language would permit. One thing I discovered during the conversation: that Herr Von Hofrath was a devout man. His remarks indicated this emphatically. A healthful tone pervaded all his words, and I knew his thoughts were genuine. How I loved the noble-hearted old man!

Dinner and its appendages over, we returned to the sitting-room. The stranger went up to a small table on which several books were lying, and took up one of them. "Blank!" he exclaimed, turning to Theresa: "what is this waiting for?"

"For your *imprimatur*," answered the maiden. "It is to be my album. You come in good time to put down the first line upon the first page." She took the book as she spoke, opened to the page, and said, "Proceed."

The countenance of the stranger assumed a thoughtful aspect. He took a pencil, and without hesitation traced the following lines. I translate them into English at the expense of both beauty and force of expression:

"THE ALBUM OF THERESA.

" Begun' and ' Ended,' two brief words, contain
The whole of what it is and is to be;
Farther than this all prophecy is vain;
Our eyes are blinded; we can not foresee
The shadowy future; yet perhaps 't were well
On its uncertain incidents awhile to dwell!"

"Your name! your name!" said Theresa, as he handed

her back the volume; "you must seal what you say." He took the book again, and in fair, distinct characters, wrote ·

"Goethe.

l had no time to express my admiration or astonishment on beholding the rising wonder of Germany; for the professor coming up exclaimed : "Wolfgang, something more Theresa will require of you than a half-dozen lines, scored by way of imprint on the titlepage. Come, be not a miser of your thoughts."

The poet took the book again, cast an almost mournful smile upon the maiden, and selecting another page, wrote as follows :

> "Strange are the thoughts that swell
>   Full in the breast —
> Thoughts that no longer dwell
>   Calmly at rest.
> They rise, they rise, be they mournful or glad,
> Like the sum of existence, both joyous and sad ;
> While the thoughtless laugh and sport and are gay,
> The sorrowing heart bleeds afresh every day ;
> Still the whirl goes round and round,
> Now 't is the happy laugh, then comes the plaintive sound ;
> Mingling, mingling joy and sorrow —
> To-day 't is joy, 't is wo to-morrow :
> And time rolls on, 'till our brief life has passed,
> And the grave closes over ALL at last."

"Wolfgang," said the professor, seriously, after reading what the other had written, "this is well ; nay, it is beautiful. But it is incomplete."

"Finish it; I pray you finish it," said Goethe, sadly : "T please your once loved pupil, finish it."

The old man, thus invoked, took the album, and leaving a short space, continued as follows :

> "Such is the history of existence *here*,
> Brief as it is, and incomplete, and vain,
> Not worth the living for, could we not look
> *Beyond*, and grasp existence infinite.

Without the promise of a life to come,
There's naught indeed to cheer the heart of man,
For all is dark within and gloom without.
E'en the brief sunshine of a happy day
Brings but the thought that when the morrow comes
Clouds will obscure the whole, and damp the joys
Just rising in the bosom. Is it so?
Is life so cheerless? Is it really naught?—
Without the promise, yes; but, thanks to GOD,
The promise stands for ever firm and sure—
'I am the resurrection and the life,
Believe in me, though dead yet shalt thou live.'
Existence, then, is not an idle dream,
If 't is probation for the life to come;
For here we're fitted for another world—
Fitted for weal or wo—how dread the thought!
And now we see why life's so full of change,
Of blended shades of joy, and pain, and sorrow;
Why we are tried, our bosoms torn, our hearts
Broken and crushed; were there no sorrows here,
Who would aspire to heaven, or seek the joys
That flow perennial from the throne of GOD?
Compared with which earth's glories are but dross.
Blest then be life, mysterious life: and blest
Be GOD who gave it; who created man
For wisest purposes. Nor farther ask,
But humbly seek his favor; learn of him,
And if you would be happy, DO HIS WILL."

The old man closed the book, and handed it with a solemn air to his young friend. The latter read what had been written with serious attention : then turning toward the professor, he drew himself up to his full height, and laying his hand impressively upon the arm of the other, exclaimed with dignity, " Doctor, do not misinterpret me: I BELIEVE."

XII.

I BELIEVE! Those words were full of meaning; and in every situation, under every trial, in the midst of scenes the most exciting, I have remembered them. Strange to say, the first lesson which I learned in Germany, the land of mystical philosophy, of wild theories, and of wilder doubts, was BE-

LIEF; and that too from the most remarkable individual, every way considered, of whom Germany could boast. But did Goethe *believe?* I will not vouch for it; I am only confident of his assertion that he did; and I will not think that he was a man to palter. But for my purpose it was of no consequence, so long as the exclamation was evidence of his opinion. And had I wandered so far to learn the simple lesson from *him?* Yes. And now, just as the German is ascending to his zenith, I, so many years his junior—I, who have had the same glowing energy, the same healthful, hopeful ambition, the same unchanging, determined aspirations—I must stop short when I have scarce entered the lists. I see the door closed upon me just as I essay to cross the threshold. The pitcher is broken at the fountain, and the wheel is broken at the cistern, before a draught of the refreshing waters is conveyed to me; and when the reward of past struggles and of present exertions appears to be close at hand, I am called away, to be here no more. GOD forgive me for this momentary murmur! I know that his purposes are true, and none can question them. Come then to my aid, O sacred Faith, in this moment of my weakness, and give me strength. Teach me that although we work here, and know comparatively nothing, yet we live always; that knowledge is and ever has been progressive; that the soul of man is as capacious as his aspirations are boundless, and that he has before him duration infinite, in which to labor and to KNOW.

XIII.

THE professor and his former pupil stood face to face. It was a striking picture. I wish I could sketch it. The poet, in the exuberant maturity of early manhood, with his open brow, his lofty look, and earnest demeanor, in which one might read much hopefulness and a strong will, great energy and an untiring patience, stood self-relying and firm. The appearance of the professor was more chastened, more subdued; exhibiting equal firmness, with less determination: a higher faith, with less self-confidence. Benevolence and every Christian virtue were in his countenance. None could mistake its expression.

At this moment Theresa, who, with myself, had been an earnest witness of what was passing, broke the silence; "Herr Von Goethe," she inquired, modestly, but with firmness, "do you honor the sacraments?"

"I honor them," was the serious reply of the poet.

"But do you attend upon them, believing in their efficacy?"

"All that is holy is efficacious; all that is Christian is holy," he said.

Theresa paused, as if not satisfied, then quietly seating herself, resumed her needle. At the same time the professor invited his guest to walk into the garden, whither they proceeded

XIV.

I was left alone with Theresa. I felt embarrassed; I knew not why; I tried to think what I should say to my new acquaintance, but could find no utterance for my thoughts. To me the silence was continually becoming more awkward, when Theresa, looking up from her employment, said: "The gentleman does not care to walk in the garden; he must be fatigued. Indeed," she continued, changing the person, "you must have had a toilsome journey; and you have left your home, too. But you have friends here in Leipsic?"

"None," I replied, touched by the simplicity of her manner; "none, unless I may call your father and yourself by that title."

"And why may you not? My father bade you welcome, and by that I know he is your friend. And if he is, then am I."

There was in this something so peculiar, so different from anything I ever before observed in my intercourse with the sex, that I was puzzled. Theresa seemed neither diffident nor embarrassed; yet if ever true modesty marked one's demeanor, it certainly gave character to hers. The more I considered, the more I saw to admire; until I came to the conclusion, which a subsequent acquaintance fully sustained, that she was by nature so artless and single-minded—her heart so free from guile—that she gave expression to her real feelings, and spoke unhesitatingly as she thought.

"Were you not unhappy to leave your home and come so far?"

"No, I was eager to get away."

"Ah! I perceive," said Theresa, with seriousness, "you have lost your parents: and absence was a relief."

My heart smote me at these words, for I thought of my mother. "No, you mistake me; my parents are both living, and I love them dearly."

"And yet you were desirous to leave them?"

"I was, though not for the sake of leaving *them*."

"I shall understand you better by-and-by, perhaps," said Theresa.

"I am sure of it," I answered; "so I will only say now that I come here to prosecute my studies under the direction of your father."

"What course do you commence upon?"

"Philosophy, I think; for I am deeply interested in the great German thinkers."

"A wearisome and unprofitable pursuit," said the professor's daughter, with an almost oracular tone.

I looked at her, surprised at the remark; but perceived no change from her previous quiet manner.

"Why do you say so?" I asked, curious to know how one so young could speak upon such a subject with such self-possession.

"Because you will soon become involved in a maze of theories; unsatisfied with one, you will turn to another, and then speedily to another; and so on through the whole, until at last you will mock at all, for they will all seem to mock at you. I say so, because I witness these things every day: but I make you angry," said Theresa, quickly, seeing my face suddenly flushed. "I have spoken what you do not like; I am sorry."

It was indeed true. She *had* spoken what I liked not, and my face was flushed, but not from anger.

XV.

THERE are periods in the experience of every individual marked by a crisis—sometimes of a moral, sometimes of an intellectual, sometimes of a merely physical nature; but still a *crisis*—when it is suddenly discovered that the advance, which we have flattered ourselves we have been for years making, is an advance toward ruin; when, on a sudden, we behold, instead of beauty and fair proportion, moral hideousness and desolation; instead of the perfection of intellectual attainment, an intellect oblique, and perverted, and abandoned; when, instead of a physical frame, full of life, and health, and strength, we discover the slow but certain approach of the insidious enemy, disease. I am sure that every one who may read this page, will recognise, if not in all, yet in some part of what I have here put down, judgments which his own experience will confirm. And in the cases I have mentioned, how very suddenly does the light break upon us; and then how unerring and how plain are our convictions—how un-mistakeable is our situation—how we wonder at our blind-ness, at our stupidity, in not earlier discovering it! And it is not by any uncommon incident that we are awakened to a sense of our position. The merest trifle, the most unimpor-tant occurrence, a word, lightly spoken, breaks the spell, and the scene is changed!

XVI.

INSTANTANEOUSLY I awoke, as from a dream. A fearful reality, which I dreaded to encounter, frowned forbiddingly upon my life's fancies, and suddenly they were no more. "You will mock at all, for they all will seem to mock at you. I say so, because I witness these things every day!" Had the learned professor, or the great Goethe, or any distinguished philosopher, closed an eloquent discourse with this sentence, I doubt if it would have affected me. I should have regarded it as a part of the system of the lecturer to utter such a warn-ing; but to hear from the lips of the young Theresa so strong, so earnest, yet so simple an argument, in language so clear and forcible, without the least appearance on her part of as-sumption or display, had the extraordinary effect upon me which I have just described. It seemed like the voice of an angel pronouncing against me. I had wandered from my fatherland in search of wisdom, and was I to receive such a lesson from this maiden! Were the teachings of all the learned doctors to be set at naught for so simple a remedy? With the haughty Syrian, I was ready to exclaim: "Are not Abana and Phar-par, rivers of Damascus, better than all the waters of Israel? May I not wash in *them*, and be clean?"

I felt the impotence of the question before I could myself

frame a response. At a distance how had I regarded the great German thinkers! Close at hand, in very communion with them, how did she, the young Theresa, regard them? What a comment did the answer to this question involve! The words of the apostle now glowed before me: "Beware lest any man spoil you through philosophy and vain deceit." But if I gave up all hold upon my philosophy, I was lost. I had no other resource; I could go nowhere else.

XVII.

These thoughts passed like lightning through my brain. One minute had ticked slowly away, and the revolution was complete. Theresa sat regarding me with wonder. She could easily see that something had powerfully affected me; but farther all was a mystery. Her voice brought me back to myself.

"What have I said?—what mistake have I made?—why are you displeased?" she said.

As calmly as I could, I assured her I was not displeased, but suddenly indisposed, in a way I would hereafter explain; and, pleading fatigue, attempted to take my leave, that I might revisit my hotel. The professor at this moment came in with his guest, and positively forbade my doing so. "Your apartment has been ready for you these two weeks, and if my young friend is indisposed, he may go to it at once."

I was glad to accept his offer. I was shown to a neat and delightfully situated chamber, where everything was prepared with a due regard to comfort and convenience. I felt too agitated to think more at present. Besides, I was really weary. Early as it was, I drew the curtains and got into my bed. I fell into a disturbed and uneasy slumber, which lasted well into the following morning.

XVIII.

I DID not awake until a late hour. The day was fine, and looking from my window, I found the view delightful. The house was nearly surrounded by an extensive garden, in tasteful walks and labyrinths, at the extremity of which was a summer-house. As I enjoyed the prospect, I saw Theresa coming down an avenue, accompanied by her distinguished guest. They were in close and apparently interesting conversation, although I could not perceive anything peculiar in the manner of either. The former maintained her modest self-possession; the latter the same noble and dignified demeanor. He stopped often to examine the most minute things, to which he would call the attention of his companion. Now the variegated colors of a strange flower would arrest his steps; he would then pause, and regard with singular scrutiny the movements of a spider which had woven his mesh across the path: perhaps a butterfly would next attract him, or a bird upon the wing, or an insect in the air. Nothing seemed to escape his observation, and nothing appeared unworthy of it. Presently the two turned and entered the house. I hastened down, and in answer to the kind inquiries of all, was happy to declare myself "much better in every way."

XIX.

I HAD determined to explain to Theresa the cause of my singular conduct the previous evening, and was in hopes that she would make allusion to it. She did not, however, but

15

evidently avoided it; doubtless with a design to save my
feelings. After breakfast, the professor and his guest went
out together; the former apologizing to me for the seeming
neglect, on the ground that his engagements for the day were
imperative. I know not why, but I dreaded to be left alone
with Theresa. She, however, appeared desirous to prevent
the time from becoming irksome to me. She asked me no
questions, but herself started topics for conversation.

"I have received a gift this morning," she remarked;
"something you would be curious to see; and I think I may
show it to you, although it is not to be made public. It is
well known that our friend Goethe has been a long time engaged upon a tragedy, and that he has now nearly completed it. Last night he added, or rather inserted, a scene
in it, and he was kind enough to give me a transcript, declaring that it was half mine."

So saying, Theresa produced the manuscript, remarking: "I
believed you would be interested to read it, and here it is."

The thoughts were evidently suggested by what had passed
the day previous. What power of appropriation has that
man! As it forms a part of the same subject, I insert it here;
although it may seem a departure from the plan I have thus
far pursued, it is not really so. I copy it in the German. A
translation would spoil its beauty :

Margarete. Versprich mir Heinrich!
Fauſt.   Was ich kann!
Margarete. Nun ſag', wie haſt Du's mit der Religion?
       Du biſt ein herzlich guter Mann,
       Allein ich glaub', Du hältſt nicht viel davon.
Fauſt. Laß das, mein Kind! Du fühlſt, ich bin Dir gut ;
       Für mein Lieben ließ ich Leib und Blut,
       Will niemand ſein Gefühl und ſeine Kirche rauben.
Margarete. Das iſt nicht recht, man muß d'ran glauben!
Fauſt. Muß man?
Margarete.   Ach! wenn ich etwas auf Dich könnte!
.   Du ehrſt auch nicht die heiligen Sakramente.
Fauſt. Ich ehre ſie.

Margarete.   Doch ohne Verlangen.
    Zur Messe, zur Beichte bist Du lange nicht gegangen.
    Glaubst Du an Gott?
Faust.   Mein Liebchen, wer darf sagen,
    Ich glaub' an Gott?
    Magst Priester oder Weise fragen,
    Und ihre Antwort scheint nur Spott
    Ueber den Frager zu seyn.
Margarete. So glaubst Du nicht?
Faust. Mißhör mich nicht, Du holdes Angesicht!
    Wer darf ihn nennen?
    Und wer bekennen:
    Ich glaub' ihn.
    Wer empfinden?
    Und sich unterwinden
    Zu sagen: Ich glaub' ihn nicht.
    Der Allumfasser,
    Der Allerhalter,
    Faßt und erhält er nicht
    Dich, mich, sich selbst?
    Wölbt sich der Himmel nicht dadroben?
    Liegt die Erde nicht hierunten fest?
    Und steigen freundlich blickend
    Ewige Sterne nicht herauf?
    Schau ich nicht Aug' in Auge Dir,
    Und drängt nicht Alles
    Nach Haupt und Herzen Dir,
    Und webt in ewigem Geheimniß
    Unsichtbar sichtbar neben Dir?
    Erfüll' davon Dein Herz, so groß es ist,
    Und wenn Du ganz in dem Gefühle selig bist,
    Nenn' es dann, wie Du willst,
    Nenn's Glück! Herz! Liebe! Gott!
    Ich habe keinen Namen
    Dafür! Gefühl ist Alles;
    Natur ist Schall und Rauch,
    Umnebelnd Himmelsglut.
Margarete. Das ist alles recht schön und gut;
    Ungefähr sagt das der Pfarrer auch,
    Nur mit ein Bischen andern Worten.
Faust. Es sagen's aller Orten
    Alle Herzen unter dem himmlischen Tage,
    Jedes in seiner Sprache;
    Warum nicht in der meinen?
Margarete. Wenn man's so hört, möcht's leidlich scheinen,
    Steht aber doch immer schief darum;
    Denn du hast kein Christenthum
Faust. Lieb's Kind!

Here was the dreaded subject back again. I felt that I had not strength to grapple with it, for I knew how futile was the contest. I determined if possible to give my mind some repose; at least for a few days. After expressing my thanks, therefore, for the perusal of the manuscript, I asked Theresa if she would not take a stroll with me in the Rosenthal. She assented, and thither we proceeded.

NOTE.—The Editor of Mr. Saint Leger's memoirs trusts that he will find favor with his less literate readers, by appending a translation of the preceding extract, from the excellent prose version of "Faust" by Mr. HAYWARD.

MARGARET. Promise me, Henry!

FAUST. What I can.

MARGARET. Now, tell me: how do you feel as to religion? You are a dear, good man, but I believe you don't think much of it.

FAUST. No more of that, my child! you feel I love you: I would lay down my life for those I love, nor would I deprive any of their feeling and their church.

MARGARET. That is not right; we must believe in it.

FAUST. Must we?

MARGARET. Ah! if I had any influence over you! Besides, you do not honor the holy sacraments.

FAUST. I honor them.

MARGARET. But without desiring them. It is long since you went to mass or confession. Do you believe in GOD?

FAUST. My love, who dares say "I believe in GOD?" You may ask priests and philosophers, and their answer will appear but a mockery of the questioner.

MARGARET. You don't believe, then?

FAUST. Mistake me not, thou lovely one! Who dare name him? and who avow: "I believe in him?" Who feel—and dare to say: "I believe in him not?" The All-embracer, the All-sustainer, does he not embrace and sustain thee, me, himself? Does not the heaven arch itself there above? Lies not the earth firm here below? And do not eternal stars rise, kindly twinkling, on high? Are we not looking into each other's eyes, and is not all thronging to thy head and heart, and weaving in eternal mystery, invisibly—visibly, about thee? With it fill thy heart, big as it is; and when thou art wholly blest in the feeling, then call it what thou wilt! Call it Bliss!—Heart!—Love!—GOD! I have no name for it! Feeling is all in all. Name is sound and smoke, clouding heaven's glow.

MARGARET. That is all very fine and good. The priest says nearly the same, only with somewhat different words.

FAUST. All hearts in all places under the blessed light of day say it, each in its own language; why not in mine?

MARGARET. Thus taken, it may pass; but, for all that, there is something wrong about it, for thou hast no Christianity.

FAUST. Dear child!

END OF BOOK SECOND.

BOOK III.

’Απ’ ὄμματος βέλει φιλοίκτῳ,
Πρέπουσά θ’ ὡς ἐν γραφαῖς, προσεννέπειν
Θέλουσ·

Æschylus, Agamem, 233.

The trembling lustre of her dewy eyes,
Their grief-impassioned souls controlling;
That ennobled, modest grace,
Which the mimic pencil tries
In the imaged form to trace,
The breathing picture shows.

Εὔχομαι δ’ ἀπ’ ἐμᾶς τι
’Ελπίδος ψύθη πεσεῖν
’Ες τὸ μὴ τελεσφόρον.

Ibid., 969.

Return, oh faith, thy seat resume,
Dispel this melancholy gloom,
And to my soul thy radiant light impart.

BOOK THIRD.

I.

THERESA VON HOFRATH! how can I delineate thy character—how can I approach thee, sweet, gentle, heavenly Theresa! A sacred awe comes over me, a mysterious reluctance pervades my spirit, as I bring back the recollection of the days passed with thee. And shall I again summon those fond associations, and recall those happy hours? Can I bear to dwell upon them, and live them over? It is an agonizing happiness—a blissful torture!

II.

I AM calm, nevertheless, as I pencil these words—very calm. Why should I not be calm? The days of the years of my life are numbered; but the allotment is universal, and not to be dreaded. "Birth" and "Death" are words merely. "Change and change" define them. Even now I see the world recede; but I carry myself about with me wherever I am transported. Therefore hath Memory her portion in my immortality.

Yes, I am calm when I speak of Theresa Von Hofrath. Why should I not be calm? In her gentle conduct, in her quiet life, in the mild dignity of her nature, in her child-like simplicity, in her deep, unwavering faith, what is there, I ask, in the recollection of all these, to make my heart beat the quicker, or cause my pulse to fluctuate with an unwonted trembling?   Yes, I *am* calm; very calm!

III.

THERESA VON HOFRATH, under GOD, thou didst save my soul!   Without thee I had been lost.   Yes, I see the precipice over which I was hastening.   I see thy hand extended to save.   Which, which shall it be?   A plunge—a struggle—death; or a turning aside—a conflict—everlasting life?

Shall I see thee never more, Theresa?   Shall thy deep, earnest, soul-absorbing eyes never again meet mine? never again!   Shall heart and soul never again beat in sympathy with heart and soul, never again revel in the ecstatic elysium of a new communion?

I WILL NOT believe it, although a god should declare it to me.   Sooner will I believe that heart and soul and GOD are nothing.

IV.

BE still, rebellious tempter.   Dare not to disturb the calm current of my thoughts.   Down, ye mocking suggestions. Away, ye dark, thick, brooding fancies—hence, all! all! At any rate, your time is not *yet*.   The mysterious union of body and spirit still is, though faintly indeed does Vitality in me perform her office; but the wheel is not yet broken: I am at the helm still! therefore, Doubt, thou supple, coward slave of evil, avaunt!

I WILL that I believe.

I DO believe!

V.

Why have I to fight this battle over and over? Why this never-ceasing, never-ending wrestling, "not with flesh and blood only, but with principalities, with powers, with the rulers of darkness of this world, with the spiritual powers of evil in the heavens?"

Have, then, spirits of evil this power to assail us? Would that I were convinced of it! for though thronged by a myriad of fiends, I could glory in the contest; joyfully could struggle with anything, with all things, *out of myself;* but to find my enemy within my gates; to cherish in my bosom the viper that stings me; to be forced to keep it *there,* yet keep it *under*—ah, that is the fearful fight!

Μαχη δῆ, φαμίν, 'ἀθανατος ἐστιν ἡ τοιαύτη, καὶ φυλακῆς θαυμαστῆς δεομένη!

The world beyond is the world of reality; this, the world of shadows and of images. Yet to take leave of this commodious frame-work; to step out alone and unattended upon thy journey to ———— *where?* Has the thought no terror? Does it not bring an inner shuddering? No. *It doth?* NO!

VI.

Well, what was I to do, now that I was upon German ground, and at Leipsic? I first determined to know what was going on among the young men. Poor wretch, how I stood, beating my head against the wall, without being able to burst through the adamantine gates that kept me a prisoner! How I longed to break the shell and get at the kernel—how

I struggled to come into the light, out of this darkness! I
am aware that a class of persons will inquire : "What was
the matter with this youth? Had he not kind friends, bright
prospects, health, vigor, and sufficiency of wealth? What
did he want?" My only answer to such is, I labor but for
those who sympathize in my narrative; and if in the detail of
this true experience I come in the slightest degree to the assistance of kindred minds, struggling in similar contest, I am
content.

I was eager then for some explanation of what *was;* I
longed to KNOW. Had the alternative been placed before me,
as before the first man, " In the day thou eatest thereof thou
shalt surely die," I should have incurred the penalty without
aid of the tempter serpent or the woman. My previous intercourse with the world had thrown no light upon the mystery of living. I had thus far seen everything under constraint. Even my wild excursion to St. Kilda, the memory
of which I dearly cherished, did not help me in the difficult
point. Like the child who must break his bauble to find out
how it is put together, so I proceeded to break in pieces the
patchwork which makes up society and composes what is
ordinarily called life.

What youth has not experienced a chilling sensation when
first introduced, after leaving home, to a circle of acquaintances, whose very cheerfulness depresses him, and whose
stirring but welcome greeting causes his heart to sink low
down in his breast! But I had no such feelings. So great
was my curiosity to make acquaintance with things as they
were, without the restraint, I may say, of GOD or man, upon
my thoughts and actions, that this was the absorbing desire
of my soul. After all, considering the recluse life I had led,
and the strong passions which were seeking development
within me, this could not be wondered at.

VII.

I LIVED with Herr Von Hofrath.   I had a quiet apartment,
with a pleasant prospect from the window, and the large and
well-selected library of the professor afforded abundant occupation when I was disposed to read.   He himself was at all
times a cheerful as well as an instructive companion.

The first feeling that I enjoyed was a sense of freedom.
Not the slightest restriction was put on me.   The professor
conversed with and advised me, started new ideas, awoke in
my mind new trains of thought; but he did not attempt to
fetter me; he laid down no rules; insisted upon no condi-
tions; prescribed no limits.   He proceeded to point out what
course I should adopt, and what lecturers it was wisest to follow.   When he saw he had made a suggestion not to my
taste, he forbore to press it, but turned to something else;
there was no dictation, no air of superior knowledge or intelligence.   He treated me as a fellow-laborer, not as a child;
and while he gave me, with the most unaffected simplicity,
the benefit of his experience, he would always congratulate
me that I was young, and had the years of my life in expectation.   The importance thus given to living, had a wholesome
effect upon me, for I beheld in the professor a bright example of it.

I was not long in making friends with a good number of
my fellow students.   My several acquirements, purchased by
years of severe study, stood me in good part.   I could converse fluently in many of the modern languages, and thanks
to De Lisle, was well acquainted with ancient literature.   At
that time, there was scarcely an Englishman at Leipsic.   This
of itself enabled me to make acquaintances readily, for being

looked upon with rather an inquisitive eye, the young men were willing enough to gratify their curiosity, while they could at the same time show civility to the object of it.

So I soon came to feel at home, wherever I was, and then I went to work at my old lesson, the *what* and the *why*. My first marvel was to witness the strange way the mad fellows who called themselves students, lived. The apparent contradiction in their actions from one hour to another, and the singular mixture of chaos and order in all they undertook, struck me as inexplicable. Young men who were engaged over night in the wildest dissipation, I beheld the next morning seriously engrossed by an ethical lecture from Von Hofrath, or engaged upon some abstruse subject, requiring the most patient and attentive consideration. They would take full notes of every lecture, and afterward rewrite them in order. The wildest and most blasphemous opinions were freely bandied and discussed, and even when considered untenable, were not altogether reprobated.

Everything seemed in a formative state. Darkness brooded, while light illumined. The good and the evil, the sensual and the spiritual, the sacred and the sinful, were jumbled, discussed, pulled in pieces, and put together. Still nothing came of it, so far as I could see. Then I asked myself, What are they doing?—to what end are they living?—what will come to pass out of this?

VIII.

Among the students was one Friedrich Kauffmann, a native of Breslau. This young man happened to meet me immediately after my arrival in Leipsic, and without introduction on either side we became acquainted and were friends.

His appearance first attracted me toward him. He was

about twenty years old : his stature rather below the ordinary height; his chest and shoulders large and unwieldy; his countenance, though thoroughly German, animated. Light brown hair, inclined somewhat to curl, fell negligently over his forehead, the only beautiful feature he possessed, and that was indeed beautiful. Imagination and wit, reflection and the power of analysis, honesty and singleness of purpose, were all expressed in the clear outline. His face was ordinary; his eyes blue —not handsome, but expressive. To look at him, one would suppose that he had a head, or rather a forehead, that did not belong to him. Not that his other features were ugly or unexpressive, but because that was so perfect.

This Friedrich Kauffmann was honest. Before Heaven I believe it. He was an enthusiast without being a hypocrite, or self-deceived. He knew always what he was doing, but he was still an enthusiast. I could trust to Kauffmann, and we learned to like each other. I do not mean that I confided in him; my bitter disappointment with De Lisle had taught me a lesson; besides, with me the day had passed for all that; but I could talk and compare views, and reason, with my new friend, and hear him in return with real satisfaction, for I knew he spoke ingenuously.

There was a club at that time in Leipsic, called "THE FREE SPEAKERS." It embraced but twelve members in all. They met almost every evening at an appointed rendezvous, and uttered, or professed to utter, what was in their minds. Their motto was,

> *" Evil unspoken breeds evil.*
> *Good unspoken is barren."*

Friedrich Kauffmann was the originator and leading spirit of the society. We had not been long together before he urged me to join it. It was a select and sacred circle of true men, he said, and he could in no way show his friendship for me so much as to ask me to make one in it. I did not relish this open principle of the club, provided indeed one was really honest and lived up to it. On the other hand my curiosity prevented me from altogether declining the offer. " Tell me first " said I, " what do you mean by

> *" ' Evil unspoken breeds evil.*
> *Good unspoken is barren ?'*

I had supposed that half the victory was gained over ourselves when we confined our evil thoughts to our bosoms."

" Not so," answered Kauffmann with earnestness: " Give your evil thoughts so much as a place to harbor, and they will spin their slimy meshes over the fine framework and around the delicate tendrils of your heart and lay their eggs there, and these will hatch and breed, while you, their miserable victim, dare not let them out for lack of courage, or for fear of harm they will do to others. No; turn out the unclean spirits, and if you choose, pray for some herd of swine, that they may enter into them, and let the whole brood run violently down a steep place into the sea and be choked."

" But is it not enough that I drag these forward into my own presence and there pass sentence upon them ? Are not others made worse by the knowledge that I have within me so much that is unworthy ?"

" No, Saint Leger, it is not enough ; you can not rid yourself in this way. What says your Shakspere :

> *" ' May one be pardoned and retain the offence ?'*

" Summon the culprits into your own view. Nay, banish them, as you try to persuade yourself you have done"—

" Heaven should be my witness to that," interrupted I.

" Ay, Heaven in thy mouth, but in thy heart — the evil still grows and bristles and swells ; but say it out, with the honest purpose of riddance, to true sympathizers, to manly men. Yet stay; let me explain myself more calmly.

"I take it for granted that you have evil in you. Whether much or little, it matters not; how it came there it matters not; when it came, it matters not; that is, not for my argument. Now your moral sense (never mind about a definition for that either)—your moral sense condemns the evil; while your baser sense tempts you to the practice. I do not advocate a dissemination of your evil thoughts, neither do I advise an indiscriminate out-speaking of them to whomever you chance to meet; nor a mere babbling of words, without thought or reflection, even to a friend. For to disseminate evil, because it is in you, is monstrous; to open your heart to the simple or the scorner, is folly; to utter words without meaning, is idiocy. But I do advise to the selection of friends who have a kindred purpose; who shall be searchers after TRUTH, and with such to be a free speaker. Call it a confessional, if you will; save that the confessions are mutual, which of itself alters their character. Yet believe me, the effect upon the heart is ennobling. The good we utter is, by that act, made permanent within us, while it enriches those to whom we impart it. The evil we boldly bring to light and expose, by that act, perishes, while it has no power to corrupt. Therefore we gather strength, instead of betraying weakness, when we speak out to friendly minds what is in our hearts."

"But is there not danger," said I, "that in a society like yours, there will grow up a purpose of display, rather than of open ingenuous speech? Would it not be well to select one friend for such an object? and," I added, for the sake of provoking further discussion, "would it not be better that that one should be of the softer sex?"

"Foolish of heart," exclaimed Kauffmann, "that can not understand; or else, which I the rather judge, oh, perverse of mind! that will not; be it known that in the intercourse of two minds only (which is your first suggestion) there is induced a moral and intellectual covetousness—I call it by that name, having no better at hand—since what is uttered by either, whether of good or of evil, is not out-spoken, but confided. The friends get to be confidants, and selfishness of purpose gradually becomes paramount in both. The good is approved, to be sure, but it is at the same time hoarded up for use on proper occasions, while, if the truth were known, the evil is served much the same way."

"Well," said I, "what say you to my second suggestion, the selection of one of the other sex?"

"Are you jesting with me, fellow-student?"

"No."

"Do you seriously ask whether, instead of healthful intercourse with manly intellects, it is not better to select for the object a woman, or some mawkish love-sick girl? Why, a woman will make for you a very holy sentiment out of a wicked reality, and a kind of divine beatitude out of a wicked sentiment. She will bid you cherish your sins, so long as they be daring, high-wrought, and have a smack of the super-sensual about them; so long as you will lisp your confessions into her ear. Nay, say to a woman that you are a devil incarnate, and she will beg you to be a devil still, so long as you are a very valiant devil, and belong to her. Saint Leger, remember what I tell you; trust in MEN. Not to one, in confidence, but open your heart to true hearts. Dare to seem what you are. Resolve to be what you seem. Above all things deceive not yourself. It is the part of a fiend to deceive another; it is the part of both fiend and fool to practise a self-deception."

As Kauffmann finished speaking his eyes flashed, his chest expanded, and his whole frame appeared agitated by the intensity of his emotions. I took no notice of his excitement, but after musing a moment, replied quietly:

"My friend, I am not disposed to deny anything you have said, nor yet can I say I am ready to give entire acquiescence thereto. The discussion will do me good. I am ready for it, carry it where you will, say in it what you will. 'What man dare, I dare;' for I believe the maxim of one of your poets, that we arrive at truth through extremes, and that we must first exhaust error, and often madness, before we can reach the bright goal of peaceful wisdom. But tell me, Kauffmann —and remember that I want truth in your reply, for I think I have discovered in you one foible which it is the part of friendship to point out—tell me, have you not had some serious love-passage ere now? I believe you have. Your friend could not be brought to think as you did. You felt that she was bound to do so. You became angry; you acted foolishly; you lost her."

"You have hit the nail upon the head," interrupted the student, with a forced laugh; "not another blow; it is driven deep enough."

"Yet let the circumstance teach you a lesson," I continued; "if we really seek for and worship the Beautiful and the Good, and the Just—TO ΚΑΛΟΝ, TO ΑΓΑΘΟΝ, TO ΔΙΚΑΙΟΝ —why insist upon our doing this in one beaten way, according to one prescribed formula, by one fixed course of thought or reasoning? So long as we reach the goal, why wrangle with each other about the different routes or means of conveyance? Is not the harmony of souls a higher point to attain than the unison of souls? We must not claim that others should think with our thoughts; it is much happier if their thoughts harmonize with ours. Therefore be arbitrary with no one except yourself."

"No more now," replied Kauffmann: "we shall do each

other good. Think of my proposition for our society. I will see you to-morrow. Nay, not to-morrow," he continued, thoughtfully; "not to-morrow, but the day after. Good-by!"

We separated, and I walked slowly to the Rosenthal. This was my first serious conversation with a fellow-student, and my mind by the exercise acquired a more healthful tone. Others beside myself, then, were tortured by doubts and anxieties, with speculations and vague surmises. I was not in the wilderness alone. My heart beat with a stronger confidence ; the weight upon it was a little lightened.

IX.

BEFORE the door of Herr Von Hofrath I met Theresa. Although we were living in the same house, I had but little opportunity of becoming intimate with her during the first days of my sojourn, in consequence of the many things which required my attention, and kept me nearly all the time in the town. Besides the girl had her own round of duties, and was not always visible when I might wish to see her. As I approached the threshold, she advanced a few steps to meet me. The sight of her gave me a pleasure, I could scarcely account for, and dispelled in a moment the effect of Kauffmann's philippic. Was it not strange! How, on a sudden does the young pulse quicken! how does it falter! What a slight thing will disturb its equipoise! How different from the calm, unruffled, measured beat of the experienced heart, which only seeks repose !

Theresa advanced to meet me. "I hoped you would have returned early," she said. " My father and myself were invited to visit a friend at some little distance. We wished you to go, for you would have met many scholars ; it is now too late."

" But why did you remain?"

" I thought the empty house would make you melancholy; for you have no home-feeling here."

" I love to be alone, and to feel solitary and homeless," said I, abruptly. I do not know what put the words into my mouth, or why I spoke as I did. There is a perversity which besets us sometimes, when speaking to a woman whom we regard; we say rude things when our feelings are gentle, and cruel things when our hearts are tender. Theresa looked full at me, in her placid, earnest manner, and asked: " Why?"

I felt convicted of a falsehood. I stood abashed for a moment, and then replied, carelessly enough: " I do not know."

After this, neither spoke for several minutes. The pause was becoming awkward, but I could not break it. Theresa asked in her calm, quiet tone, " Are all Englishmen like you?"

" If they are, you are ready to pronounce them very disagreeable."

" No, but I feel disappointed."

" Why?"

" My father has always described the English character in a way that made me pleased with it, and ——"

" I will not force you to finish the sentence," said I, bitterly (what right had I to feel bitterly, instead of the young girl whose feelings I was wounding by my rudeness?) " I will finish it for you. You are sorry that the specimen you behold in me should not agree with the description."

" And yet," said Theresa, without appearing to hear my remark, " it was of your father that my father used to speak; and I thought we should be friends."

" For my own sake I shall regret it if we are not," was my cold reply; and I turned and entered the house, leaving her still near the door.

X.

THE twilight approaches.   Now it deepens into the gloaming.   Still the young girl stands where I left her.   How do I know?   Have I not stolen to my window, and, looking through the casement, watched Theresa with an indefinable uneasy apprehension?   She moves not: she does not advance: she does not retreat: she does not turn: she does not seem to stir.

Of what is she thinking?   Beneath that imperturbable placidity has that young creature *any* feeling?   If she has, how could she, so young, obtain the mastery over herself?   Perhaps she is soulless; clear and pellucid as a crystal; not heartless, but without a heart.   But then that eye, Theresa!   Not so loud! she will hear me.   How strange that her calmness should have such power upon me!   Did she look reproachfully?   Of what am I talking?   I have done nothing.   Is it singular, when the evening is so lovely, that a maiden should stand a few moments in the open air?   Perhaps she expects a friend.   It *is* so—I have it.   But then she "hoped we should be friends"—and I replied that "I should regret it if we were not."   That was very proper.   And I came away, for I was fatigued.   Yes, I am fatigued.   See! she turns to come in; will she raise her eyes to my window?   If she does, I will speak to her.   I will, positively.   She does not.   She has entered the house.

XI.

THERE are times when, as if awaking from oblivion, the thoughts and associations of a former epoch reappear—

strangely, like the shadows of the departed — and awhile tenant anew the soul; not, indeed, as lawful possessors, but as timid visitants, ready to start at the first alarm, and disappear as suddenly and mysteriously as they came : as some unfortunate, forced from his early home, now fallen into other hands, steals back, after a season, unobserved, and pensively wanders over the abode once so friendly, but which can no longer afford him a permanent shelter.

How tangible and real are these images. At the moment I commenced this page, the evening with Theresa came before me with so startling a vividness, that I involuntarily referred to it as something now occurring. Here was the window; there stood Theresa; beyond, across those meadows, was the town; this way, the pleasant walk toward the river. Were I a painter, I had not let the scene glide from me; fading, fading—so! I am no longer in the Rosenthal. Theresa is not beneath my window. But I am in the house of my fathers. This is the room in which I most delighted when a boy. I go on with my narrative, but must draw upon memory for the detail.

XII.

I HARDLY know why it was, but I expected when I went down to breakfast the next morning to see Theresa exhibit some constraint of manner toward me. But here again I was disappointed. She received me with the same gentleness, the same unaffected quietness, that had before marked her demeanor. For myself, I was piqued because she did not appear disturbed. I soon grew ashamed of so ungenerous a weakness, and reproached myself for harboring a sentiment so unworthy. Then I questioned myself of Theresa, but could summon no answer—none whatever; I only determined to

seek her friendship, and ask her what she really was: for it
seemed as if I could never make the discovery.   After breakfast I proposed a walk to her.

"I am hardly at liberty so early," she replied; "but—yes,
I will go with you."

"Neither am I at liberty, but I wish to speak with you."

"Indeed! we will set out at once."

But what was I first to say, after so formal an announcement? We walked on a few steps, when, summoning my
resolution, I exclaimed:

"Mademoiselle Theresa, I was rude to you last evening,
and I wish to crave pardon for it."

"Your manner then was not natural," said Theresa, with
some earnestness. "Explain to me why it was not?"

Again I was at loss. I felt all the conventionalism of my
education stripped from me on the instant, and by this mere
child. I had acknowledged my rudeness, and she had asked,
with earnest simplicity, of the cause. "*Why was I not natural?*"

What a question! I hesitated—commenced an answer—
stopped, and said: "I can not reply to your question satisfactorily to myself, certainly not to you. I acknowledge the
fault; it is for you to pardon it."

I paused again, but Theresa said nothing.

"After all," I added, playfully, "is not *rudeness* natural
sometimes?"

"Not in one that is true-hearted. How can it be? Not
in you, I am sure, else you would not speak of it as a fault."

"But are not faults natural to poor humanity?"

"The idea is horrible," she said; "God made man upright.
When he goes astray into sin, he does violence to his nature;
he may be led away to a returnless distance, still it is an unnatural aberration."

'You are too serious, mademoiselle."

" Call me Theresa—I like it better."

" You are too serious, Theresa.   I wish not this discussion with you, I have enough of it daily with others.   Do not let us contend about words.   I want a companion and friend.   1 said yesterday I loved to feel solitary and homeless.   It is not true.   I do not love to feel so."

"Ah, now you speak naturally," said Theresa, in her native tongue: "I shall not be disappointed—perhaps.   Only talk with me in French no longer; it is the language of the hollow-hearted.   You can speak our honest German."

" Not so well as you the French ; but I will attempt it, if it will make us better acquainted."

" We shall find that out by-and-by ; but first will you tell me why you came here to Leipsic ?"

" To finish an education which at times I am sorry was ever begun."

"If it is to go on with a bad business, you do right to be sorry; if to perfect a good one, you are wrong."

I was amazed at the turn our discourse was taking. Had the professor's young daughter assumed to be my mentor ? No, not so; she exhibited neither the tone nor the manner of a teacher or adviser.   Her voice was sweet, her manner gentle, yet both so self-possessed that I was puzzled.

I felt that the conventional language of compliment which is always used by our sex to the other,. would be entirely out of place.   It was the work of a moment to compare Theresa with every other woman I had seen.   She was unlike every other.   What should I do?—adapt my manner to hers ? yield to her influence ? My pride of opinion was discomposed. I hesitated to yield.   Should I not rather cloak myself in it, and go on my way ?   Theresa perceived my hesitation.

"Why this unrest?" she asked; "let us converse no more, if you are disquieted."

This was uttered in a tone so soft, yet firm, that it reached my heart. I have said the day had passed for my confiding, but I should have made one exception. I could confide in Theresa. Heretofore I had been interested in the sex from a desire to understand *them*. I had sought their confidence without giving my own. How completely were the tables turned! I was about to open my soul to her, while she yet remained to me a mystery. The resolution was taken, and kept.

Very briefly, yet pertinently, I went over my life. I did so abruptly and without preface, for I felt annoyed at what I was doing. It seemed foolish—weak—unphilosophical—anything but characteristic. But I was committed. Theresa had the whole. I laugh sometimes when I think how suddenly I gave up my heart's secret thoughts and struggles: gave them up without exchange; unconditionally; no reserve; no keeping back at all. Yes, she had the whole. Why do the tears start at the recollection of that morning? I wipe them away, but they come again.

XIII.

THERESA listened to my recital, and when I had finished, said, with her usual gentleness, "It is better to speak, when what we conceal disturbs us. I would not without reflection say what I think of your history; but is it not action that you most require? You are true in heart, honest in purpose; will not a practical life bring you to what you were?"

"And must I go *back*, Theresa?"

"Certainly, if you would be happy. Have you not forsaken your early faith?"

' Because it no longer sustained me."

" Because you no longer trusted !"

" Are you happy ?"

" I am ; but I have longings which may not, I suppose, be satisfied here. Let us say no more now. We may say too much at first. We become known to each other better when we speak what is called forth by a more familiar intercourse."

We returned to the house. I was relieved. I felt that I was a better being. I took my way to the town with a stronger confidence in myself and in what I hoped to be. I was desirous to speak with Kauffmann, but it lacked a day of the time appointed for our interview. I was late for the lecture, and so strolled about Leipsic.

XIV.

A few evenings before, I had been introduced to a young man whose daily habits and manners were so peculiar, whose uttered sentiments were so startling, that he received from his fellow-students the *sobriquet* of Mephistophiles. His real name was Wolfgang Hegewisch. There had been a dance on the evening referred to, in the suburbs of the town; not by people of the better class, certainly, but at the same time not of an objectionable character. A great many students were there, many of whom had sweethearts in the company. The general order of things was convivial, and the most complete hilarity reigned throughout. Pursuing my habit of seeing what was passing, I had accompanied an acquaintance to the place. I went as a mere looker-on, and took no part in the amusements of the evening.

My notice was presently attracted by a person apparently about five-and-twenty, standing in one corner of the room. He was tall, swarthy, or rather sallow, with a high, command-

ing forehead, a deep-sunken, fixed black eye, a large Roman
nose, small mouth and thin lips, and was spare in person,
though well enough formed. He stood with folded arms,
watching the merry-makers. There was something revolting
in the expression of his countenance. He appeared to take
a fiendish satisfaction in the weaknesses or the foibles of humanity; and these he evidently thought were exhibited in the
scene before him. As I had declined both the dance and the
waltz, my companion declared in a jesting way that he would
present me to Mephistophiles—meaning Hegewisch. I assented, and we were introduced. I bowed civilly, and received an emphatic nod in return. I forbore to start a conversation, and my new friend showed no signs of doing so.
After standing near him a few minutes, I turned away, not a
word having been said on either side. I saw nothing further
of this man during the evening, but became curious to
know more of him. No one could give any satisfactory information in reply to my questions, though I inquired the
next morning of almost every one I knew.

"He is our Mephistophiles," said one. "He is the devil
himself," said another. "Beware of him," cried a third. At
that moment the gaunt form of Hegewisch glided by, and as
his glittering eye passed over the group who stood canvassing
his character, the young men instinctively shrank from it.

"Good health and a better occupation to you, gentlemen,"
he exclaimed, in a tone of mocking irony.

"Did I not tell you so?" said young Ludwig Melcherson.

"Nonsense," chimed in a new-comer. "Can you not let a
man rest in peace? What has become of our honest German
liberalism? Because Hegewisch neither carouses with you
nor plays with you; because he will neither fence nor smoke;
because he refuses wine, and beer, and spirits, and runs not
after the women; because, in short, he never *does* anything

that you can complain of, he must be a devil! Very good reasoning, among such precious saints as you!"

"But how does he look?—what does he say? Answer me, Karl," cried Melcherson.

"How would *you* look, Herr Ludwig, if everybody pointed toward you and called you fiend? Come, come, fellow-students, let us have no more of this. Am I not right? 'Give the devil his due.' Let us drink to a better appreciation of Wolfgang Hegewisch."

The company gave enthusiastic assent, and dispersed better satisfied with themselves and with the object of their vituperation. What I had heard, however, only increased my curiosity to know the man; but since, I had not met him.

XV.

I HAVE thus gone back a little, to explain what occurred the morning of my interview with Theresa, after I came into the town. I said, I took a stroll about Leipsic; I extended my walk to a remote part of the city. As I crossed a narrow street, I heard behind me, "A truant so soon, Herr Saint Leger!" I turned and beheld Hegewisch in the doorway of a small house on the cross street, a little way from the main avenue. He wore a long dressing-gown, buckled around his waist, which gave to his figure even a more gaunt appearance than was natural. I went toward him.

"My friend of the ball-room, I believe?"

"The same," I replied.

"I have long wished to see an Englishman, and they tell me you are one."

"'A cat may look on a king.' You have liberty to survey me for any reasonable period."

"I see you are disposed to be accommodating; that has its

corresponding effect upon me. Pray walk into my apartments; that is, if you are willing to be questioned."

" I certainly am: for I calculate upon obtaining more than
I give."

" Ah, I have heard that there were some sensible men
among the English; I begin to think it true."

" And I have heard there is nothing like common sense in
all Germany, and I begin to think that true."

" A hit! that was just what I was coming to. I feared you
had not found it out. But pray tell me, since you know so
much, what in the devil's name sent you here?"

" I can't answer to such an adjuration."

" Pshaw! 'tis only a habit I have, when pleased. Don't be
afraid; the devil won't harm good children. So, why do you
come to Germany?"

" To make the acquaintance of such rare fellows as yourself."

" Good; come in, then." And I went into the apartments
of Wolfgang Hegewisch.

" Here I eat, there I sleep," said the student, pointing first
to one room and then to the other. The sleeping-room, adjoining the one we first entered, was narrow, and contained a
small iron bedstead, a straw bed, some quilts, but no pillows;
not a chair, nor table, nor mirror; nothing but the little bedstead, and the straw bed, and the patched quilts. The other
apartment was better apparelled; there were chairs, and a
table, and an old secretary, on one side; a large shelf of books
on the other; a laboratory filled with chemical apparatus occupied the third, and along the fourth, where the windows did
not prevent, were hung up odds and ends of almost everything;
stuffed birds, a death's head and marrow-bones, crossed as in
the old pictures; a dried snake or so, a young crocodile, and
a brace of lizards; an old gun, two or three antique helmets

and head-pieces, in short, it seemed as if the ingenuity of the occupant had been racked to assemble the most incongruous mass of revolting objects.

"Here I eat, there I sleep," repeated Wolfgang Hegewisch.

"If I had the selection, I should invert the proposition, and say, There I eat, here I sleep; but every one to his taste,"

"I am glad to find you liberal. I will prove to you by-and-by that I am right in the disposition of these rooms. In the meantime, it is the dinner-hour for honest men. You will stay?"

I nodded assent.

"Katrine, Katrine," shouted the student—a stout serving-girl entered—"Dinner."

No cloth was spread, but a coarse dinner of the most ordinary description was served, without wine of any kind, or even beer. There was but one course, and it was passed through rapidly, and in silence.

"You don't smoke?" said Hegewisch.

"No."

"Nor drink?"

"When there is nothing to drink, no."

"And you have no vices?"

"Certainly not."

"Bah! you are joking."

"At least I have none to *speak* of," said I.

"Nay, answer," said the student, in a louder tone, "have you no vice?—do not your senses, on some single point, in some slight, unmentionable matter, enslave your spirit? Answer me there."

I began to think I was conversing with a madman; but put on a look of composure, and said, calmly, "I answer—no."

"Then why—this time I say in Heaven's name—young man, are you here? Is it to lose all that you have that may be called virtue—which, by the way, is mere sound, only sound—and acquire all that may be called depravity?   That's not sound; that is the real, genuine base-metal."

"If you will talk less like a madman I shall be happy to converse with you."

"Don't go; don't go; excuse me; I will be quite sane; I am not at all dangerous.   Give me your hand; 'tis pleasant once in a while to come across such an innocent fellow as yourself.   I wonder what will become of you.   I hope—yet 'tis folly to hope—but I do hope to see you dead and decently interred before you are of my age—five-and-twenty."

" Why ?"

" That is cool.   Because I like you.   I liked you the day you first came among us.   I liked you at the hob and nob down yonder.   I like you here; I don't want to see you when the fire in your soul has been extinguished."

Hegewisch uttered these last words in a tone so gentle, that I started, almost believing some one else had spoken.   I looked at him with astonishment; his eyes had lost what now seemed their unnatural mocking expression, and exhibited signs of the deepest melancholy.

"I do not understand you.   Let us have some explanation."

" To a certain age," he continued, resuming his accustomed manner, " we chase the hope-phantom with an ardor which one would think inspired by some divinity.   God! who could imagine that the hero-youth should turn out but a drivelling snob.   Look at him, all his hopes, his expectations, his aspirations, his swelling ambition, pride, energy, resolution! all— all turned to—what?   Perhaps to bestiality; to gross selfishness; or possibly, escaping these, to teaching the A B C to some little copy of himself, who will come forward, feel a sentiment and a hope, and in his turn beget children and bring them up to perpetuate the race. We are taught, we learn—for what? to teach others: and they others; and so on, *ad infinitum;* faugh! 'tis a sorry affair. But what can we do; 'tis useless to complain. Have we not passions? do they not lead or drive us—if you will have it so—to the devil? Well, can we resist? Yes, you say. Do we resist? No. Why not? because we love sin? Nonsense! Because we love pleasure, enjoyment, instant gratification.

"So I enjoy what comes to me: do you for that call me a wretch? Granted. Do you claim to be virtuous? Granted. But what makes me the wretch and you the saint? Circumstances, physical conformation, position, opportunity, etc., etc., etc. Therefore, if I had been you, I should have been you. If I were you I should be you; nothing else can be made of it. Then we come straight to the question: '*Who maketh you to differ?*'

"Perhaps this is a ground you do not wish to occupy. Now it is just the ground, were I a saint, that I would plant myself upon. I would place my back to the wall and fortify myself with: 'Whom He did predestinate them he also called.' 'Who shall lay anything to the charge of God's elect? It is God that justifieth.' 'Shall the thing formed say to Him that formed it, why hast thou made me thus? Hath not the potter power over the clay, of the same lump to make one vessel unto honor and another unto dishonor?' What can a poor devil like me reply to that? How can I screen myself? What can I say, except: 'My fathers have eaten sour grapes, and the children's teeth are set on edge.'"

Hegewisch paused. His manner was bitter and defying; he seemed determined to argue himself into a belief of what he knew was false.

I took up the subject. "You complain then," said I, "that we can not be what we desire to be. Is that it?"

"No. I complain that we can not desire to be what we ought to desire to be · and that circumstances beyond our control have effected this."

"And therefore you are not to suffer "

"Exactly."

"The same argument would clear the highwayman an assassin."

"I know it."

"Then you would object to punishment."

"As punishment, I do, but not as a preventive. A scamp picks my pocket. I would have him shut up that he may pick no more pockets."

"But do you not admit any connection between sin and suffering ?

"I do not admit the existence of what you term sin. Guilt there may be, and misery there is; but sin is as impossible as holiness; uncontrollable circumstances produce both. Every action is produced by a motive; that motive is powerful enough to produce it, or it would not produce it; therefore there is no sin."

"You admit that sin exists, but insist that none commit sin ? What an absurdity."

"I admit that sin (*i. e.*, the principle of evil) exists, but that it can be imputed to none. Neither can holiness, according to your scripture. Do what we may, we are but unprofitable servants."

"Well, then, I meet you on your own ground : your argument proves too much. If I may not blame the wretch who murders his neighbor, although murder be a sin, you can not impute any blame for his punishment here, or for retribution hereafter. If he can not sin, the avenger can not sin. So you are back to the same point, after a fruitless round of sophism. You would better exclaim with the Mussulman, 'What is. is ;

what must be, must be.' You say the sinner ought not to be punished, but he is punished nevertheless; and as sin can be imputed to none, we can blame none for his punishment. Such is the constitution of things; and it is a necessary con stitution; and if necessary, it is right.'

"Well enough reasoned. But nevertheless I will quarrel with it. You doom the offender. But tell me WHO—WHAT placed this principle of evil in the world?"

"I do not know. I only know it is here, and that we must make the best of it."

"Must not some Power, infinitely controlling, have done this?"

"I do not know: I admit, that I can not understand it. It transcends our reason. Why then question about it? Tell me," continued I, "why does fire cause agony to the exposed flesh; why does water strangle the bold swimmer? why does the swift air carry pestilence, or the hurricane in its course devastation? why does a blow injure our frame, or hunger weaken, or thirst torture it? why do we need clothes to protect from heat and cold? why are we weak when young and decrepit when old? Answer me these, and I will tell why misery is entailed upon sin, and why sin exists. I take you on your ground, and on your ground I expose your sophism."

"Stop there!" said Hegewisch; "we have gone far enough. What fools are we, to babble in this way."

"Not so, if we get at the truth at last."

"Truth!" interrupted my companion: "truth! So you have fallen into our German cant, and are a 'seeker after truth?' Why do n't you practise truth? why do n't you live truth? Why the devil do you go about eternally seeking, with your mouth full of our mystical jargon, which it would puzzle a fiend to understand?"

"You are right, Herr Hegewisch. Let us commence forthwith." 17

"Bah!   I am not in that catagory.   I am only an adviser ;
the practice is for you.   I am irreclaimable.   Good-by now,
but come again and see me."

So ended my first interview with Wolfgang Hegewisch.

XVI.

"Why had I come to Germany ?"   It was strange enough
that Theresa and Wolfgang Hegewisch should each ask me
the question ; and deprecate, although in different terms, my
present course.

What was that to Theresa or to Hegewisch ?   Why should
either presume to dictate to me ?   A moment's consideration
put at rest this movement of weak pride.   I became calm.
I determined to subject myself to the most rigorous discipline ;
what friend or enemy, sycophant or scoffer, said, should be
weighed carefully, and the result passed to my benefit.   Such,
and many more resolves of similar import, were made, while
with renewed courage I girded myself for the trial.   But,
words—words—how they troubled me ! how I tried to dis-
encumber myself of the schoolman's terms, and to translate
them into language that could be apprehended.   At first I
could not imagine in what I was baffled; and when I came
to discover that it was by sounds merely, I took courage.

XVII.

Whatever I did, wherever I went, the meager anatomy
of Hegewisch haunted me.   In the lecture-room, among the
students, in my walks, awake, asleep, or in revery—there
were those glittering black eyes, and that scornful face, and
that gaunt figure.   Sometimes the countenance would present
itself in the softened melancholy, in which for a moment I be-

held it when in his apartment; and then, it appeared in such mournful depression that I could hardly restrain my own emotion. In one situation only was I free from the illusion. In the society of Theresa nothing could abstract me from the influence of her presence. No apparition haunted me then. I breathed the pure atmosphere which surrounded her, and felt that a new life was beginning within me. If ever lived upon this earth a sinless being, save only the ONE in whom we trust, it seems to me that Theresa was sinless. So it was that in her company I found peace of mind ever after the day in which I gave her my confidence. But away from her, and Hegewisch appeared. Why was I so beset?

XVIII.

I EXPECTED at the appointed time to see Kauffmann. Strange to say, he had absented himself from Leipsic, and had not been seen since the day we had our last conversation. Hegewisch, I often encountered. This was a relief, for the real spectre drove away the imaginary one. He always greeted me whenever we met; sometimes cordially, sometimes abruptly. Once in a while I would find him discoursing to a group of students, seemingly attentive listeners, who, though fascinated by his presence, were evidently startled and almost terror-stricken by what he said. On such occasions I invariably joined the company, and Hegewisch would as invariably bring his harangue to sudden conclusion, and leave us. In this way some two weeks ran on, when, all at once, Hegewisch disappeared. I felt my interest still more excited by the circumstance · and after a lapse of a few days, being unable longer to restrain myself—for his shadow haunted me more than ever—I determined to go to his apartments and inquire there I was warranted in so doing, by his request that I would again see him. I proceeded to his rooms. I found him within. He was seated in a chair at his old secretary, reading a manuscript. He started suddenly upon my entrance, thrust the writing hastily into a drawer, and without rising, exclaimed: "You are welcome. I am glad you have come."

I looked at him attentively, and was struck with the change. His eyes were more sunken, his face more sallow, his cheek more emaciated.

"You have been ill; you are ill," I said, almost abruptly.

"I have been—I am," was the reply.

"Why did you not send for me?" I inquired, for something told me that my sympathy would scarcely be repulsed.

"You have come in good time," replied Hegewisch. "Sooner I could not have seen you. I am better."

"Indeed. Have you been so ill?"

"Yes; and how this cowardly frame of ours shrinks and trembles and grows puny, under the attack of the Destroyer. Death I would meet and not tremble, but it is his advance-guard, with its Parthian warfare, cutting one off by piece-meal, that disturbs me."

"And is that all that disturbs you, Wolfgang Hegewisch?" I demanded, in a tone which gave evidence that I felt deeply for him.

"I am no longer disturbed by anything. Mind, and body, a wreck—a ruin."

"Say not so," I cried; "say not so! Only rouse yourself; invoke the slumbering faculties of your being, make Memory do her part, Hope her part, Faith her part, Patience her part, and you are saved."

"Memory!" muttered the student; "GREAT FATHER, does he speak of memory—does he commend me to the poison ——"

"Not without the antidote."

"Saint Leger," said Hegewisch, recovering himself at the

sound of my voice, and rising with dignity from his seat to approach me; "Saint Leger, do not attempt to comfort me. My spirit is tossed upon a stormy sea, where tempests rage continually, and there is no hope of a calmer season, but rather apprehension of a deeper and more terrible gloom! Do not think to comfort me."

"I will; I came for that purpose; you shall be comforted!" I exclaimed, repressing with difficulty the emotions which filled my bosom.

The eyes of Hegewisch grew moist, but he struggled to prevent any evidence of feeling. It would not do. In spite of every effort a large tear formed in each of those strange eyes, and overflowed the lids and rolled down.

"Weak, weak, weak!" whispered he, wiping away the drops. "Let the hour hasten; let death come before I am quite imbecile."

"Will you not be calm and hear me? Will you not say what distresses you? Speak to your friend?"

"It is written here," said Hegewisch, laying his hand upon his heart. "It is written here, with a pen of iron."

"What is written? Why speak in riddles? Why not heed my request?"

"Listen to me, then," said the student. "Perhaps it will relieve me to probe the wound. You are the first human being that my heart has warmed toward, since—since——it became stone. Will you hearken? Do you care to hear the story of one who has cursed the day in which he was born?"

I expressed an eager assent, and without further hesitation the student, after drawing his chair nearer to mine, commenced.

XIX.

THE STORY OF WOLFGANG HEGEWISCH.

I WAS born on the Rhine; it is of no consequence to mention the place; the events I narrate are of too recent occurrence to give them their locality.   I am the elder of two
brothers.   My father was the Baron ———.   I no longer use
the name or title, but have taken instead my second name,
Hegewisch, which was that of my maternal ancestor.

My childhood and youth were very joyous.   My disposition
was trustful and sanguine; my nature open and confiding,
and my temper not unamiable.

No two were ever more unlike than my brother and myself.   He was cunning and stealthy; shrewd and vindictive;
full of malice and of treachery.   In our childhood even, he
envied me the privileges of the first-born, and as we grew
older his envy merged into a subtle and revengeful hate,
which became more and more dangerous, as it was manifested
the less openly.   All this, however, but little affected my happiness.   My heart overflowed with benevolence toward all;
and I regarded the conduct of my brother only as childish ill-
humor or youthful caprice.   I did not know his real character, or the depth of depravity it had already reached.

I was the favorite of both my father and my mother.   My
brother gave them continual uneasiness, by the early manifestation of many unhappy traits of character.

My days ran pleasantly.   I had a fondness for manly exercises and for books.   My education was attended to with care.
and it was so admirably planned that I can not look back upon
a single day of study with unpleasant reminiscences.

How could I fail of being happy? My brother as we grew up took more pains to conceal his feelings. He practised a ready dissimulation and affected a strong regard for me. Thus were confirmed my most favorable impressions of his conduct, and we advanced pleasantly enough together. Only I could not love him. I had never thoughtfully reflected upon his nature. I had never seriously condemned him, yet I shrunk from his society. My greatest error was a neglect of my reflective powers. There was much to excuse this; and I have been fearfully rewarded for this sin of omission; but the future was all so bright, the present all so happy, that it will not appear strange that I took everything upon trust and allowed nothing to detract from the felicity in which I moved, and which I saw before me. Yet I was not negligent of study. On the contrary, I delighted in learning. I even applied myself severely, and in doing so was happy.

But I did not reflect practically, nor apply the lessons which I daily gleaned from books to my own case. Indeed, I thought not of myself. To be sure, I loved to be happy; but it was an impulsive natural desire which involved no selfishness. For I sought always to make those near me happy, and herein found my greatest pleasure. Can you imagine a more desirable state of being? Had it not some resemblance to that of Eden?

Caspar—this brother of mine—I must make my story brief—he, the while, was not idle. He read and pondered; he was up early and late, not with the zeal of one who loved his labor, but with the assiduousness of a slave under his task-master. The more he learned, the kinder was his bearing toward every one, until even the baron and my mother began to hope that he was redeeming his good name. Still, while his manner was becoming so amiable, his eye was more full of craft and his movements more stealthy.

With the servants and retainers, Caspar could gain no popularity. In spite of constant and persevering endeavors to win their favor, he was regarded with unvarying dislike. For this, Caspar hated me, but he smothered his feelings, and affected to look up to me with the consideration which belongs to the elder brother.

There was one person only with whom he appeared to have confidential intercourse. This was a priest named Hegel, belonging to a monastery a few miles distant. He was not of the severe and self-denying class who are crafty and remorseless from principle, and fortify themselves in deeds of darkness by apt quotations of scripture; yet reject with scorn the claims of sensualism, and crush with iron step the promptings of the appetite. This Father Hegel knew nothing of privation or self-denial. He was in appearance just the priest that has been described so often, fat and rubicund. But here the common analogy ended. He seemed good-natured, but at heart was arbitrary and cruel: too indolent to be ambitious, he contented himself with being a tyrant wherever he could tyrannize. He had a great deal of low cunning, low malice, low vindictiveness. He ministered to his passions whenever he could do so with safety, and when he could not, he turned their forces in some other direction.

With this monk Caspar was very intimate. He brought him often to his room in the castle, and many and long were their secret conferences. Their intimacy commenced when Caspar was about sixteen, and I, therefore, nearly eighteen The baron regarded it with strong distaste, for he had been educated a protestant, and his good sense would have condemned it under any circumstances. But somehow, the more intimate Caspar and Father Hegel became, the more amiable was Caspar. The monk took every occasion to ingratiate himself with the baron and my mother, and sought especially to propitiate me. His words were full of charity. He spoke of Caspar as one whose morbid feelings had made him moody and discontented. He admitted that he had taken pains to gain my brother's confidence, in order, if possible, to influence him by the strong force of Christian precept and example, and he was happy to find that his labor was not altogether in vain. Caspar had improved; his feelings were becoming natural; he regarded his former unhappy state of mind with abhorrence; he believed he was no longer under the influence of the " Prince of the Power of the Air." Not that he had sought to proselyte him; no—he only wished to withdraw him for a season from himself, and the rest he would leave to the " Good Shepherd of Souls."

Such was the tenor of Father Hegel's discourse to my mother, to the baron, and to me. Who could help being influenced by it when the evidence of amendment was seen from day to day? Caspar grew more kind and amiable; the monk more saint-like and devoted.

I say not that my father was satisfied. Quite the contrary. For he was a man of ready intellect, who had seen much of the world, and knew what faith to put in the professions of such men as Father Hegel; but balancing the apparent improvement in Caspar against the danger to arise from the means used, he doubtless thought it best not to interfere. My mother felt greater hope; and for myself, I was pleased at the change, although I could not overcome the instinctive repugnance which I felt when my brother, in apparent kindness, put his arm in mine, or laid his hand, with seeming affection, on my shoulder. By all the other inmates of the castle the monk was held in detestation. Notwithstanding all his efforts to gain favor, he was absolutely hated. There is a singular straightforwardness in the capacities of many of the humbler classes, which, like the peculiar appreciation of children, recognises at once the pretender and the hypocrite. It was so here; and Caspar and the monk found themselves foiled where they had doubtless expected the least opposition.

Hegewisch paused. He remained silent several minutes. At last he said: "Why do I hesitate? Why linger on the threshold? Why dread to approach the subject? Do my thoughts ever wander from it? My right hand has forgot her cunning, but *I* shall forget this—never"

X X.   .

THE student resumed. "I have been reading," he said, in a quiet tone, seemingly unconscious that he was wandering from his subject, "I have been reading a few passages of Claudian, and these lines strike me with more force this morning than ever before. They state pertinently the matter which disturbs me and makes me a denier." Hegewisch read in a low but collected voice:

> "SÆPE mihi dubiam traxit sententia mentem,
>   Curarent Superi terras, an nullus inesset
>   Rector, et incerto fluerent mortalia casu.
>   Nam cum dispositi quæsissim fœdera mundi,
>   Præscriptosque mari fines, annisque meatus,
>   Et lucis noctisque vires: tunc omnia rebar
>   Consilio firmati DEI—
>   Sed cum *res hominum* tanta caligine volvi
>   Aspicerem, lætosque diu florere nocentes,
>   Vexarique pios, rursus Inbefacta cadebat
>   Religio."

He closed the book and looked at me inquiringly.

"The Bible," I said, "is full of this subject. It does not slide over nor evade it. We read in direct terms of the apparent injustice of GOD's management of the affairs of men.

"'The wicked in his pride doth persecute the poor.'

"'For the wicked boasteth of his heart's desire.'

" ' There is a just man that perisheth in his righteousness, and there is a wicked man that prolongeth his life in his wickedness.'

" ' Wherefore do the wicked live, become old, yea are mighty in power ?'

" Yet how distinctly are we assured of the great and final result. How surely and how confidently does the Bible speak in vindication of the ways of God to man.

" ' Though a sinner do evil a hundred times, and his days be prolonged, yet surely I know it shall be well with them that fear God, which fear before him.'

" ' But it shall not be well with the wicked.'

" ' Thou renderest to every man according to his work.' "

" I have no patience with the subject," interrupted Hegewisch, bitterly. " Nor can I ——"

The student stopped suddenly, and with a strong effort at self-control, he exclaimed, in a hoarse whisper, while a perceptible shudder passed across his frame : " I have blasphemed enough."

" You have forgotten the narrative," said I, gently, without noticing his emotion. " Pray finish it now, before I leave you."

" The narrative," repeated Hegewisch, clasping his hands across his forehead, " The narrative ! Ah, yes, I recollect; but where was I ? Oh ! I remember that too. Pardon me if I have detained you ; but those lines from Claudian. Yes, they were running in my head."

Thereupon he continued :

A few leagues from ——, and still farther up the Rhine, stood the castle of the ancient lords of Richstein. A house at that time famous as well for its long ancestry as for the wealth and influence which were centred in its then present possessor. This personage had married late in life, and was blessed with a single child, a daughter, to soothe the asperities of declining age.   The lord of Richstein and my father were friends. And it was understood between them that the elder son of the baron should wed the young Meta of Richstein.   Both were then in infancy.   The little Meta being nearly three years my junior.

Time rolled along: the children saw much of each other, but when together were quite too young to form any serious intimacy.   Before Meta reached her tenth year, the lord of Richstein was summoned to his last rest.   And in the year following, the same tomb closed upon his wife.   Thus was Meta left, at a tender age, an orphan, an heiress, and the sole representative of an ancient and noble house.

The death of the lord and the lady of Richstein struck me with terror; but the impression soon wore away, and when I learned that Meta was to be removed to another part of the country, and to receive her education under the direction of her aunt, the much respected and beloved patroness of the holy abbey of Rennewart, I rejoiced that she would have an adequate protector, without thinking how prejudicial the re ·moval might be to my own prospects.

In short, I indulged in no dreams of the future; I cared for none.   The idea of marriage had never seriously entered my head.   I had no worldly cunning, nor policy, nor shrewdness. I was satisfied with home and my means of enjoyment, and of course was happy.

I do not remember whether I bade Meta adieu; probably I did not.   She was kept in deep mourning, and was shut in the castle after her mother's death until she went to her aunt. And before a twelvemonth passed, new scenes and associations had doubtless led us quite to forget each other.

Only my father did not lose sight of the proposed alliance. He kept up a formal correspondence with the lady patroness,

which was productive of a letter every six months, in which
the baron inquired, in courtly phrase, after the condition of
the holy abbey, the welfare of the lady patroness, and the
health of the young lady of Richstein. Every six months
answer was returned in like parlance, that the condition of
the holy abbey of Rennewart (Laus Deo) was satisfactory, the
welfare of the lady patroness was perfect, and the health of
the young lady of Richstein was good. Nothing occurred for
years to disturb the uniform current of events. Meta and
myself had not met since the young girl left Richstein. Still
our betrothment was held as settled by both the lady patroness
and my father. I was about twenty. To this period I have
given a brief outline of my history, and of that of my brother,
and I have gone back only to make my story intelligible.

I was about twenty. One morning, as I was engaged in
my own room, collating favorite passages from Æschylus,
some one knocked at the door. I uttered some word of admission, and Caspar entered. He came close to me, and I
observed, for the first time, that his countenance was pale,
and that he had the appearance of extreme dejection. I asked
him to sit down, but he shook his head despairingly. I inquired what troubled him, and this too he declined. I could
do no more, so I remained silent till he should speak.

"My brother," said he at last, in a low, pathetic tone, "my
dear brother, I am the most miserable of creatures!"

Astounded at such an announcement from one usually so
calm and self-possessed, I was for the moment unable to reply.

"I am, believe me—I am, Wolfgang," continued Caspar;
"and you are the only one to whom I can go; you—who
will prove my enemy and my ruin!"

"For the love of Heaven," I exclaimed, "what mean you,
Caspar, and why do you speak with such horrid significance?"

"'Tis true—too true! Say—tell me, Wolfgang, may I reveal the secret of my soul to you?"

I looked him anxiously in the face, but said nothing.

"I must, I will tell it to you, although it make certain my destruction. Know that I love Meta of Richstein—your Meta—and that my love is returned—that she loves me! I have uttered it; kill me if you will, for life is a burden to me! I will not prove a traitor to my brother; I can not live without her."

"Is that all, Caspar? Does your distress centre in this?" said I, in a lively tone. "If so, take the girl and welcome; I wish you joy of her. Long may you live in the old castle of Richstein, and your descendants after you. So compose yourself, and for once in your life look cheerful and happy."

He stood amazed. "Are you in earnest, brother?" he cried, "or are you sporting with my feelings?"

"In earnest—certainly. Come, I will sign, seal, and deliver. Prepare your documents. How can I be in love with a girl I have never seen since she was a child?" .

"But the castle," interposed Caspar, timidly, "and the large tenures, the baronies, and ——"

"All, everything goes with the bride," interrupted I; "so say no more about it, or I shall begin to think you care more for them than for your lady-love."

He winced a little under this remark, but took no notice of it.

"Documents in writing," continued he, musingly, "are certainly unnecessary, when there is as yet no vested right. Nay, in this case the right can scarcely be called inchoate, or contingent even; still, Wolfgang, as the world views things so strangely, and as none of us can read the future, may I trouble you, since you kindly offer it, to say something in writing to the effect that you relinquish all claim to the hand of Meta ?"

I hesitated. My suggestion had been made playfully, and here was a serious request for a written relinquishment. I could not but look upon Caspar as acting with his accustomed selfishness, and all my former antipathy toward him revived. But as I was anxious to be rid of him, I took a pen, and wrote, thus :

" My brother Caspar, having become attached to the Lady Meta, of Richstein, and she reciprocating the attachment, I freely resign all claim to the hand of the Lady Meta which I may have in consequence of any betrothment by our respective parents."

This I signed and handed to Caspar. He read it, changed color, stammered, and looked at me suspiciously.

" Is it not satisfactory ?" said I, sharply.

" O ! yes," he said, " only I would suggest a trifling alteration, to save Meta from all embarrassment."

" I shall make no alteration. Take the paper, or not, just as you choose. As I have said, I resign the whole to you. I mean what I say. It is done !" Such was my answer. He ventured no more, but thanking me with assumed humility, hastened from the room.

The longer I thought of this occurrence the more mysterious it seemed. I did not doubt a moment that Caspar was influenced by ambitious and mercenary motives, but I wondered how he could have managed to meet with Meta, while she was at such a distance, and bring affairs to so serious an issue. However, I soon dismissed the matter from my mind.

After this, Caspar was away from us much of the time. Father Hegel came rarely to visit him, and it seemed that their intercourse was becoming less intimate.

Months passed. The spring was gone, and summer was setting in. I had prepared for several pedestrian excursions along the Rhine and into the regions adjacent. These journeys were made quite at random, pursuing as I did no fixed plan of travel, but allowing the caprice of the moment to lead me this way or that. In one of these hap-hazard excursions I strayed away as far as the old town of Rhineck. Fatigued by exercise, I stopped at the first inn that presented itself, and securing with difficulty a small chamber, immediately retired. I know not how long I slept, I was awakened by a whispering near me, and opening my eyes, I perceived a stream of light across my apartment, which came from a crevice in the partition against which my bed was placed. The sound which had disturbed me was continued from the other room. The parties were seated close to the crevice, and I was so near that I could hear them distinctly.

"Are you sure that it was he?"

"Yes, quite sure."

"But was he coming here, do you think?"

"How do I know? I only know that I saw him. But if he was coming here, he has no idea that Meta is at the chateau. Besides, I have told you over and over again that Wolfgang cares not for the girl."

I could hear Father Hegel in a low, vulgar, discordant laugh, while I recognised in his companion my brother Caspar. "The young cub has no love for carnage till he has lapped blood; so the youth knows not the volcano which he carries within him till his passions are roused. Let Wolfgang meet the girl of Richstein, and then good-by to your claim!"

"I do not think so. What Wolfgang has said he will abide by."

"When he discovers the cheat you have put upon him?"

"It will then be too late."

I could hear noth.ng further, for the parties changed their position, and shortly after left the room.

I slept no more that night. I saw that a plot was laid to ensnare an innocent girl, and that I had been made to play a part in it. New light dawned upon me. I felt older by years than when I laid down. I could now appreciate the shrewdness of Caspar, and understand the selfishness of his nature. Everything was clear to me.

There it was—the change from youth to man; the new energy, the awakened purpose, the first practical development; the harnessing in to the train that sweeps round the earth, laden with every imaginable object of hope, and every imaginable desire of the heart!

I rose early. I expected to meet and confront my brother, and was prepared to do it. This was not to be, however. He and his companion had taken their departure before I left my chamber, and no one about the inn could tell me whither they went. My next thought was to seek for Meta; but where was she to be found? Occupied with the idea, I started forth, and walked on mechanically till I came to the town-gate. Producing my passport, I went through, and continued my stroll until I was entirely away from the suburbs, and surrounded only by pleasant green fields, through which were frequent lanes leading to the river. I turned down one of these, which led me presently to a spacious old mansion, situated a little distance from the water, and surrounded by a high wall. The entrance was protected by a large gate. As I came up, I saw a little boy upon the outside struggling to open it. He had apparently strayed out and in some way got through the gate, but was unable to get back. Finding his struggles of no avail, he began to cry. I ran forward, and opening the gate, took him in my arms and carried him inside. At the same moment, a girl came bounding down the path, and ran

18

to the spot where I was standing with the boy. I never yet forgot a countenance, where the lineaments had become formed, and I recognised instantly in the beautiful and blooming creature before me the young Meta of Richstein.

With remarkable grace and self-possession, yet with becoming modesty, she thanked me for the trouble I had taken with her little charge, who, she said, was placed under her care for a few minutes, and ran off unperceived, alarming her for his safety. I saw that I was not known, and I could not resist the temptation of preserving my incognito. Indeed, I knew not what to say or how to announce myself. The longer I hesitated the more difficult it seemed.

It was a strange meeting between two betrothed. Destiny had thrown us together in the delightful season when the air was balmy, and nature smiling. The water spirits upon the bosom of Father Rhine seemed sporting, and nymphs and fauns and fairies to be revelling in the fields and through the bowers and around the wells and fountains of the old chateau.

And I thought of my renunciation, and wished I had not written and signed it; and I was glad that I had framed it so cautiously, and wondered what would be the end of the history; and revolving all these things, I was standing still, gazing upon Meta, but taking no notice of what she said, nor of anything else. There I stood, looking, and saying nothing.

How long I remained in this way I do not know. I believe Meta spoke, and asked if I was ill, or something of the sort, but I am not positive. When I recovered from my trance, she was standing, as much enrapted as I had been. Memory was summoned to its office, and a dim reminiscence was flitting across her mind. But the shadows threw no certain trace across the vista of the past; the glimmering disclosed only the same dim reminiscence. Meta was the first to speak.

"Excuse me : You come, I presume, to call on the baroness ; but your countenance seems so familiar that I must ask if I have not had the pleasure of seeing you before ?"

"I have been often in Rhineck, but never at the chateau."

"Nay, it can not have been in the town; but your countenance *is* familiar. You are some friend of our family ?"

"Then we may have met at Rennewart ?"

"At Rennewart ; no. But this shows that you know me."

"Yes, I do know you, Meta of Richstein," said I, slowly, and sadly. "I only hope that you may not remember me."

"It is the young Baron of———," she exclaimed, suddenly, with a look first of terror and then of scorn. "What would he here ?"

The air, just before so genial, became oppressive ; nature turned her smiles into frowns. The water spirits ceased their sports and plunged down to their caverns in the bottom of the river, and the nymphs and fauns and fairies left off revelling and fled noiselessly away into the dark recesses of the woods.

How different my first and second trance ! Her voice brought me to my senses. She repeated in the same disdainful tone her question.

"What would you here?"

"I would expose a base and premeditated fraud upon myself and you. I would prove that we are the victims of an outrageous plot. I would clear myself from aspersions which I believe have been cast upon me, and explain whatever may seem to you deserving of censure."

"Of censure !" exclaimed Meta, scornfully. "So it is but a trifling matter for censure when a nobleman of an ancient and honorable lineage basely insults an unprotected maiden over whose destiny he has control, through a compact of their parents, by bartering away his claim to her hand as he would the service of a bondsman, and at the same time adding indignity to insult by mentioning as a reason for it his preference for another!"

"False, false—all false. You have been deceived; and I have been traduced."

"Spare your hypocritical excuses," interrupted Meta, drawing a paper from her bosom; "read that and begone!"

She handed me the paper. It was the same that I had given to Caspar. I opened it, and to my astonishment read as follows:—

"My brother Caspar: Having become attached to the Lady *Myra* of *Eberstein*, and she reciprocating the attachment, I freely resign *in your favor* all claim to the hand of the Lady Meta, which I may have in consequence of any betrothment by our respective parents."

A feeling of transport welled up within me, as I looked on this convincing proof of my brother's treachery. Not the sudden discovery of so wretched a crime in him could restrain it. I remained calm, however, and after reading the writing twice over to mark carefully the alterations, I handed it back.

"Well," said Meta, indignantly, "what have you to say?"

"That the writing is a forgery."

"Do you deny your signature?"

"No; but if you will listen to me a few moments, I will prove the forgery to you."

"I will listen."

My explanation was short, but explicit. I detailed with exactness what occurred at the interview between Caspar and myself, so that Meta could understand that it was solely on her account that I had signed anything. I described Caspar's earnestness and apparent sincerity. I narrated all he had said of her attachment to him, and the wretchedness which the betrothment with me was causing both.

I then came to the paper which I had myself written and signed. I bade Meta examine it carefully. I pointed out distinctly the several forgeries: first, where, by a new punctuation and a capital, I was made to address Caspar instead of naming him; second, the alteration of "Meta" to "Myra;" third, the change of "Richstein" to "Eberstein," and fourth, the addition at the end of a line where a space was left, of "in your favor." The alterations were made with extraordinary skill, but were nevertheless apparent to a practised eye.

I next told Meta the conversation I overheard at the inn, and the resolution I took of seeking her out and vindicating myself, though at the expense of exposing a brother's guilt.

She was overwhelmed by my disclosures. We had remained standing all the time, she listening to me earnestly, while her face was at one moment completely crimsoned and the next deadly pale. As I pointed to the alterations in the paper, we stood still closer together, she holding one side of it and I the other. And I perceived her hands tremble and her eyes droop and her lips quiver as she discovered the irresistible proofs of the conspiracy. How my heart warmed toward her as she stood agitated by conflicting emotions; how I cursed my previous indifference; how I wondered that I could have so long abstained from seeing and knowing the one with whom my destiny had been linked; how was I now touched by her extreme loveliness, her dignity, her grace, her modesty, her spirit, her pride, and lofty bearing; how on a sudden did every perfection of womanhood seem to shine in her. She folded the paper, handed it to me, and said in a low but emphatic tone: "I am satisfied. You will accompany me to the chateau that I may introduce you to the baroness."

I assented, and we went on together. Meta declining with

kindness my offer of assistance. On the way she informed me that the baroness was her cousin, whose husband had died some years since, and that she had been in the habit of spending some portion of each year with her.

The reaction upon the discovery of injustice done to an innocent party is not generally of a pleasing nature, but I am sure our walk to the chateau was a happy one.

I know not how it was, but although we scarcely spoke to each other, yet insensibly we slackened our pace, and were moving very slowly along the path. Somehow we walked very near together, although Meta had declined taking my arm — and I began to think that I was her protector, and it seemed as if I could feel down in the depths of my heart, that her spirit was receiving support from mine; and then all nature was gay again, the undines reappeared, and the nymphs and fauns and fairies were sporting as gayly as ever.

Arrived at the chateau, I was ushered in, and Meta left me, to inform her cousin of my coming. More than an hour elapsed before either appeared. After that Meta and the baroness entered together. Meta said nothing, but the baroness greeted me with great kindness. It was evident that she had heard the history of the deceit practised upon me. After a while she took occasion to refer to it. She told me that Caspar had for several years been a frequent visiter at the chateau; that he had introduced to the lady of Rennewart and to herself a monk for whom he claimed a superior sanctity and holiness: this of course was Father Hegel; that I was represented as having apostatized from the true faith (I never had been a Romanist), and was reckless and unprincipled in an extreme degree. As a proof of the last portion, it was stated that I had never thought even of inquiring for Meta or of seeing her, and that I would not hesitate to sell my claim to her hand.

These insinuations were made gradually and quietly; not to Meta, for no opportunity was given for it; but to the baroness and the lady of Rennewart. After a season, they had been convinced, and had promised Caspar that if he obtained proof of my indifference, they would, with the consent of Meta, and of my father, consider him the betrothed. He was finally allowed several interviews with Meta, in which I was traduced in the vilest manner; and to crown the whole, he had called that very morning and left my written renunciation. He had not as yet produced any consent from my father, but had promised to do so shortly. The baroness went on to say, that she hoped I would add nothing to what I had already communicated, that she felt satisfied of my honor and integrity, and that Caspar had always excited in her mind distrust and apprehension. She concluded by informing me that he was expected to return and dine at the chateau, and requested me to take such steps as to receiving him as I should think proper.

The baroness had scarcely concluded, when approaching footsteps were heard in the great hall, and Casper was ushered into the room. He stopped quickly on seeing me, looked at Meta and at the baroness, and turned pale. He did not speak, nor show any other mark of excitement, but maintained his position, as if determined to be addressed before accosting any one. It was too much for me. I rose and came close to him:

"Caspar," I said, "you are henceforth no brother of mine. Never again speak to or approach me. For the first and last time I heap opprobrium upon you. I am compelled to do it in my own defence. I call you forger, liar, knave. Your plans are frustrated, your plot discovered, and you disgraced."

Before I had done speaking, his countenance had resumed its natural cool, sardonic expression. When I concluded, he

glanced calmly around the room, gazed for a moment at the
baroness and at Meta, whose looks told plainly what were
their feelings, and then cast his eyes upon me, with an expression of mingled curiosity and scorn.   Suddenly he nodded
his head, as if satisfied with the scrutiny, muttered slowly to
himself " The monk was right;" turned on his heel, and left
the apartment.

The departure of Caspar was a great relief to all.   So
speedy a termination of the interview, especially when we
believed it to be decisive, removed a load of anxiety which, in
spite of everything, weighed upon us.   Meta continued silent,
but I knew she felt happy and tranquil, because I myself felt
so.   The baroness, however, had enough to converse about.
She taxed my patience by narrating with particularity Caspar's
course from the commencement of her acquaintance with him.
" She could now see why he had said such and such a thing.
and done so and so; she was sure Meta never cared for him;
that Meta would say so herself," and so on; until at last I
ventured to suggest that the subject might be unpleasant to
the Lady Meta, (her words were daggers to me ;) whereupon
the baroness remembered she had forgotten something or
other in her haste to receive me, and begged me to excuse
her presence.   I was left alone with Meta.

How it gladdened my soul that I had never seriously thought
of her as my betrothed; for my heart was left free and un-
trammelled by any previous association, and I could feel like
approaching her as if we had never been the subject of compact or conference.   All the unhappy influences of a betrothment were thus obviated, while the circumstances connected
with Caspar's villany insensibly drew us to each other.   After
the baroness left the room, we took a stroll together upon the
bank of the river.   We spoke not one word of the incidents
of the morning; we conversed about ordinary and casual

things. Very little served to entertain us, for we were satisfied with each other.

Day after day passed, and found me still at the chateau. Day after day I lingered in the enjoyment of Meta's society, and dreaded lest any change should break the spell which held me.

Those are halcyon days,—continued Hegewisch, after a pause,—the days of the first wish of love; the days when the object is found, and the wish becomes a sensation; the days when as yet no words are spoken, but when in their place is that indescribable something in the look, the manner, the conduct of each toward the other, which is perfectly appreciated, yet not quite understood; which leaves room for delicious doubts, and exquisite half-formed hopes, and gentle fears, and sweet questionings of the heart.

But I must on! May the Power which is mightier than I give me strength for this last trial.

XXI.

Hegewisch was silent several minutes, apparently nerving himself for the recital; then his countenance grew animated, his eyes gleamed with a strange fire, and he exclaimed in a bitter tone :

> ——" Nessun maggior dolore,
> Che ricordarsi del tempo felice
> Nella miseria."

The Florentine was in the right when he wrote those lines. No, there is no greater anguish; but there is a point beyond that—yes!—where no anguish, nor sorrow, nor torment comes; because there is nothing within by which to feel them any more, where all is dead. Dead! what more horrible conception! what so dreadful a reality! Vitality, but no life; mind, thought, memory, but no h. pe, no apprehension, no joy, no pang!   Why did not the Ghibelline put *that* into his Divine Comedy?

Life! shall I tell you what it is?   Ah, would it were what so many make it: a pumping of air in and out of the lungs; a covering of the nakedness, to the prevention of shame; eating lest the body fall away; sleeping o' nights, from wearisomeness of the flesh!—then were man indeed somewhat better than a beast.   But to have pining wants which gnaw the soul, and for which no provision has been made; to love, and feel that love lasts only so long as life; to labor, and know that the grave closes upon all results of toil; to enjoy, and be conscious that time withers up the sources of our bliss; to be miserable, and feel that death may not release us; to undergo all the mad pleasures of earth, and all the remorse which their indulgence brings; to feel in prosperity that nothing can secure against change, and to recognise in adversity no hope —Ha! ha! that—*that* is life!   What a precious boon to that poor praying beggar, man!   But in me the god of this world and the GOD of the other world are both baffled, for *I* am DEAD!

—He paused, leaned back in his chair, covered his face with his hands, and groaned aloud.   Thus far he had run on with a frantic rapidity, which showed that his reason was unsettled. I had thought it best not to interrupt him, although he grew every moment more wildly excited.   But the reaction came now; and with exhaustion came reason and calmness, and a profound melancholy.

Saint Leger—he said, in a subdued tone—heed not my ravings.   Look upon me, and behold a desolated ruin.   My spirit and my body are fit companions.   Ah, when shall the end be?   I will go on with my story, truthfully, word for word.   Perhaps you will discover wherein I have sinned.

Would that you could, for it would be a relief t feel I had deserved my doom! The fiend who is dragging me to perdition could then no longer tempt me to blaspheme the Holy Ghost.

—He shuddered as he uttered these words, and I feared he was again becoming excited; but he preserved his composure, and presently went on:

After several days, I left the chateau to return home. My parting with Meta was one of the happiest moments of my life. We had not spoken one word of our feelings for each other during my stay—positively, not one word; but we had talked of almost everything in the wide world; we had exchanged thoughts and sympathies, and, strange to say, our feelings were in exact harmony. The endless, boundless world of the imaginative and the imaginable! Pleasant is it when we find in another the echo of what we feel and are; but how much higher the enjoyment when we can appreciate in such a one the feelings which we ourselves do not possess, and thus enter, soul with soul, into the sweet exchange of spiritual harmonies! By not reducing our feelings to the point of mere self-enjoyment, we experience a growing happiness, the reverse of what those lovers feel who allow the flame to die by what it feeds on, and who in this way are exposed to the curse of a double selfishness. To sustain the life of the affections, we require a companion, not a counterpart; and they are blessed who mistake not one for the other.

I said that my parting with Meta was one of the happiest moments of my life; for, like the miser, I wanted time and opportunity to tell over my treasures, and hug the remembrance of all that I had gained closer to my bosom. Besides, it seemed to me that our intercourse during a separation would be kept up with all the charm of a refined spirituality; and then we should enjoy that mysterious influence which

those who love do have over one another when absent, and
which is more precious to the soul than all the delights of a
closer, sensible union. Thus I took leave of the baroness,
and bade Meta adieu, and went on my way; a halo of bliss
surrounded me; I dwelt in a world of ecstasy. What a
sweet separation ! what happy hours of exquisite memories !

XXII.

How opposite all this to the stern, unyielding, practical,
which for ever unremittingly does labor, laboring; or to the
iron necessity that fills the stomachs of the starving by robbery
or theft; or to the condition of the sick one, languishing
and ready to die; or to that of the bold blasphemer of
Almighty God.

XXIII.

WHEN I reached my home I found Caspar already there.
According to my resolution, I passed him without notice. Believing, however, that he had not practised upon my father, I
scorned to repeat to him what had occurred.

I had but just got to my own apartment, on the first day
of my return home, when he opened the door and came in.

"Wolfgang," said he, with an ingenuous air, "you are a
more sensible fellow than I ever gave you credit for being.
You have outwitted two shrewd heads, and how the deuce
you found us out I can not imagine. You are reserved, eh ?
and regard me with offended dignity ? Nay, do not frown;
do not draw back. Listen to me. I fell in love with Meta.
You look indignant. Well, then, I will 'speak the truth and
shame the devil.' I fell in love with the Castle of Richstein
and its dependencies, and old baronies and tenures. Now
strategy is commendable in the race for a fair maiden. I at-

tempted it with you, and I have been foiled : had I succeeded, you would have been foiled. But here is my hand; for once I am frank with you. I bear you no malice for the savage words you hurled at me the other day. Be as good a Christian as I am : forgive and forget."

It was with difficulty that I could preserve my self-possession during this insulting harangue. When it was concluded, I waved my hand and bade him begone.

"Have you nothing to say to my offer of amity?" he inquired.

"Nothing except that I believe you are as treacherous in the offer as you were in the fraud you attempted to practise. For the sake of our parents, I am content to pass you as I would a stranger. Expect nothing more. Come not near me or mine ; cross not my path ; practise on me no more, or by the blood that is now boiling in my veins, I will crush you as I would a reptile beneath my heel."

'Fool," exclaimed Caspar, "I was prepared to yield what fate had wrested from me ; but as you defy and threaten me, look to yourself. You have roused a demon within me which I was willing enough should slumber. Look to yourself; for the evil day comes to you and yours. Remember the word I utter now — *Revenge.*"

He went out in a passion, and departed from the castle : it was a month before I saw him again; then he had resumed his usual manner, only he was more quiet and taciturn. We met as strangers, having no intercourse whatever. It thus became necessary that the baron should understand what had passed between us. I gave him an account of the whole affair. He was almost prostrated at the recital; the forgery touched him to the quick. For a time he was in the deepest agony: no one can portray his feelings. His first intention was to banish Caspar for ever from his roof; but I interposed.

My kind and gentle mother also interceded, and it was settled that he might remain. Caspar, however, could not but
observe the change which had taken place in the castle. Every eye was averted as he passed, and every look told strongly of dislike and contempt.

This seemed not to affect him; he preserved the same habits of careless and hardened indifference. And so we lived
another year.

Remorseless, the wheel of time sweeps onward. Now
heavily creaking, it moves with a duller pace than the snail.
Again it hastens majestically with a thunder-speed. Anon
the wheel flies round and round with impress as light as the
footprint of the swift Camilla. But remorseless always, for it
is driven by Destiny.

Speak I not an illusion? Moves the hand upon the dial, slow
or fast, as I suffer or am happy? Does the sun stand still on
Gibeon while I groan under the torture of the rack? or hastens it down behind the groves of Vallombrosa as I hang in
ecstasy on the lips of my beloved? And yet it is thus our
feelings give character to the world about us; to time and to
eternity. And it is thus that I can understand an *eternal hell*.

—He continued to moralize, like a man desiring to gain
time before submitting to some painful operation. I did not
interrupt him, and at length he came back to his story:

Well, another year was gone. I had passed it profitably;
I had become a man. During the period, Meta and I had
spoken to each other of our love. It did not make me the
less happy, for although my heaven of bliss faded mysteriously away, it left a terrestrial paradise in its place more natural,
and therefore I should say happier, in an earthly state. For
it yields a more desirable existence in a world where joy and
sorrow are to be shared by trusting and trustful hearts.

What therefore nature ordains, who should gainsay? Ah,

I had no wish to gainsay it, when I could pour out my whole soul in impassioned accents, and receive in return the treasures of *her* heart.

How we talked, and hoped, and planned! what rich contributions were levied upon the future! What images of bliss did we see in all coming time, and how did we paint the golden hours, when closely united, never to be separated in life, earth would become to us an Elysium! All that I had ever hoped for or imagined, all that poets had ever painted, or minstrels sung, I found in the soul of my betrothed.

Gladly would I linger here over that happy year. A lifetime of love was crowded into it.

I was now a man, and began to feel stirring within me that leaven of unrest which after a certain period, for some strange purpose, works in the human breast unceasingly, urging to action and to toil. This did not disturb my soul's passion — my love for Meta; it rather gave it force and manliness. But I felt that there was something to be seen and known beyond the petty boundary of my own principality. I had a healthful curiosity to visit other countries, that I might return with more expanded ideas, with a larger benevolence, with a fuller view of humanity, so that I might better understand my true relation with the world. I became fully possessed with this desire. Meta, whose love was not bounded by narrow selfishness, and who entered into all my thoughts, encouraged me in my plan. The baron, my father, approved of it, and my dear mother would not say nay, although she shook her head mournfully, and her eyes would fill with tears whenever I mentioned the subject.

Twenty-one years six months and thirteen days of life had I lived, *eighteen years and five months* had lived Meta, when I set out for the old castle of Richstein, to bid her adieu before I hastened on my voyage. There were feastings at the castle, and there was wassail among the neighboring lords, and among the retainers and dependents of Richstein, for the lady Meta had returned to her ancestral house, thenceforth to be her home. With her had come the lady of Rennewart, a proper companion and guide for a young maiden under these newly assumed honors.

We met as lovers should meet. We—[here the student stopped, his voice was difficult; his face exhibited the deepest despair] parted—as lovers should part [he ejaculated, after an effort]: Twenty-one years and six months and thirteen days lived I; eighteen years and five months lived Meta, *and no more time lived we;* no more—no more! There stopped the hands upon the dial-plate. Let death and hell rejoice—they were victorious.

It is of no consequence where I voyaged. But, in brief, let me say, that I visited the Americas, and doubled the cape, where two oceans sweep together. I went among nations unenlightened and barbarous, and visited countries civilized and refined. I passed to the gorgeous East, and trod the precincts of the Holy Land. My tour was not, as my rambles about home had been, desultory. I planned it with care. Two years was the time I allowed for my absence, and I allotted a certain period to each division of my journey. Upon the map, Meta and I had marked where I would probably be at such and such a time, so that we might keep up a close union of ideas.

I passed first, young Englishman, to your country, and there learned what was liberty; therefore I liked your nation. From England I sailed upon my voyage.

Meta and I had one source of distress. This was the long time that must intervene in hearing from each other. In England I could receive frequent intelligence, but, my voyage commenced, a long period would elapse before we should hear again. She, however, was to send letters in advance to the places I was expected to touch at or visit, and I, in return, promised to write by every opportunity.

During the first twelve months after leaving England I heard from Meta four times, and from my home as often. For the next six months I could not expect to hear from her, owing to the infrequency of my route; but I comforted myself with the thought that, after that time, I should be continually approaching home, and should hear often of the welfare of those I loved.

I came at last to Constantinople. My pilgrimage seemed drawing to a close. I could now at least communicate directly with my fatherland. I was confident of finding a large budget at the Prussian embassy. But I went and found nothing. I knew there was some mistake, and so inquired again. Still nothing. I asked once more, with great particularity. Nothing—nothing at all.

I never felt heart-sick before, but I tried to sustain courage. In the disturbed state of Europe what wonder if packages should miscarry; but how could so many have miscarried? After all, I did not know how to despair; my heart was naturally buoyant, and I could not augur ill of the future, for the future had never deceived me. I stayed nearly a month in the city of the Moslem, hoping each day that I should hear news from home, but none came. So, after hurrying rapidly through Greece, I sailed for Leghorn, where I was sure of hearing something. And I did hear. There was one letter waiting my arrival at the commercial house to whose care all communications for me were to be addressed. *One* letter, directed in a strange hand, was, by the confidential clerk—a withered old man with a bald head and dull gray eyes—given to me; and, taking it, I retired in haste from the counting-room, and gaining the street, I walked slowly toward my hotel. I had the letter in my hand all the time. I looked at it often on the way, but did not open it.

I reached my hotel; went to my apartment; bolted the door; I laid aside my cap and cloak, and sat down. Still the letter remained unopened. In one instant I could know my fate. I took a long breath, broke away the seal, and tore open the sheet. . . . . . My father was dead, that was all. Meta—was safe!

The letter was written by a friend of the family, announcing the sudden death of my father, and urging my immediate return. It was dated more than six months previous, and stated that duplicates would be sent to every place at which I might be supposed to touch. The letter was short, but it spoke of my mother as too overwhelmed by the event to write to me. My friends were generally well. A post-scriptum, however, added, that a courier had just arrived from Richstein, announcing the decease of the lady of Rennewart.

In thirty minutes I was *en route* for Germany. I paused neither night nor day. When horses gave out I changed them. I had no rest nor refreshment except what I took in my carriage. Night and day, day and night, I hurried on. At length, one morning, as the gray dawn began to streak over the east, I arrived at a little town about five leagues from Richstein. There I stopped and ordered breakfast and fresh horses. So far, excitement had kept me up; but now I felt the need of something to sustain me.

I ate breakfast; I can swear that I did. I remember it with distinctness; but my heart throbbed loudly all the time. Again I was on the road, and it would soon bring me to the castle of Richstein.

My heart beat louder and louder. I was tempted to ask some questions of one of the postillions, but refrained. The Rhine flowed along placidly, as of yore, and through the trees I could discern the towers of Richstein standing out cheerfully in the morning sun.

I drove up the main avenue, and getting out before I reached the castle, I bade the postillions wait for me. Hastening down a private path which led to a secret entrance to the castle, I gained the main hall, where I encountered one of the old servants, whom I at once recognised. " Where," said I, "is your mistress? where is the lady Meta?"

The old man's countenance fell; his voice faltered, but he made out to answer: "In her own apartment, sir; next to the library."

I bounded up the stairway; I passed through the narrow hall; I reached Meta's room; I flung open the door. Meta was sitting unoccupied, looking out at the window. She seemed just as beautiful and as blooming as when I left her. Rapturously I called out her name and ran toward her. She turned upon me an unmeaning look, started from her seat, and ran to the other end of the room. Oh, GOD! what did it mean!

I called to Meta again. I repeated my own name, and asked her if she did not know me. She screamed aloud at the sound of my voice, and falling on her knees, began praying piteously for mercy. "No! no!" she exclaimed, "I will never speak of Wolfgang again!—I will only pray for him! I *must* pray for him—I WILL pray for him!—though you beat me, murder me, give me that hateful thing to drink— pray for him I will! but nothing more! nothing more!" And then she burst into tears, and went on weeping so sadly, that I knew not what to do. Oh, merciful CREATOR! the truth burst upon me—my Meta was *mad*. But I had still to know the worst—still to feel the iron enter deeper into my soul.

The door opened, and Caspar entered. 'Soho, Mr

Knight-Errant!" he exclaimed; "you have returned, eh? I have no objections to greeting you at the proper time and in the proper place, but you must not come here into my wife's apartment!"

I did not tremble, nor turn pale; I grew composed. My heart ceased to beat loudly, and fell back into its customary measured pulsation. I saw it all, and stood firm. "Is Meta your wife?" said I, sternly.

"She is," said the other; "and the sooner you leave this room, the better. She is very nervous, as you perceive, and your presence is particularly disagreeable to her."

"Wretch—devil—hell-hound!" said I, fiercely, "your life is in danger!"

The villain smiled contemptuously and placed his hand upon his dagger, which he half unsheathed.

"Nay, draw it; I say to you that I will NOT leave this room!"

"We shall see," said Caspar; and going out he returned presently with three or four men servants.

"Put that man out from here, and turn him from the castle."

"The man who touches me at this moment, shall look for his soul in eternity the next."

The men did not stir.

"And as for you," I said, turning to Caspar, "do as I bid you: draw your dagger; defend yourself the best way you can; for your time is short.'

So saying, I rushed upon him, twisted the dagger from his hand, and seizing him in my arms, swung him round and round as if he were a plaything, and hurled him through the lattice-work clear out of the window, to the pavement below. By Heaven, I did! I hurled him out upon the stone-work as I would toss a biscuit overboard into the sea.

I glanced round and said, "Whose turn next? who wants to follow?"

The room was vacant in a trice.

I turned to look for Meta. She had crept up into the corner of the room, and was crouching behind some drapery that lay there. I touched her. She looked up at me with her once beautiful but now wild eyes, and exclaimed piteously, "Oh, do not, do not come so near me! I have seen you in dreams, and in visions, and in the voice of waters, and have prayed for your soul's welfare, my beloved!" And then she burst into tears again. I could endure this no longer. I took my betrothed in my arms. I went down the staircase and out at the secret entrance, and traversed the private path until I came to the carriage. I placed Meta in it, and getting in myself, took her in my arms, and ordered the postillions to drive swiftly to ——. They obeyed. The wheels flew round; the distance was rapidly passed. Meta slumbered upon my breast as sweetly as an infant.

At length the walls of my paternal mansion were in sight. The wanderer had returned from his pilgrimage, and had brought home his bride. Presently we reached the castle. I was in my mother's arms. I know not how. The whole household were almost instantly around me, and received me as one restored from the dead. Meta was carried sleeping to a quiet chamber, and there I watched her. I did not sleep.

She slept peacefully for several hours. I did not leave her an instant during the time. At last she awoke. With what eagerness I had waited for that moment; but, alas! I was to be disappointed; her reason had not returned. When I spoke to her, she commenced weeping, as if her heart would break. The burden of all she said was, that she had prayed for me, that she would pray for me and for the welfare of my soul; then she implored my forgiveness, and again cried piteously for mercy.

I was distracted. How I bore my anguish I know not. My mother came in. At the sight of her, Meta was soothed. She nestled her face in my mother's bosom, and was tranquil.

On the first opportunity I sought an explanation. The baroness could give none. She could only say that after my departure everything went on happily and well until the death of my father, which had occurred suddenly about seven months previous; and that the lady of Rennewart had died under a similar attack on the succeeding day. My mother was so overwhelmed by the dreadful affliction, that for some months she was unable to leave her room; and when she did come out, she learned that Caspar had espoused the lady Meta; that they were privately married, a dispensation having been procured for that purpose. She had not seen Caspar since the death of the baron, and upon going to Richstein to visit the lady Meta, she was refused admittance upon some frivolous excuse. This was all my mother could tell me. Would you believe it, that in this enlightened age, and in this enlightened country, such an outrage could have been committed so secretly, and so surely? But two devils planned it, and hell gloried in the plot.

How my heart was crushed, day by day, I need not tell you. To see my betrothed, apparently in health, fair and beautiful as ever, and yet, a maniac or an imbecile! How can I sit so calmly and tell all this! Why will not my heart bleed!— why can I not feel!

I watched over Meta almost every moment, and when I was not with her, my mother took my place.

I gave not a thought about the fate of Caspar, but news found its way to the castle, that he had been taken up bleeding and insensible, and that, although he was severely hurt, his injuries were not considered fatal. I was not the destroyer of my brother. I am thankful now that it was so. Then I did not care.

Weeks passed on. Sometimes I would take hope, from Meta's becoming more quiet than usual. She would look at me with an almost natural expression, and then would commence weeping violently, insisting, as usual, that she would pray for me. At last she fell sick. It was a blessed relief, for I could alleviate her physical suffering, although I could not minister to the troubles of her soul.

A burning fever attacked her. Her strength was prostrated. A celebrated physician, my father's friend, was called in. He took great interest in the case, and watched it with sedulous attention. It was a pleasure to see him at the bedside of his patient: so careful, so discriminating, so judicious. To this physician, this friend, I had given no word of explanation; but I saw that he knew all.

One morning, after paying his usual visit, he called me into another room. "I think it best," said he, "to advise you that a crisis will soon take place in the disease under which the lady Meta is languishing: probably to-morrow, perhaps to-night. If she comes out of her present state with her reason restored, she will not again lose it, but—she will die. She can not survive many days. If, on the contrary, she comes out of it with a dull and settled melancholy, she will recover; but she will always remain in imbecility."

I was again seized with terror. I turned away, and went back to Meta's chamber. She was in a deep slumber. I knelt by her bedside, and prayed that her reason might come back to her, and that she might die.

The sleep continued through the night. During the whole time I sat by her and watched. The disease had done its office upon that lovely handiwork of God. There were the sunken eye, and the pale, thin cheek, and the pallid brow; yet these were not half so appalling as were all the marks of life and health, and fresh, living beauty, which she had retained at the expense of a soul in ruins.

The morning came, and she still slumbered. I gazed at her by the light of day, and thought I saw a change on her countenance; calmness, and quietude, were there.

No one was in the room save Meta and I. At length she breathed heavily and opened her eyes. I trembled so much that my knees shook together. She looked faintly around, as if the place were unfamiliar, and then fixed her eyes upon me. A thrill of pain seemed to dart through her, and then a ray of joy illumined her wan face. She raised her hands, and extended them toward me. "Thank God," she murmured, and swooned away. When she came to herself she was very weak, but she was tranquil. She could scarcely speak, but I saw that she was happy. I bent over her, and she whispered, and called me Wolfgang. She asked where she was, and when I had come back, and whether I had been all the time well.

She had no recollection of anything unhappy or unpleasant respecting herself, and I thanked Heaven for this drop of real mercy. She said she had been ill, dreadfully ill, for months; and had been tormented with horrible dreams and visions, too horrible to think of, or to mention, but that she felt better now. This was all she said.

I feared, as her sense became clearer, that the truth would dawn upon her: but it was not so. She continued to speak of her long illness, dating its commencement from the sudden death of the lady of Rennewart—the last event she recollected.

She continued nearly without change for several days. She was extremely weak, but daily gained a little strength. Still, she herself had no hope of recovering. She would hold my hand for hours, and, when too feeble to converse, gaze at me as if her soul was drinking in delight.

Oh, happy unconsciousness! Oh, blessed memory, that for once forgot its office!

"This is not the promised consummation, Wolfgang, dearest," said Meta to me one evening. "But what matters it? our spirits are wedded. And, if I precede you to the bright world beyond, your soul will find out mine: and then we shall never part again. No voyaging, then, Wolfgang, no voyaging, then!"

My heart was bursting. I leaned my head upon her pillow in agony.

"Nay, this is unkind. The strong should have confidence. But ah, I see! God, in mercy, when he takes away our strength, bestows upon us faith."

"Do you remember, Wolfgang, those happy hours at Rhineck? In a little while we shall be spending happier seasons than those. I believe it. I know it," she continued, while her countenance grew bright with the radiance of heaven.

"You will not be very happy, dear Wolfgang, when I am gone; but a little while, and then, we part no more—no more. Here now, upon the borders of the other world, I feel that there was no earth, no dross, in my love for you; and this is why I know we shall be one hereafter."

For a few days Meta continued to gain strength, slowly, and I began to hope : hope? to fear, rather; for how could I ever name to her the dreadful truth. I forced the subject from my mind, and gave myself entirely to that suffering angel.

Even the physician seemed as if he thought his prediction might prove false. But it was not to be. Two weeks had elapsed, when one morning Meta complained of faintness. Upon examination it was found that internal hemorrhage had commenced, caused by the violence of the fever. All that skill could suggest was put in requisition to check the attack, but it was of no avail; she died—she died sweetly, gently, lovingly, in the morning, while the sun was beaming brightly, and the river was running placidly on its course; when birds were singing and the world was alive to cheerfulness and joy.

It was a time for her to die. I held her hand clasped tenderly in mine, when the spirit left its home; and then, I had only the hand, but no Meta—ah, God ! no Meta.

—Hegewisch remained for some time silent, and then went on in a different tone and with the air of one relieved from a dreaded task :

I had yet to sustain another shock. My kind physician sought an early opportunity to speak to me in private.

" My young friend," said he, "from the bottom of my soul I pity you. What I am about to say, you must hear, and, if you can, forget. I was your father's early friend and companion. We were together always. I attended him upon his death-bed. I tell you—you, his son—that the baron died by *poison*."

"And the Lady of Rennewart ?" said I convulsively.

" In the same way, without doubt. I did not attend her."

" And Caspar ?"

" We have said *enough*. Adieu."

Here was room for a world of horrible surmises. So long as Meta lived, I thought only of her. Under the pressure of this horror, a new feeling took possession of me : it was a desire for vengeance.

I dared not deliberately imbrue my hands in a brother's blood ; so I turned all my hate upon his coadjutor and abet ter, Father Hegel.   I did not try further to solve the mystery connected with the late terrible events.   I guessed enough. And therefore my revenge sought out the monk.

I deliberated upon many plans, but in none could I please myself.   I tried to invent some new and devilish torture to which to subject his vile body while I should stand gloating over the spectacle.   I thought of seizing him secretly, and starving him slowly to death.   No scheme which man or fiend could suggest, did I fail to turn over in my mind.   At length I determined to kill him before the very altar, while he was offering, with his unholy breath, some prayer to Heaven. Then I could send his soul to hell — doubly damned by hypocritical offerings to the GOD he was mocking.

The monk was accustomed on certain occasions to celebrate mass at a chapel near our castle.   I watched for the time and for the season ; both came ; and I sat out one morning to perform the sacrifice.   I was late in gaining the chapel, and as I came up I perceived a crowd around the entrance. I made my way hastily to it, and beheld Father Hegel lying in the agonies of death.   He had fallen in a fit of apoplexy. There he lay, his sensual features full of blood, while the distortions of his countenance showed his agony.   In a few moments he was no more ; and I was cheated of my revenge. I did not rave till then.   I turned away, and before the temple and the altar cursed God.   I rejected all belief in a Savior, and blasphemed the Holy Ghost.   Hell was not black enough to darken my heart.   I had borne everything till now — and now, everything was insupportable.   I ran with incredible swiftness back to the castle.   I gained *her* room.   I locked myself in — I threw myself upon her bed.   I grew wild and delirious; I began to be in pain ; I flung the door open and shouted for help.   My mother and several of the servants came.   That night the fever attacked me, and for weeks I was prostrate under its burning rage. I could never have recovered without the attention of a tender parent and devoted physician.   Yet I did recover, but, as you see me, with these hollow cheeks—this 'repulsive countenance—these sunken eyes.

I determined to leave my home, for the fiend followed me wherever I went, whispering that Caspar lived. So I took leave of my mother—one bright, moonlight night, when she was fast asleep—by kissing her many, many times. You know she was the only one left who cared for me : but—I went on my way. I have spent most of the time since at the universities. I do not know why, but study and toil of mind are best for me. Once my mother discovered where I was, and I had to go back with her, but I made my escape, and came here to Leipsic.

I have tried very hard to *feel*. I have wished that something might excite me; that my life might be in danger, so that, instinctively, I should put forth my strength to save it. I avoid no danger; I keep open house ; here is my treasury, [the student pulled out a drawer, without lock or key, nearly filled with gold pieces] but nobody robs the strange fellow, ha—ha—ha! They are afraid of me. I sleep in yonder ; and sometimes I lay all night and think of Meta and myself at the old chateau. And my heart seems less dead—and then, I sleep—to wake, always the same—always the same. Now leave me !

I took my departure in silence.

Thus ends the story of Wolfgang Hegewisch.

END OF BOOK THIRD.

BOOK IV.

'Ω ΦΙΛΕΠΑΝ τε καὶ ἄλλοι θεοί, δοίητέ μοι καλῶ γενέσθαι τἄνδοθεν, τἄξωθεν δὲ ὅσα ἔχω, τοῖς ἐντὸς εἶναί μοι φίλια.

PHŒDRUS, 279, B.

Oh thou beloved Universal Numen, and ye other Divinities, grant that I may become more beautiful within, and that whatever of externals I may possess may be all in harmony with my inward (spiritual) being.

BOOK FOURTH.

I.

THE casement is open. The delicious perfume of summer finds its way hither unbidden. The still, solemn pines tower up in the twilight. Across the Avon the new forest stands lonely and silent. The river runs between, dark and deep, always flowing; season after season, year after year, age after age, flowing on; an emblem of permanence and of change.

II.

I FEEL like labor. Go to! I will spoil this beautiful twilight.—Thomas, bring candles. . . . . .

Now comes the moth to seek destruction in the flame. Hark: the cricket is chirping its unvaried note; the nightingale whistles his sweet but melancholy strain. The owl and bat, the fire-fly and will-o'-the-wisp, they too are busy enough.

Where is the lively squirrel that has been springing all day from bough to bough? where the pigeon and the hawk? where the lark and the vulture, the linnet and the eagle, the coney and the fox?

The snake no longer glides across the path, and the toad has found a resting-place. But the owl hoots from the treo

and the bat flits crazily through the gloaming; the fire-fly
and will-o'-the-wisp—see! there they sparkle and flicker
and brighten again!

"Where is GOD my MAKER, who giveth songs in the night?"

III.

READER, who hast borne me company thus far, if indeed
you have entertained a sympathy in this narrative, then let us
rest a moment here.

Perhaps you are young, and if you *are* young, stand up,
and bless GOD that just at this very instant, you are brought
to a pause.

Bring out your hopes and look at them. Look at them;
but not through a Claude-Lorraine glass. Look at them, and
tell me, do they belong to the petty future of earth, or to
the infinite of another life? Can you not answer? Alas!
what an unhappy thought that you know not yourself; that
you should be always journeying on with—a stranger—
yourself a stranger to you, and you a stranger to yourself!
an awful companionship. Great GOD, what if you be destined
to live thus for ever!

Perhaps, you are no longer young. Nevertheless, you
have hopes—yes, hopes, still.

Bring out your hopes and look at them. Look at them;
but not through the dark vapor of disappointment or despair.
Nay, shake not your head so gloomily: but arouse; and do
you too thank GOD that you are brought for a while to this
stand-still, as the world rushes on and leaves you. Do not
be impatient: do not say to me, "Hands off! I must over-
take my comrades yonder; see how they get the start of me."
Stay, something better is in store for you than this unnatural
race which you are running; and what balm is there in that

word " better!" Let it continue always better—and how will you approximate by-and-by to the TO BEATIΣTON!

Come, then, youth and man and maiden; come and sit down with me, as the evening deepens into night. There—I have put out the candles—and the moth is safe.

Let us bring out our hopes and look at them. Let us do it in a cheerful, hopeful, heartfelt way. Thank GOD we are here yet, safe upon the earth; and the earth *does* seem safe to man; the enduring earth, the kind mother, the patient nurse, which yields us sustenance and supports our life. While we talk of a BEYOND, we would not forget thee, pro-lific Parent, with thy changing seasons; glorifying and renew-ing thy days in the hoar-frosts of winter, in the balmy breath of spring, in the triumphant maturity of summer, and in the fading glories of the fall. Earth, we bless thee. Surely we may bless thee, if the CREATOR pronounced thee good. Shall we not forgive thee the bearing of a few thorns and thistles for all the fruit which we have pressed from thy bosom, or shall we complain, that in the sweat of our face we have to till the ground, since it yieldeth us her strength *by* tilling?

But to our hopes: these hopes shall indicate our destiny. Arrest and cut off all that are anchored here; strip the heart of the vain promptings which flutter around it; silence the busy whisperings of passion and self-love; then tell me—youth, man, maiden—what have we remaining? Is there a void—an utter void—left in these hearts of ours? nothing possessed, nothing enjoyed, no residuum but the bitter ashes? Is it even with us " as when a hungry man dreameth, and be-hold he eateth: but he awaketh, and his soul is empty: or as when a thirsty man dreameth, and behold he drinketh; but he awaketh, and behold he is faint, and his soul hath appetite?" Then indeed have we made shipwreck when the voyage has scarce commenced, and we have only to look to it that such shipwreck be not irreparable. To the work—quick, quick! that the voyage may NOT be lost.

But arrest and cut off and silence these whisperings and promptings and hopes, and do our hearts still beat with their usual time? Do we behold a broad expanse beyond the extreme limits of the actual? Is our gaze into this expanse only rendered brighter and clearer by the cutting away of the superfluous foliage? and can we with a lofty look and courageous heart and trustful spirit, lay our hands upon our breast and feel the Infinite stirring within us? Youth, man, maiden, I give you joy if this be so; for then indeed are we safe; safe, though the possibilities which surround us are fearful to contemplate; though we may not control the hour or the circumstance; though grief may be preparing for us a potion in the same cup from which we have drank delights and joys; though everything about us seem dark and unpropitious; though everything be dark and unpropitious, yet are we safe—*safe*.

Farewell, youth, man, maiden! Perhaps we shall meet in another world; perhaps we may then call to mind how, for a few moments, upon the banks of the Avon, in gentle Warwickshire, we stopped and communed together.

IV.

WHAT had become of Kauffmann? I was to meet him on the second day after our interview; several weeks had elapsed and he had not made his appearance. At first I wondered at his prolonged absence, but I soon became so interested in Wolfgang Hegewisch and by the society of Theresa Von Hofrath, to say nothing of studies which I pursued systematically under the learned professor, that I had almost forgotten Kauffmann, and his company of Free Speakers.

One morning after breakfast I was seated in my own room. Whether I was thinking of my last evening's conversation with Theresa, or of the Latin thesis upon which I was engaged, I can not tell. I had accomplished little or nothing, although I had been an hour at my task. My door was open, I held my pen in my hand, and a partly finished sentence, began half an hour before, had dried in upon my paper, together with sundry attempted continuations, which had been corrected, written over, and dashed out. I heard a step upon the stairway, and then a step through the hall, then a step into my room; a bold, manly, hopeful, straight-forward step; but I did not look up, I did not feel like looking up; for just at that moment the strong elastic physique of the step was discordant to my feelings; so I held my head over the paper, brought my pen to a line with the sheet, and was about changing a participle into a gerund by way of emendation, when I received a friendly blow upon the shoulder, and at the same time a hand was held out for me to shake. Then I looked up—it was Friedrich Kauffmann.

"I see I must announce myself—my name is Kauffmann, once a friend to you ——"

"Now a friend *of* me," interrupted I, laughing. "How could you expect to be recognised after running away, staying away, and breaking an engagement?"

"Spem bonam certamque reporto,"

said he, in a cheerful tone.

"Se non è vero è ben trovato,"

returned I, looking him full in the face, and discovering that hope was indeed in the ascendant there.

"How you are metamorphosed; what has happened to you? Give me your hand again. You are happier than you were; better than you were, your mind is in health; it was not in health when we separated. Kauffmann, I rejoice with you; pray tell me what has produced this change?"

Kauffmann's countenance assumed a serious expression. It was evident he had something to communicate. Shutting the door, he proceeded to seat himself close by me.

"Saint Leger, I have settled in my own mind a matter that has always perplexed it."

"Well."

"It is the relation of the sexes to each other."

"Ay!"

"So sure am I that I am right, that I do not fear to tell you all."

"Pray go on."

"I will. Do you remember our last discussion? Do you not recollect—some wizard must have put it into your head —you told me I had had in my time a love affair, and had quarrelled with my friend because she would not yield to me?"

"Yes."

"Saint Leger, every word was true; true *verbatim et liter-atim*. And had you struck me to the earth I should not have been more astounded.

"'Surely,' said I, 'something must be wrong in what I have done, if a mere acquaintance lights upon it in this way.' So I went home and locked myself into my room, and I said, after I had turned the key: 'Friedrich Kauffmann, thou goest not out hence till thou hast sifted thyself as wheat. Self-confident though thou art, thou shalt yield if thou ought to yield;' and I communed with my heart, and I tried to commune with God; I brought to mind everything that took place at that last interview—that unfortunate interview, between Margaret and myself. I weighed everything truthfully. I had done the same before, but in different scales. Then I thought of creation and life, and happiness and unhappiness, and what should cause the one and the other; and I asked myself, To fit us for a hereafter, must we of necessity suffer—always suffer? Dare I blame my Maker before I have searched in myself for cause of censure? And so I came—standing up alone before God—to believe, and to feel, and to know, that much as I had loved Margaret, I had not loved her aright, or thought of her aright, or treated her aright; and then a new light broke in upon me, and I unlocked the door and ran out, and earth was bright. The next day I had seen Margaret and all was explained."

"But the relation of the sexes?" said I.

"I intended that for another interview, when we both have more leisure. I come now on a special mission."

"Nay, but I am curious to have a synopsis at least of your theory."

"Very briefly, then, it is this: The most perfect spiritual happiness consists in the spiritual union of a man and woman, just as the most perfect domestic felicity consists in a well-adapted temporal union. How rare y are both kinds blended! How are we taught, from youth up, that man's province is command, and woman's submission! Is it not absolutely absurd to suppose the Creator should make one sex to be in subjection to the other? the good God to ordain and perpetuate an eternal tyranny! Besides, is it not folly to suppose friendship can exist except between beings mutually free? The spiritual union makes the perfect life. And there can not be spiritual *union* where one spirit is the master spirit and the other the subservient spirit. I spurn the cant idea of our times, that difference in sex is an organization of earth, with reference only to the continuance of the race. So sure as there is another life, will male and female be so through eternity; they are destined to seek and find happiness in each other; together to fill the object of creation, perfection in unity. But I can stay no longer at present; I came to engage you for this evening."

"But Margaret and yourself, and this perfect life, including the spiritual and the domestic, are they so happily blended that you have no fears of another ——"

"None; fellow-student, none," interrupted Kauffmann, rapidly. "Saint Leger, had I not felt sure of your sympathy in this matter, my lips had been closed," he said, suspiciously.

"You have it: believe me, you have it, my friend. And, if your theory requires a little more perfect development at your hands before I embrace it, remember I am not the less rejoiced at the renewal of your hopes."

"I believe you; take my hand; and now say, will you be at my rooms at seven, precisely?"

"For what?"

"To accompany me to a meeting of the Free Speakers."

"I fear I must decline: on the whole, I can not join your company."

"Oh, Father Jupiter!

> 'Proh superi! quantum mortalia pectora cæcæ
> Noctis habent!'

Who asks thee to join us! What a cautious, calculating wretch you are. But you are an Englishman, and I will not condemn you for the vandalism that is part of your nature. Know then that I have obtained the consent of our society, that you, undeserving as you are, should be present on one of our mystical nights, when you will see no one but the scribe, and hear all that your ears shall catch. This is a distinction never before granted to living man. By Heaven, we refused Goethe himself, who wanted, as a matter of curiosity, to be present on one occasion."

"Say no more; I go, and thank you, upon my knees, for the privilege.   Will that do?"

"Yes.   Live well."

And so saying, Friedrich Kauffmann left the apartment, with the same elastic, cheerful step, with which he entered it. I rose, and looked out into the garden.   I beheld Theresa in a small arbor, engaged in securing a vine which had broken loose from its fastening.   Snatching up the thesis, I tore it into a hundred pieces, and the next minute I was assisting Theresa to train the vine.

V.

I concluded to go with Kauffmann to the " mystical meeting."   At the appointed hour I was at his rooms, and we set out together.

"Have you no instructions to give me," said I, " before we enter ?   How am I to act ?—what shall I do ?"

" You are not to act, and you are to do nothing but listen with all your ears."

"And what is the meaning of ' mystical night' ? "

" The night when we speak ' unsight, unseen,' and treat generally of hidden things.   We then venture often upon daring suggestions, not to say assertions, believing that some truth will be heaved up among the error."

" But who is truth-sifter to the society ?"

" Hush ! we shall get into a discussion, and it will spoil my sybiline tranquillity.   Besides, here we are at the door.   Go in at the entrance; you are expected.   You will find the scribe in his seat, and a vacant chair for you ; take it, and say nothing."

" But you ?"

" I enter from another direction.   You will not see me again to-night.   Farewell."

VI.

I PUSHED through the door, and found myself in a dark, narrow passage. I had nothing to do but stumble along till I came to the end of it, which I did presently, and discovering another door, I opened that, and found myself in a room of moderate size, tolerably well lighted, containing twelve little chapels or recesses, across which curtains were suspended from the ceiling, so that the occupant could remain unseen.

In the centre sat the scribe, with a large book upon a desk before him. Near him was a vacant chair, the only one to be seen. I marched in and took my seat, with as much nonchalance of manner as I could assume. The scribe did not appear to observe my entrance; he did not look up, or alter a muscle of his countenance. Not supposing that I was literally limited to the use of my ears, I took the liberty of casting my eyes around this strange apartment. Directly over the door at which I entered was inscribed, in large letters:

"Worship God."

Upon the wall opposite the door was the following:

ELEMENTS.	NATURE.	COMPLEXION.	PLANETS.
Water.	Cold and moist.	Phlegm.	Venus and Mars.
Fire.	Hot and dry.	Choler.	Sol and Mars.
Earth.	Cold and dry.	Melancholy.	Saturn and Mercury.
Air.	Hot and moist.	Sanguine.	Jupiter.

Over the scribe's table I read:

Chascedin, Asaphim, Chatumim, Mecasphim, Gajarim.

Qui contemplatione creaturarum cognobit creatorem.

There was also an inscription at the top of the curtains, over each recess, such as:

Renounce — Renounce.

Love, but desire not.

Enjoy, but seek not to possess.

Be tranquil — be tranquil.

Grapple with and unmask yourself.

Dare to be wise.

Nothing without its equivalent.

Every action shall have its recompense.

Every procedure shall have its vindication.

Always a result.

Are you contented with yourself?

It will be the same story to-morrow.

Looking through the room, I could see nothing but the curtains before the recesses, the scribe, and the scribe's desk.

In a few minutes the mystical meeting commenced by the scribe's striking upon the desk with a small hammer. I was all attention, and prepared to take my friend's advice and use my ears. Presently a voice was heard from behind one of the curtains:

FIRST VOICE: No one can be better than the being he worships; therefore worship the Perfect Being.

SECOND VOICE: He who fulfils what he designs not, is a machine; he who fulfils not what he designs, is a driveller.

THIRD VOICE: Deity can not sin, because Deity can not be tempted. For with *what* could Deity be tempted? What could Deity gain by sinning? Man, poor wretch! is badly enough off: he carries both Deity and devil in his bosom. He has every temptation to sin, and every inducement to keep from sin. The temptation is pressing, close at hand; the inducement is weak, afar off. Therefore a man who in the midst of besetting temptations still preserves his integrity, is the greatest possible object of moral contemplation.

FOURTH VOICE: True enough. For angels are but milk-sops, after all. An angel would be all the better for a good night's carouse in honest Moritz's wine-cellar; even to the ruffling of some of his feathers. What a sorry appearance, though, would the dreadful next morning bring! But your Man—*he* is the creature!

FIFTH VOICE: And your devil is more of a milk-and-water affair than your angel. One looks on, smiling and good-tempered; the other, grinning, and grimacing, and whimpering—an inverted dog-in-the-manger; caught himself, he snarls because everything created is not caught. Verily, the devil *is* a milk-sop.

SIXTH VOICE: No more, gentlemen, of what does not concern us. I would speak of man. GOD created man perfect. The Tempter gave him a hint of the pleasure of sin; man took the hint, yielded to the Tempter, and gulped sin like a flood. A perfect being could not have yielded; therefore GOD did not create man perfect, for he carried within him the elements of imperfection: the power to sin.

SEVENTH VOICE: That is masterly! Now let us know for whose sake was man made; for the sake of GOD the creator, or for the sake of man the created? If the former, it seems to have been a bungling piece of business; if the latter, why worry the poor devil with your moral salves and cataplasms, your nostrums, salts, and smelling-bottles? Let him have his own way if a free agent; and beyond all, let him have his own way of having his own way, say I.

EIGHTH VOICE: Gentlefolks, pray forbear; we are certainly getting beyond our depth. We shall have to mount stilts at this rate. Therefore seek helps. Remember the proverb: "A dwarf on the shoulders of a giant can see farther than the giant himself."

Ninth Voice: Still, let me be the giant. I would find another giant, and mount him.

Tenth Voice: Verily, this is a strange assemblage! Behold an illustration of the old saying: "Children, fools, and drunken men, speak truth."

Eleventh Voice: How of drunken men?

Tenth Voice: "*In vino veritas.*"

Twelfth Voice: I am truth! I am pale and slender, but unchangeable; I am poor, needy, and a wanderer; I can promise nothing, for nothing comes of promises. Whoso gives me shelter gains nothing here; nay, he loses much: the excitement of false images, false shows, false honors, false symbols, false words, false deeds. The man who shelters me must lose all this.

First Voice: A word, neighbor, about this same truth. Why is this commodity subject to so much alloy, when of all commodities it is most injured by alloy? Why is it necessary to make truth palatable by a seasoning of make-believes? Why is it considered a mark of wisdom to conceal our thoughts, and a mark of folly to expose them? Why is it, as our brother has said, that but three classes stand charged with telling truth: children, fools, and drunken men?

Second Voice: I will have none of you, Mistress Truth! What could I do with you, naked as you come to me? Clothe yourself with the befitting and graceful drapery of prevarication, and you may perhaps pass current with us. But to take you as you are—I would as soon walk about naked myself.

Third Voice: Nay, but strip man of all his vanities, and what is *he?* Take from him what sin has entailed upon him, and what is he? Relieve him from the care of maintaining life; the care of providing clothes, food, and a place to sleep, to eat, and to rest in; the care of preserving life and of enjoying life; from education, and the need of education; and you arrest all the busy occupations of humanity, and make man ——

Fourth Voice (interrupting): Go on, brother; work away at man; you have but just began. Strip him of *all* his vanities; strip him of his follies; strip him of his deceits; strip him of his pretences and his shows; strip him of his feelings; strip him of his thoughts; strip him of himself—then what is he? Pshaw! man is as his Creator intended him to be; a capital chap, after all, is man. Go on and prosper, mad fellow!

Fifth Voice: Not so fast: cease this trifling, and be serious, for the feelings we are now cherishing are defining the spiritual world in which we shall live for ever.

Sixth Voice: True. How many lives are going on at this moment together—how many hearts are now beating with a stirring selfishness!

Seventh Voice: And the man who revolves about himself as a centre is a lost man.

Eighth Voice: Why are you not better?

Ninth Voice: Why am I not worse? Answer me that!

Tenth Voice; After all, is there not something unendurable in man's condition?—groaning under laws which he had no voice in enacting, and forced to live with instincts, and passions, and desires, and impulses, which he had no agency in creating. Surely man is not himself.

Eleventh Voice: Hearken to me. You err greatly. Man may or may not be himself; but man is only himself when necessity no longer binds him; but necessity always binds the sensuous man. It is when his moral nature asserts its superiority that man fears no necessity; for he rises superior to necessity.

Twelfth Voice: Well spoken.

VII.

I HAVE put down enough of what passed at the mystical meeting of the Free Speakers, to convey some idea of their proceedings; these went on without intermission for two hours, during which the wildest ideas were started, while often the best sentiments were uttered. The medley was truly an odd one. At length the scribe struck with his hammer upon the desk. Silence succeeded. The scribe then rose, and turned to leave the room. As a matter of prudence, I thought it best to follow; so I pushed on after him, but he disappeared at a side-door. I marched straight into the street. And thus ended my first and last visit to the Mystical Society of the Free Speakers of Leipsic.

VIII.

SAY what we may, assume what we please, as to the relative position of man and woman, it is an important era in our lives (I speak for my kind) when we first begin, not only to be susceptible to female influence, but to require it as a want of the soul. For it is then that the errors of the heart levy their first fearful contribution, to be continued through all time, and, for aught I know, through all beyond. It is then that the passions are either brought into subjection or become tyrants, and lead perhaps to interminable perdition. Certain it is, at all events, that there are wonderful changes in his spiritual relations, unseen it may be, but none the less real, which man owes to the influence of woman.

It is not easy to describe this influence, for we lack the

psychological terms by which to describe it. It is not objective, positive, or opposing, but rather pervading; entering
upon the slightest occasion into the inner sanctuary of the
soul, and purifying by its presence the whole inner life.

Take, for example, a happy surprise. You come unexpectedly upon one you love—perhaps you have not acknowledged to yourself that you do love—and feel a delicious,
thrilling, quickening of the heart. To this succeeds tranquillity and a subdued happiness, while you are sensible that there
is a mysterious something which surrounds your friend, as
with a soft, delightful zephyr. It meets you, fills you, and
leads you captive. You linger, enchained by a spell which
you have no desire to break, and everything is forgotten in
the absorbing delight of that moment. Now I care not how
depraved the man may be, I care not how sensual, how deeply
steeped in sin : for the time being, and while under such an
influence, he is pure. It may not be lasting, but for the moment this influence is effectual.

Can we explain this magnetism? No, nor can we explain,
although we may understand, the same power in its higher and
more important relations.

This much I had written, almost unconsciously, after glancing over the account of my interview with Kauffmann. It
fell from me like a soliloquy, yet I hesitate to erase it : on the
whole, I will let it remain.

As for myself, the influence of the sex upon me began
early and has continued—always. Whether or not it was
peculiar, the reader may judge. I will to speak truth of my
self. God only knows (I say it with reverence) how difficult
is the task; for it is not every one who is familiar with his
own experience.

IX.

I FIND it difficult, in this part of my narrative, to select from the many interesting occurrences which transpired during my stay at Leipsic, those which had a controlling influence over me.   Unless, however, I adhere to my resolution of detailing these alone, I shall swell my MS. to an inconvenient size.

X.

DAY after day the glories of my new philosophy faded gradually away, while I no longer experienced the sustaining power of my former belief.   Still, I was not altogether beyond its reach.   Unconsciously I found myself falling back upon the truths of revelation, while at times the remembrance of a mother's prayers and earnest exhortations came over me with such force that I was melted to tears.   But these were momentary influences.   My general state of mind was chaotic. To be sure, the instruction I gained in my several studies was not lost upon me; but it did not reach my heart.

I had confided in Theresa, and that saved me.   How little I felt this at the time!   how little indeed do we ever feel the importance of events while they are taking place!   And do you account it puerile, this confiding that I speak of?   Are you made of such stern stuff that you can not understand it? Look back a little; turn your heart inside out, and see if you can not find the remains—perhaps scorched to ashes, but still the remains—of some such feelings.   Withered, blasted suppressed, neglected, trampled on, they may be; but they have been there. And did it ever occur to you that what seems now so insignificant in your eyes will one day assume an air of imposing magnitude, and what seems now so vast and important will presently dwarf into mere littleness ?

From Theresa—the spiritual, heaven-minded Theresa—I learned the value of the practical. Without her appearing in the least aware of it, Theresa's soul had upon mine a remarkable effect. During my various occupations, amid the changes of the new life I was leading, in moments of weakness and temptation, in times of depression and exaltation, in all these, dear Theresa, thou wert my safeguard and my life. Instead of her spirit reposing upon mine, my spirit found repose in hers. I began by degrees to think more of what Kauffmann had said. I felt that I had within me a strength of soul and purpose able to cope with the mighty; yet I daily renewed my strength from the heart of that young girl !

Yes, in my struggles after a healthful state of life—I say it with truth—Theresa Von Hofrath was my chief, perhaps, sole assistant; and this, apparently, without any design. There was a charm in her very being which touched and swayed and subdued me.

But how shall express my feelings for Theresa ! May I not better say I had no feelings for her ! she was not so much a particular object of thought and attention ; she rather gave life and tone and character to all my thoughts. What liberty is to a people, she was to me. As liberty is nothing positive, but only a favorable *status*, so the influence of Theresa produced in me a moral *status*, of a nature best adapted to the circumstances by which I was surrounded. What was developed by all this we shall see.

X I.

AFTER a full deliberation; after patiently wearing out a twelvemonth in bewildering my brain with German metaphysics; after listening to lecture upon lecture, and system upon system; I concluded deliberately and decidedly, that my sojourn in Leipsic had not brought about, and would not bring about, the desired result.

I had come to Germany a demi-god. My watchwords were, "no subservience to opinion," "no limits to human wisdom," "consult Nature in all her modes," and so forth. My mouth was filled with vain arguments; for vain I knew them to be; that is, I felt a consciousness, in that *lower* deep below the lowest deep, that I was all wrong; that I was dreaming, and should one day awake to a sense of my real condition. Then when I came among the learned doctors, and lecturers, and schoolmen—solemn mockers and grave triflers—and found how they were all pulling and turning and mystifying, with their = + and —, I=I, and "no man must *must*"—when I found that my old question was not answered, and no result came of all this foolery—I felt assured that I had missed my mark. From this I sometimes found relief in taking up a volume of my Lord Bacon. Often could I clear my brain from the mists that thickened around it by perusing the plain and intelligible lessons of wisdom which that mighty mind had left to the world. In the same way I could shut out strange visions of the frightful demons of the Hartz—those hideous and unnatural creations of the German poets—by reading the Midsummer Night's Dream, or the Masque of Comus. In Germany I learned to appreciate the philosophy and the poetry of my own land.

XII.

I **KEPT** on studying, and perplexing my brain.   Besides the public lectures, I continued to enjoy the private instruction of Von Hofrath; and his lessons were not of a nature to be forgotten.   But lectures and lessons were not what I desired —were not what I needed.   As I have said, after I had been in Leipsic a twelvemonth, I still found that what troubled me in England troubled me in Germany : the *actual*, the *practical*, the *what* and the *why*.   The students made no advance, it seemed to me, in these.   Each professor had a theory of his own and powerfully advocated it.   At times I almost pined for my English home, and for English scenes.   I recollected the matter-of-fact events of my life with the greatest pleasure, and called to mind, with surprising minuteness, the associations of my childhood.   When I thought of my former feelings, and contrasted them with my present bewildered state, which was becoming daily more bewildered, I decided that I had nothing to do but to throw my philosophy overboard, and take in for ballast what I best could.

Thus from a religiously educated youth I became a freethinker, and from a free-thinker I came to be a kind of worldling.   All this time, I believe I earnestly desired to think aright; and so far as my actions were concerned, I had no special reason to reproach myself.   After all, my spirit experienced some relief from being let down from the clouds, even at the risk of grovelling on the earth.   So I determined to give up the chase after an unintelligible mysticism, although I should be accused of falling from my high estate, and of exhibiting a low and unworthy degradation.

The professor, who had taken care not to dictate to me during what he was pleased to call my transition state, watched this change with interest. He regarded me, in a degree, as a skilful and experienced physician regards a patient who, though apparently sick unto death, he feels confident will at length rally under judicious treatment. Herr Von Hofrath was too sagacious a minister to the mind diseased to interfere with a rule equally applicable to soul and body—*wait on Nature*. His motto was, assist where you can, but be sure you do not retard by injudicious interference. When I was ready to condemn my whole routine of labors, he would say, complacently: " Well, well; it is something to have got so far as that; but not too fast; take care lest while you gather up the tares you root up also the wheat with them."

" Especially," I would add, " if I can not tell the tares from the wheat."

" By their fruit ye shall know them; therefore wait."

" How long?"

" Till you have done asking questions. Now come with me; I am reading Shakspere's King John. I wish to use your copy. Come, you shall read to me."

Such was the considerate manner of the professor during this miserable period of my life.

XIII.

THERESA, always sweet and gentle, grew even more sweet and gentle when she perceived my restlessness and discontent. Every word she uttered came from her heart, and her heart always beat true. She would assure me with so much confidence that I should yet enjoy peace of mind, she would calm my impatience with so much tenderness, that I almost believed her.

How shall I picture Theresa as I wish? To do this I should detail exactly what passed between us. I acknowledge that I can not perform the task. The scenes glide away, and I can not grasp them. When I would do so, Proteus-like, they change and fade and vanish altogether.

Something out of ourselves engrossed us always, and the hours passed imperceptibly. As the strong ask not themselves whether they are in health, so it never occurred to us to ask if we were happy. What a character was hers! She had no bashful timidity, yet a rare appreciation of what belonged to her sex. She was so truthful and so earnest that she stopped just this side of heroism; she was not an enthusiast either: she was too thoughtful, too gentle, too considerate.

Theresa and I were friends. If friends, what had we in common? A desire for happiness. So we talked and walked and read and studied together. But we never spoke of the feelings we entertained of each other. I doubt if we did entertain feelings to speak of; had we done so, the universal soul-pervading influence of her spiritual, would have been narrowed down to the individual and the positive. Then we should have been in love; *in love :* a specious term, which, like the paradise of fools, has never been bounded or defined. Not that I disbelieve in the phrase, but what to believe in it I do not exactly know. That true love can exist without friendship is impossible : indeed I believe that it must rest upon friendship or it will die. And friendship can be predicated only of hearts which are congenial, whose currents flow and harmonize together.

But to return. The idea of loving Theresa—as the word is usually employed—of claiming her for mine and mine only, was what I never thought of, and if I had thought of it, the idea would have distressed me. No: much as we were

thrown together — and our communion was uninterrupted — I
never entertained a wish that Theresa should be to me more
than she then was   The thought of drawing her to myself
and calling her mine only, seemed sacrilege. Was our companionship then so entirely spiritual? It seems so; and
when I thought of it I believed I had divined what Kauffmann
labored so hard upon: " The true relation of the sexes."   I
began to think that the world had gone on hitherto all wrong;
that the social condition of man was founded upon error, and
that a false idea of this relation was at the bottom of the
trouble. I said to myself, if in the resurrection they neither
marry nor are given in marriage, why may there not be examples of the same spiritual companionship here on the earth?
and why should not such examples become universal?

In this way my ideas wandered, resting first on one hypothesis, then on another, while my opinions continued unsettled.

XIV.

But, shall I confess it, there were times when in the society
of Theresa, my heart craved something different from her;
when I yearned for the *mortal* Psyche; when the Venus
Aphrodite, not the Venus Urania, seemed to inspire me. I
pined for some exquisite "creature of earth's mould," who
should unite purity with her mortality, who should possess
the embroidered girdle which fills the beholder with love and
desire, who should excite feelings entirely different from
those I entertained toward Theresa. Some being who should
realize to me the happiness of an earthly passion, and afford
the enjoyment of an interested affection.

At length I longed to love as the children of earth love.

And this longing, did it make any difference in my feelings
for Theresa? None whatever. She was still the same to

me. In these new heart developments her influence was as effectual as it ever had been. It softened and purified and spiritualized these very earthly longings, it neither destroyed nor suppressed them.

As for Theresa herself, notwithstanding all our intercourse, I never could get quite to the bottom of her heart. I know not what I should have found there ; but sometimes I thought the discovery would make me happy.

XV.

RETURNING one afternoon from the town, I found a note traced in a female hand, requesting me to come to the lodgings of Wolfgang Hegewisch. Since the interview in which he had given me his history I had been frequently to see him. At times I found him convalescing, and again, worse ; he was however evidently growing weaker, and I watched him with much solicitude. When he desired me to stay I remained, and when he was not in the mood for conversation I shorten-ed my visits. By thus humoring his feelings, my society be-gan, as I thought, to have a happy effect upon him. The last time I had seen him, he seemed in better spirits than usual, and a natural cheerfulness of manner prevailed, which com-pletely metamorphosed the unfortunate misanthrope. I could not help remarking to Hegewisch the agreeable change.

"Yes, my friend," replied he, "I *have* changed ; thank GOD, my deliverance is near."

"What do you mean ?"

He put his hand upon his heart, shook his head, and with a faint but not mournful smile replied :

"Something here tells me that a few days will release me from the world. Is not that a cause for cheerfulness ? Of late my mind has been clearer. I owe you much for it.

I have looked over my life and feel that since *that fearful event,* a frenzy has possessed me. What I have done, what I have said, what I have thought, in that frenzy, I scarcely know, but I am confident my Maker will not hold me accountable for it. I have considered lately that, since I can look only upon the course of events as they happen on the earth, and do not know what will be the administration of things hereafter, I have not regarded the whole circumference of my being, and that I have complained too soon. Do you wonder, after what I have experienced, that, now my brain is clear and my mind calm, death should be a great release to me."

"No."

"You speak like a friend; without affectation, but with kindness. Hear me. I shall never leave this room. But I would bid the world farewell with cheerfulness and with dignity; resignation I have not to practise. The days of my youth return to me, and I feel that innocent buoyancy of heart which I used to enjoy. Does this not betoken a happy future? Were not the words of my Meta prophetic? A few days and I shall know. I have sent for my mother. She will be here to-night. My kind physician — my father's tried friend — is already here; he insists upon remaining with me although he admits that there is no hope. I would bid you adieu. You touched my heart when I believed it lifeless. You have befriended me much every way. Would that I could befriend you in return. Listen to me. Leave this place; break off your present mode of life. You *think* too much, you do not perform, although performance is your province. You will become crazed here; you know enough of books, at least for the present; strike out into the world; interest yourself in its pursuits; mingle in practical life even at the expense of mingling in its follies. Return to free, happy England. You can serve your fellow men in some way. It is time you made the attempt. Apply your energies in that direction. My friend, I speak with the august prescience of a dying man, when I say to you, Shake off this chronic dream-life and ACT. Farewell!"

I was deeply affected. "I can not leave you so," I said, after a silence of some minutes. "I will not leave you until you have promised to send for me if you are worse. Do not refuse."

"I will promise, but do not come. You will almost make me feel a pang at parting."

XVI.

FROM what passed at this interview, I felt that it would be an intrusion again to visit Hegewisch, unless summoned. I looked daily with a feverish anxiety for the promised message. It is not easy to describe with what trepidation I opened the note of which I have spoken. From its contents I could gather nothing. I have the note in my drawer; it is in a woman's hand, certainly, though the characters are traced hurriedly, and without much distinctness:

"Will Herr Saint Leger die Gefälligkeit haben und vorzufragen, No. —. — Straße."—"Will Mr. Saint Leger have the kindness to come to No. —, —— Street."

I left the house and hurried to the town. I turned down this street and across that, threading my way into the remote section where Hegewisch had his lodgings, until, anxious and out of breath, I arrived at the door. I did not stop at the entrance, but passed directly up stairs, without meeting any one. Coming to his apartment, I knocked gently. There was no response. I knocked again: no answer. I opened the door and entered; the room was vacant. I cast my eyes toward the apartment of which Hegewisch had said, with bitterness, "There I sleep." The door into it was open, and there indeed I discovered Wolfgang Hegewisch, partly raised upon the bed, which had been moved into the centre of the narrow chamber. On one side, and with her arm under the head of her dying son, sat the baroness; upon the other, regarding the young man's countenance with discriminating solicitude, stood his friend and physician.

As I approached nearer, Hegewisch turned his eyes toward me, and smiled his recognition. This caused his mother to turn around. I heard my name pronounced feebly by my friend. The baroness rose hastily, came toward me, took my hand, drew me to the other side of the room, and burst into tears. I could not remain unmoved. I tried in vain to prevent the signs of my emotion. What was I to do? what could I do to comfort the afflicted mother? At this moment the physician entered. He addressed her kindly, but with firmness:

"Madam, how can you give way to the force of your grief, when by so doing you cause your son such pain? As for myself, his calm and dignified, I may say his heavenly composure, fills my breast with a happiness, unusual, and not easily accounted for. I pray you be calm."

By this time I had recovered sufficiently to join with the physician in endeavoring to assuage her anguish. She made a strong effort to become self-possessed.

"It is not this single blow," said she, "that so unnerves me; it is this in the succession of horrid events, crowning all, and crushing by its added weight the little strength that remained to me."

I inquired how my friend was The physician shook his head. "Alas! he may die at any moment. The renewal of the spasms must overpower him. He made me promise to send for you before it was too late. You may go in. He is so calm, that I have no fear of his being excited."

I proceeded to the bed-side, followed by the physician and the baroness. "Oh, Father of Mercies!" murmured I, "what have become of those days of happy wooing on the banks of the Rhine? *Is* there anything tangible in the awful past! *Should* life to man be made up of such contradictions!"

I took the hand of Hegewisch. He had scarce strength to return the slight pressure I gave it. But that smile again illumined his countenance with an expression delightful to contemplate.

"You see I have kept my promise. I feel a dreadful weight removed from my heart. 1 am happy. I am calm too. Were it not for my mother, I should not have a shadow crossing my spirit. I say again, remember not what I have uttered in my wild moments. My griefs have been greater than I could bear; but now — ah, now — Meta — at last my Meta beckons me hence."

"Mother — mother!" he whispered, suddenly dropping my hand, and gasping for breath.

She flew to his side. The spasms had returned.

"Meta, dear Meta! Gently, mother — gently. Lo! I see — . . . .

He was dead.

I could do nothing in that awful moment.

XVII.

At a subsequent interview I narrated to the afflicted parent all that I had known of her son. I had to tell the story over and over again. In some way she discovered that I was the only one who had regarded him kindly, and her gratitude knew no bounds.

XVIII.

The remains of the young Baron of —— rest in the sombre tomb of his fathers, at the old castle on the Rhine. The baroness still survives. Solitary and desolate-hearted she waits with resignation the summons to follow her husband and her son.

And Caspar? He, too, lives—lives in the Castle of Richstein, in possession of wealth and influence and power. Full of life, and in the midst of his days, he prosecutes his selfish plans—successfully. But he is God-forsaken, and abhorred by man.

He also waits the summons.

Have I digressed too much in narrating the story of Wolfgang Hegewisch? I trow not. It impressed me. It conveyed its lesson, and therefore I record it.

XIX.

The months and the seasons glided on. I was not always to live in Leipsic; not always to be a student, and I knew it. Scenes of action which lay before me, though far in the distance, began to assume a real aspect. Away from my country, I had the opportunity of viewing it from a new point of observation. I began to reflect upon its constitution, its manners, its customs, its laws. Occasionally my blood would quicken as ambitious desires and fancies floated through my brain, while something whispered that I was dreaming away my life. Whispered? Heavens! At times the words of the

dying student: "Shake off this chronic dream-life and act!"
rang in my ears as if sounded by the trumpet of the archan-
gel; while the quiet earnest question of Theresa: "Is it not
action that you most require?" penetrated my heart, leaving
a deep dull pang there.

I could endure it no longer, and just as I had resolved to
break away from Leipsic, I received this letter:

"LONDON, May 10, 17—.

"WHY do I write to you when it is too late? Why do I
remind you of your promised aid when I am beyond the reach
of aid? It is because my heart is bursting, and I must have
one solace; that of telling you all. Oh! my kinsman, pity
me. My father is dead. He died in that fearful island; a
place to me of abominations. He died and left me—how can
I blister the page by naming it—the affianced of Count
Vautrey! I know not how it was. I know not how it is.
My mind is confused; my heart is dead; I, myself am nothing
—*nothing*. When I wrote to you a long, long time since, I
expected, from several strange hints which I had received
from Count Vautrey, to have been forced to put myself under
the protection of my English friends. But the threatened
catastrophe passed away. Years ran by, happy years to me,
ah! never to return; but I can not allude to happiness now.
A few months ago, I was hastily summoned to my father. I
hurried away to St. Kilda, and found him on his death-bed.
He was suffering patiently, and was so dreadfully changed
that I scarcely recognised him; he had deferred sending for
me till the last moment.

"It was evident that he must die. My father—die! But
whom, think you, found I as his attendant?—Laurent De
Vautrey!—I did not understand it. I can not now understand it; but so it was. My father's manner to me was kind
and tender. He would call me often to his bedside, appa-

ently with the intention of communicating something, and then, as if unable to speak, would caress me tenderly, and bid me sit by his side. He grew weaker and weaker. I longed to know what was in his heart. I dreaded to know, too, for something told me it had reference to Vautrey and myself. One evening he seemed more feeble than usual. He beckoned me to come to him; I obeyed, but he did not speak. At last I addressed him: 'Dear father, tell me what is on your mind; it concerns me, I know. Do not fear, I will receive it as your wish.' He started as if an adder had stung him. Then he tried to smile, then he looked sadly and shook his head. 'Speak, I implore you,' I cried. 'Name your wishes, and you will find in me an obedient child.' 'My daughter,' was the response—and my father's voice grew husky as he spoke: 'My daughter, you must wed Count Vautrey.' I neither shrieked nor started; I did not change color nor faint; I did not fall prostrate; I stood erect; I stood firm; but—do not think I rave—could the entire misery of a lifetime the most miserable be concentrated upon one single instant, and the heart steeped in it, scarcely should it equal the wo which that brief sentence brought upon me! 'I will,' was my firm and almost sudden response. My father was startled, but not deceived; he knew the effort which those two brief words had cost me. 'Do you not,' he demanded, 'seek to know ——' 'Not one word. Oh, my father! it is enough that I know it to be necessary, else you would not have commanded it.' 'I would not. But let me tell you ——' 'Spare me—spare me,' again interrupted I. 'Let my time be devoted to making your sufferings lighter; forget me, I shall do well enough, by-and-by.' I muttered the last words to myself, but my father still surveyed me anxiously. Presently he said: 'Shall I call Laurent here?' 'If you please.' Count Vautrey was summoned. My father pronounced us affianced, and I hurried to my apartment. Then—oh! then, I gave loose to my feelings, not by tears and lamentations— these were denied to me; but by—oh God! I dare not speak of the horrors of that awful night. About midnight, I was told that my father was dying. I hurried to his bedside, but it was too late. He did not recognise me, and after a few moments he ceased to breathe.

"I will not attempt to describe my situation, or what I suffered. I left St. Kilda and came directly hither. I made it a stipulated condition with Count Vautrey, that he should leave me to myself until the time fixed by my father for the nuptials. Nuptials! I fear to tell you where I am going. I know that you are a Saint Leger, and that you would hasten to relieve me. But I will not be relieved. I too am a Saint Leger. I have promised that I will wed Count Vautrey, and by Heaven I will keep my vow. How fearlessly I write; but ah! my kinsman, there are times when this iron resolution bends and quivers like the pliant reed, and I, a very woman, weep, and weep, until it should seem that I had wept my heart away. Oh God! what shall I do. I will keep my promise to my father. He had a fearful reason for exacting it. Something mysterious, and dark, and inexplicable, is connected with all this. But come fate — come destiny—the sacrifice is ready. Farewell.

"LEILA SAINT LEGER."

X X.

AGAIN, at a crisis in my existence, did a letter from Leila bring me back to myself. There was a certain something about that letter which conveyed the idea to me more forcibly than the former one, that Leila regarded me as a kinsman merely. Strange to say, at this time the discovery did not

disappoint or grieve me. What had become of those enthusiastic feelings which I experienced at St. Kilda? Where
were the transports which I enjoyed when, gazing at the
sparkling stars from the summit of Hirta, I thought of Leila,
and Leila only? Again I exclaimed: Shall there ever be
anything tangible in the awful past? and some fiend whispered, Never! and I shuddered and prayed. But the letter
served its office. It roused me. It disenchanted me. I read
and re-read it, in hopes that something in it would throw light
upon her residence. But I looked in vain. I carried it to
Theresa, and asked her advice—women are so quick-witted
in such matters.

Theresa perused the letter carefully, then raised her eyes
to mine, and said: " The case is pitiable; how wrong the
decision! Do you know if she loves somebody?"

" I do not."

" It seems to me that her heart is interested. So passionate; so determined; alas! with such feelings, if she has
lived in the world—and you say she has—she has been interested; her heart is occupied."

" Why do you think so, Theresa?"

" How can it be otherwise? Who can resist necessity?
It rules everywhere; hunger demands food at the point of
the stiletto; weariness woos the balmy breath of sleep on the
dizzy height where the slightest misstep would be fatal; the
body seeks and must have its accustomed exercise or it loses
its accustomed strength; and the giant passions which inhabit
around the soul, they must have scope and exercise and food,
or they prowl within and ravage and devastate and lay waste
there. There is no armor against that which is ordained."

" You give strange attributes to your sex."

" Attributes!" said Theresa, with more warmth than I had
ever seen her exhibit; " how dearly does woman pay for all

her attributes. If her mind is strong, it frets and chafes because it is cramped and confined to the narrow sphere which man has chosen to allot to it. If alas! her soul is passionate, how surely will it be consumed within her, or become the subject of injury and abuse. If she is loving and trustful, how is she doomed to disappointment or disgust. If her heart yearns for the companionship of man, how chilled and crushed does that heart become, when she finds that man treats her as a plaything rather than as a companion. If she scorn the trammels with which her sex are confined, she encounters misapprehension and the severest censure. Rebellious, she is coerced; submissive, she is by turns caressed and trampled upon. To wait and not murmur; to expect and not complain; to live and move and have her being, as if she lived not, moved not, and had no being; to be sacrificed, to suffer, to be silent—this is the destiny of woman."

"Theresa! where did you gather such strange conclusions?"

"Here," she said, laying her hand upon her heart and looking at me in her earnest manner, yet just as tranquil, as composed, as ever. "I do not say that I have experienced," she continued; "but my spirit teaches me that I speak truth."

"How do you remain so calm always? Why are you never excited? What power do you invoke to maintain such serenity?"

"The power of the soul is in itself; it does not need human appliances. I seek the aid of the MOST HIGH to sustain it."

"Theresa, have you loved?"

There—I had asked a question which I had been waiting for an opportunity to put ever since I first saw my friend. Twenty times at least I had it on my lips and each time I lacked the courage to speak out. Now I had spoken. What a bold home thrust! What a direct downright not-to-be-escaped interrogatory to one who, when she spoke, always uttered truth.

"Theresa, have you loved?" She directed her calm blue eye upon mine, and its gaze seemed to search my being. In that eye I could read little, save perhaps a slight, almost imperceptible, look of scorn; no—not scorn—but rather an enduring self-relying look which at times resembles scorn. Her brow appeared broader, her countenance nobler; but she did not speak, and in this way we sat looking at each other. I had committed myself, and could not recede. I repeated the question. "Have you loved?"

The eye of the maiden changed again—that strange calm imperturbable eye!—and became almost mournful, as she uttered with quiet distinctness, "No."

I took a long, deep breath; perhaps, in the excitement of the moment, respiration had unconsciously been checked; this would account for the relief I experienced, for I did feel relieved. I was reproached too for my rudeness; and I hastened to ask forgiveness.

"Pardon me, Theresa; it was very uncivil; but I could not resist the impulse."

"It was not right; but you can not tease me," said Theresa, gently. "Let us speak of your relative. You should do your utmost to save her from so dreadful a fate."

I proceeded in the conversation with a light heart. "Do you really think I should interfere?"

"I think you should seek your cousin and endeavor to alter her decision. When the happiness of a young creature is staked upon such a certain issue it seems dreadful to allow it to come to pass. Behold an opportunity for you to act; set about it. See what you can do."

XXI.

HERE our conference was interrupted. I retired to my room. In a short time I had finished three letters; one to my father, one to my mother, and one to Hubert Moncrieff.

In the letter to my father, I asked permission to leave Leipsic and make a tour of the continent; this had been promised me when I left England, and I ventured to suggest that the time had arrived when I could best profit by the permission.

To my mother I wrote a letter full of questions. I asked an explanation of the singular life which my aunt Alice led — it was always a forbidden theme at home; I begged for an account of her history; and I inquired about Wilfred Saint Leger, and Leila, and Laurent de Vautrey.

To Hubert I wrote, as I suppose young men usually write to each other. I challenged him to come over and accompany me in my travels. I gave a glowing description of what we should hear and see and do. I spoke of our friendship, our congeniality of feeling, etc., etc., and wound up with a reference to our exciting voyage to St. Kilda. In a post-script, I inquired if he had heard anything more of the Wœdallah or his daughter, and in a *nota-bene*, asked, "What of Vautrey; did you ever hear anything further of him?"

After I had despatched these letters, I felt more at ease. I did not doubt that my father would consent to the proposed tour, as its advantage was advocated by the professor, who certified in an ample manner to the proficiency I had made as a student. Besides, I had nearly attained my majority : in another month I should be one-and-twenty.

XXII.

I WAITED patiently for answers. Hubert's came first. Youth best sympathizes with youth. My postscript and *nota-bene* were first noticed. He had a long story of the death of the Wœdallah; of the sudden appearance one night of the "beautiful Leila," at Glencoe, attended only by her servants; of a long conference with the earl, his father, of which he could discover nothing; of her leaving the next day; and of his endeavors to ascertain (on my account, as he assured me) whither she was gone. He could find out nothing, discover nothing, except that Margaret, who was acquainted with everything, Heaven only knew how, had inadvertently spoken of Leila as living at Dresden, that he had affected not to notice the remark, and had afterward tried to find out something more, but in vain. That he knew nothing of Vautrey at all; but rumor had associated his name with that of the fair Leila.

Hubert regretted that he could not join me in the proposed tour, but the thing was impossible; the whole house was in uproar preparing for two bridals. His sister Margaret was to be married to a young English nobleman, and his brother Francis, on the same day, to the Lady Annie, now sole heiress of Glenross. "So you see," continued the letter, "the fates keep me here, when I would a thousand times rather be away with you. We must bide our time; but we will have a scamper together yet. By the way, old Christie often inquires for you. He says ye are a 'lad of mickle spirit, only a bit whittie-whattieing like; mair the pity, puir fellow.' I will write you again after these confounded—pshaw, I mean these happy—bridals are over.   Good-by."

At the bottom of the sheet was a single line, in an exquisitely neat hand, " Do not forget Ella."

How much good that letter did me!   How it opened the door to my pent spirit!   How suddenly it revived all the exciting scenes I witnessed in the highlands!   And how distinctly it brought back the captivating Ella Moncrieff!   Besides, I learned where Leila was ; at least I was not inclined to doubt the correctness of the information.

XXIII.

In a few days letters from home came.   I eagerly ran over the package : my father's first, and looked far enough to see that my request was granted, and then, without stopping to read it, the one from my mother.   It was like all her letters, anxiously affectionate, showing the strong and ever-watchful solicitude of parental affection.   In reply to my queries, she said no one could account for the malady (so my mother termed it) of the Lady Alice; that in her youth she enjoyed all that station, wealth, beauty, and a remarkable intellect, could bring; that she was universally sought after and courted ; but was from childhood possessed of strange eccentricities ; her head was filled with plots, adventures, and tales of chivalrous deeds ; she was always playing some strange part in some strange performance ; she hated men as a race, or rather despised them ; she believed them all to be unreliable and corrupt, and when young took delight in humbling the haughtiest; and by degrees she excluded herself from the world, until, by habitual indulgence in her mode of life, she became what she then was.   Singular scenes were said to have transpired between Wilfred Saint Leger and herself and also between her and Wilfred the younger. On one occasion, it was understood that she had plunged a dagger into the breast of the father, declaring he should die rather than disgrace his name; and the wound came near proving fatal. On another, she threatened the son with a like vengeance, unless he abandoned his irregular life. Wilfred the younger was the father of Leila Saint Leger, about whom I had inquired, and of whom she could tell me nothing; except that her father was dead, she living with a relative somewhere on the continent, and engaged to marry the Count de Vautrey, of whom she knew very little. When a small boy he had spent a few weeks at Bertold Castle, in company with one of her kinsmen, a Moncrieff; and that the child at that early age inspired every one with aversion, not to say hatred. She knew nothing of his residence.

My vague associations connected with this man were not mere dreams after all, said I to myself, as I finished reading the letter. Strange that in my infancy he should have been for a season under the same roof with me, and that we should have met as we did; and conjecture, with its shapeless, unformed images began to fill my brain, and I was fast sinking into a mazy revery, when I remembered that my father's letter remained unread. I took it up, and as it is short, will give it to the reader of these memoirs:

" My Dear Son : I consent to your proposed tour, and am satisfied, by what I learn from the good doctor, with your proficiency while at Leipsic. As you are now a man, and are henceforth to think and act for yourself, I have no wish to fetter or restrain you. I have no fear that you will forget your sense of accountability to Almighty God, or the claims of conscience; for I have confidence in your principles, and in your uprightness of character. Enclosed you will find a bill of exchange on —— for £—, and a letter of credit on the same house unlimited. Your mother writes by this post. I pray God's blessing to rest upon you.

"From your affectionate father,

"GUY H. S. SAINT LEGER.

"P. S.—Trust no Frenchman—believe in no French woman. France has been a curse to our nation, and Frenchmen and French women a curse to our family.

"G. H. S. St. L."

XXIV.

IF ever captive felt lightness of heart when his chains were struck off and he set at liberty, after breathing the noisome atmosphere of a dungeon; if ever convalescent was cheered by the pleasant sunlight and the refreshing breeze, after the confinement of a long and dangerous sickness; if ever mariner, tempest-tossed for months, hailed with transport the sight of the green earth: then did I feel lightness of heart, then was I cheered, transported, at the prospect of this change of life. How the blood went galloping through my veins! I will pack to-day, and will set off to-morrow. Now for life! Pleasure, I will grasp you yet! Change, novelty, new scenes, new actions, freedom—ay, freedom! freedom for anything—by Heaven, I will shut out all but this purpose! I *will* live a while without the interference of that surly weight that hangs like lead about my heart. Up and out into life! Already is my appetite sharpened for adventure; already a thousand tumultuous thoughts crowd upon me.

Italy! I shall see thy soft skies; I shall revel in thy classic groves, delightful Tuscany; I shall wander through thy ruins, Eternal City. Spain! how sweet the anticipation of thy beauties! Already I see thy sunny plains and stately palm-groves, thy orange-walks, and thy delicious gardens. I hear the soft music of the evening guitar ; and now, the tinkling of the muleteer's bell greets my ear. 'Tis evening ; the maidens of Andalusia are on the balconies, listening to the impassioned serenade. I come! I will soon see this birth-place of passion —this home of love !

What if the heart become cold ?— what if the cheek wrinkle and the eye grow dim ? Youth! let me but enjoy youth! Give me but the experience of joy, passion, love, jealousy, hate ; let me see beauty, and call it mine ; let me clutch what looks so glittering ; baubles they may be, but let me have them in my hand ! Let me see, and know, and feel, instead of taking upon trust, what doth and what doth not perish with the using. Then approach, ye ministers of fate, and do your worst with me !

XXV.

In the midst of a rhapsody which I attempt now to describe, the door opened gently, and Theresa Von Hofrath entered. The fever-current was calmed; the exciting visions of pleasure dissolved apace ; only my heart continued to beat quickly as before, yet with a heavier pulsation. The letters lay before me ; I was gazing at them. Theresa came a few steps toward me and stopped. I advanced to meet her.

" I have letters from home at last."

" And can you go ?" asked Theresa.

" Yes."

" Oh, how happy I am to hear it! Now all will be well. And you can go ?"

" Yes."

Theresa's countenance actually lighted with happiness ; her whole manner changed she was almost enthusiastic in her hopes for me. It seemed as if I had never half appreciated her. A strange feeling oppressed me; I came near bursting into tears. I never could account satisfactorily for the peculiar moods that at times come over us. There is a subtle spirit within, which acts unexpectedly upon the instant, baffling, and contradicting, and defying all form, all habit, all rule, and all philosophy; a remnant of some brighter period of the soul, vindicating, by its potency, the hypothesis of a time anterior, when form, and habit, and rule, and philosophy, were unknown.

While I stood oppressed by strange feelings, Theresa had left the room.

XXVI.

IN two days I was ready to quit Leipsic. I was to go into the town in the evening, to be ready for the schnell-post, which was to start the next morning. The professor insisted on accompanying me to the hotel.

Yes, everything was ready; and, with my cloak across my arm, I turned to meet Theresa, who was coming to the door. I took her hand; a cheerful "Good-by!" passed my lips; it was echoed by her. The professor had reached the carriage, and I hastened to join him.

I did not look back to see Theresa again !

END OF BOOK FOURTH.

BOOK V.

Στείχοντα δ' αὐτόφορτον οἰκείᾳ σάγῃ
Ἐς Ἄργος, ὥσπερ δεῦρ' ἀπεζύγην πόδας,
Ἀγνὼς πρὸς ἀγνῶτ' εἶπε συμβαλὼν ἀνὴρ,
Ἐξιστορήσας καὶ σαφηνίσας ὁδόν.

ÆSCHYLUS, Chœph., 662

Occasions of my own called me to Argos.
——————— Onward as I travelled
I met a man unknown, myself to him
Unknown; he courteous questioned me how far
I journeyed, and informed me of my way.

Φεῦ· ταχεῖά γ' ἦλθε χρησμῶν πρᾶξις ——
Ζεὺς ἀπέσκηψεν τελευτὴν θεσφάτων.

ÆSCHYLUS, Persæ, 735.

With what a winged course the oracles
Haste their completion!   With the lightning's speed
Jove on this man hath hurled his threatened vengeance.

BOOK FIFTH

I.

Daybreak throughout Germany is the hour for breakfast.

At daybreak on the morning of the twelfth of May, 17—, I was seated at the table of the Weiss-Schwan in Leipsic, in company with several persons who were on that morning to take the schnell-post for Dresden.

What sent me to Dresden?

The hope of rescuing Leila Saint Leger from Laurent de Vautrey.

How was I to effect this even if I could find her, which was doubtful enough?

I did not stop to answer the question. I determined to trust to the hour and to the circumstance. Full of new projects and plans without number, I made a hasty breakfast, and rising from the table, paced up and down the hall while waiting the arrival of the ponderous vehicle which was to transport us to the capital of Saxony.

Mine host, perceiving that I had done poor justice to the morning meal, insisted that I should strengthen myself with a glass of schnapps, which it would have been discourteous to refuse; after which, and purely as a matter of self-defence, to prevent further interruption, I lighted my meerschaum and resumed my walk.

At length a noise resembling the sound of distant thunder was heard, and shortly after, drawn by some ten or twelve crazy horses, the schnell-post came rumbling down the street.

By means of kicks and screams and the free use of the whip, with the added force of sundry oaths made up of a *patois*, which would have done credit to the dispersed builders of Babel, the bedlam-looking steeds were finally persuaded to stand still.

I bade my host farewell, and distributing a few groschens among the civil attendants, mounted the ladder, meerschaum in hand, and after a short journey arrived safe — inside.

Another set-to then commenced. The kicks and screams, and whip, and oaths, were plied with an impartial distribution; and presently at the rattling pace of four miles the hour we took leave of the "bookshelf" of Germany.

II.

AND who were "we," who with one accord had sought a common destination on that morning?

At first, owing to the dense vapor of tobacco smoke, I was unable to satisfy myself on that point, but as we left the town, the air had a freer course through the windows, and I found opportunity to inspect my fellow-travellers.

There were five besides myself inside; how many were in front and rear and upon the top I do not know; but the inside contained just six, including me. There could be no mistake about it, for I counted my companions several times.

They were for the most part substantial looking Dutchmen, with staid appearance and civil demeanor. Your German is a humane and a polite man. He does not possess that busy politeness which under cover of a benevolent assiduity, scrutinizes your dress, even to the most minute portion of it;

which pries into the very recesses of your pocket; which values each article of your luggage, and puts a price even upon your own importance; but on the contrary, his is that unostentatious, unobtrusive civility which permits every one to enjoy his own quiet after his own fashion, and busy himself with his own reflections without interruption; which answers a proper question with candor, without following up the advantage by seeking to gratify an idle curiosity.

III

One—two—three—four. I stuck at the fifth man each time. Not that I made any mistake in the count; there *were* five beside myself; but this fifth personage baffled all my conjectures as to his nation, kindred, language, or occupation. The four were Dutch; I was sure enough of that. Not that tney were just alike, for one might have been a professor, another a dealer in laces, the third a manufacturer of porcelain, the fourth a stadtholder, but all Germans, not a doubt of it.

This fifth man, he was my *vis-à-vis*, how could I help looking at him?

Presently he dropped asleep; then I looked at him the more steadily. In the first place it was quite impossible for me to conjecture his age. One could make him appear almost any number of years old from twenty up to forty-five. The marks with which anxieties or disappointments or press ing cares encircle the face, the forehead, the eyes, the mouth, could be distinctly traced on the countenance of the sleeper—strange that such heartache characters should be in circles instead of sharp angles and straight lines—but then the mouth even in slumber seemed to set these lines at defiance. It was an honest mouth, from each corner round to the *em-*

bouchure; but for all that the lips were compressed; whether
in the self-relying honesty of a pure heart, or in stern resolution, or in bitter endurance, I could not determine. The
character of the face told forty-five; a something distinct
from that, partaking of innocence and simplicity, said twenty.
But little could be seen of the forehead, for an immense
quantity of tangled light hair inclining to red, was shook over
it in most uncouth disorder. The nose was large and
ugly; the face was well enough, if it had not been for the
nose, but the mouth redeemed the whole. I had not as yet a
chance at the eyes.

As to his dress, it was somewhere between a gentleman's
and that of a gentleman's valet. It was nearly threadbare:
that belonged not to the gentleman; it was in slovenly order:
that partook not of the valet. In cut and fashion it resembled
the costume of no one country in particular, but appeared to
be a sort of medley, made up for the sake of a compromise,
of the fashions of a dozen different nations.

After glancing over the dress, I went back to the face again.

With what different feelings do we regard a person sleeping and the same person awake! The defenceless character
of the situation disarms us of that depreciating spirit with
which we are apt to scrutinize the unknown and the stranger.

IV.

As the schnell-post descended a steep hill a few miles out
of Leipsic, it dashed across a small bridge with such a tremendous jolt that my neighbor opposite was startled from his
slumber. He hastily replaced the cap upon his head, which
had some time before fallen off, and as he did so, caught my
eye; I suppose there was something in it which provoked

speech, for, although not quite awake, he muttered, in a low voice :

"Ich bin über dem großen Lärmen aufgewacht. Ich habe vergangene Nacht nicht gut geschlafen."

And then, as if suddenly attracted by the beauty of the morning, he thrust his head out of the window, took a glance up and down, snuffed in the fresh air, looked half angrily toward the smokers (I had laid aside the meerschaum), then out of the window again, then once more at me.

" I believe I am awake now," he continued, in German.

" It is a fine morning," said I.

" Too fine to be shut up in this filthy place. At the bottom of the next hill let's have a run; what say you ?"

" With all my heart."

And so, on coming to a hill, we got out and proceeded on foot in advance of our conveyance. We ran on for some time in silence, until we had gained considerably on the schnell-post, when we stopped on a small mound by the roadside, to take breath. My companion turned and surveyed me with an amusing scrutiny. I say amusing, for shrewdness and simplicity were so mingled in the expression of his face, that one knew not what to make of it. I now got sight of his eyes : they were of light-gray, not large, yet expressive of humor, pathos, deep feeling, and, as I have said, shrewdness and simplicity. At length he commenced, as follows :

" Ne venez vous pas de France ?"

" Je viens de Leipsic."

" Mais où allez vous si vite ?"

" En Dresden, comme vous voyez."

He looked around and gazed at the prospect; taking off his cap, he ran his fingers through his hair, shook his head, took two or three long breaths, as if to drink in the air, and then exclaimed :

"Cuan puro y saludable es el aire del campo!"

"En el campo," continued I, "es donde se disfruta la verdadera libertad; yo me ahogo, encerrado en el interior del pueblo."

My new acquaintance turned again to survey the landscape, and his eye happening to fall upon a quaint-looking old building, not far from the roadside, he attacked me with the following:

"Questa casa è fabbricata a modo di castello."

To which I replied: "Oltre modo. Di grazia non mi romper la testa."

The other looked full in my face, and, with an easy, pleasant smile, exclaimed, in pure English:

"When did you leave home?"

"Longer ago than I care to remember."

"You are English!"

"And you are —"

"A scape-grace whom any country would be ashamed to own," interrupted the other, good-humoredly.

"And what do you mean by a scape-grace?"

"Me!"

"That is talking in a circle."

"No. You have only to get acquainted with me to know the meaning of both terms."

"How do you make that appear?"

"Wait till we *are* acquainted, and it will appear as plain as the hill of Howth."

"I have caught you—Irish?"

"And my name is Robert Macklorne."

"Mine is William Henry Saint Leger.

"William Henry Saint Leger, let us abandon that cursed vehicle and go to Dresden on foot; but stay, we shall know each other in a few hours; we come for the noon-meal

(Mittag essen) to the toll-gate. The keeper has a handsome rosy-cheeked daughter, with flaxen hair and light blue eyes. I say it in all innocence; we will make a halt at the toll-house; your luggage shall go on to your hotel at Dresden; for myself, I am not encumbered with the article; but see, they are making signs to us;" (for while we were talking, the schnell-post had gone quietly along, and had now reached the top of the hill;) "let us run;" and off we sprang for a race up the ascent. We stopped a moment at a small hut on the summit, and obtained a draught of sour wine; then mounted to the inside, and the schnell-post rolled on.

It was a grateful exercise, that of talking in my native tongue to one equally familiar with it. While at Leipsic I do not remember to have conversed in English with one of my countrymen. And what little of the language I did occasionally speak, was entirely out of the conversational way.

V.

I was not long in forming an opinion of my Irish friend. Possessing by nature an extreme impatience of everything like restraint, he had indulged his love of license until it be-came a sort of vagabondism. His story was told in a few words. He was a younger son; his family of limited means; and, consid-ered a precocious youth, he was sent to Trinity college, which, the discipline proving irksome, he abandoned in a couple of years, resolved to see the world, after the fashion of poor Goldsmith. He accordingly set out, with ten pounds in his pocket—all he could induce his friends to trust him with—and, stimulated by an inordinate desire for novelty, and aided by a surprising facility in acquiring languages, he went from country to country, enjoying with a natural ingen-uousness, not to say childishness of heart, every new scene, and entering into the sports and pleasures with which the moment chanced to surround him. In this way he had repeatedly traversed every nation of Europe, selecting ordinarily the most unfrequented routes, and visiting the most secluded and out of the way places.

Macklorne was a solitary being. He had both friends and relations, but he was nevertheless emphatically alone in the world. Did he nurse an affected wretchedness? did he deplore the unlucky fate which had sent him forth with a keen relish for novelty and change, with an exquisite taste, a delicate ear, and a nice appreciation of the beautiful in nature and in art, and yet had withheld the means of enjoying these? Not a jot. He set his fate at defiance; not by gloomily folding his arms, contracting his brow and feeding upon dark fancies; not by turning misanthrope and sneering at humanity; but by a resolute, good-humored and persevering indifference to everything concerning himself, which after all is often the token of a superior will. There was something in his singleness of heart that stood in the place of the shrewdest penetration; one could not be a half hour in his company without feeling it, and there was that about his society that made you think better of yourself and more kindly of all the world.

VI.

The half way house between Leipsic and Dresden is nearly thirty miles from either place, and just one half of the day was employed in reaching it. Long before we came to it, however, I had determined to adopt the suggestion of Macklorne and turn pedestrian for the rest of the distance. I was moved to this by several reasons. In the first place I was delighted with my companion: what a contrast with the

characters I had left behind me ! I was charmed, too, with
the idea of taking to the road in the very extreme of liberty and
license; and I believed Macklorne, who was familiar with
Dresden, might aid me in the object of my journey thither.

VII.

A SUDDEN turn in the road, just as the traveller begins to
fear that he has been misinformed as to the proximity of the
half way house, discovers, close at hand, the house itself. At
this point the postillion invariably gets up another agitation
among his cattle, preparatory, and indeed essential to the excitement of bringing them to a halt. At five minutes before
twelve we were safely deposited on the north side of the toll-
gate. In five minutes more we were summoned to dinner.
My new friend was recognised by the host as an old acquaintance; and the flaxen-haired, blue-eyed Catharine readily presented either cheek for his salutation. I was then brought
forward, and should have been allowed a similar favor, so
current was an introduction from Macklorne, had I cared to
avail myself of it. I do not know how it is, but a kiss has
always seemed to me a sacred seal of a sacred feeling, and
I have looked upon the custom of extending it indiscriminate-
ly with repugnance. But Catharine had no time to listen to any
such philosophical apology, for the guests were now nearly all
seated, and she was the only attendant. I have ever since
remembered that simple-hearted maid with a kindly feeling.
She seemed to find her recompense in suiting all. With a
pleased alacrity she anticipated every wish before it was expressed; and the smile of satisfaction, when she had procured for you whatever you desired, came from her heart.

The dinner was plain but neat. We were hungry, and the
leberwurst, the kartoffel-salat, and good home-brewed ale,

served literally to gladden our spirits.   Dinner over, the passengers lighted their pipes, the schnell-post rattled to the door,
and with a sympathizing German guttural, giving token of a
general inward satisfaction, the party set off again.

VIII.

As I stood with Macklorne watching the retiring vehicle, I
felt for the first time in years an absolute and unbounded
sense of freedom.   Presently we strolled out to take a view
of the scenery.   I was struck with its beauty,   The turnpike
wound through a delightful valley, and at this spot the ground
upon our left rose gradually higher and higher, until it reached a considerable elevation.   The hill, to the very summit,
was cut into terraces, and laid out in luxuriant vineyards. To
the right the country was undulating, and covered with immense grain-fields.   The whole had the appearance of an extended garden.   Indeed, it was a sight rarely to be met with,
even in the most cultivated regions.   Doubtless it had required years of toil, from the rising to the setting of the sun,
to elaborate such an exquisite picture of human industry.

We strolled through the vineyards up the ascent.   Thence
we could see several red-roofed cottages scattered around,
and here and there we encountered a Saxon peasant at his
labor.   His coarse but well-mended garments spoke in praise
of the "gute frau," while his honest look, and quiet eye, in
which beamed no restless light of education, exhibited an entire contentment with his lot of ceaseless plodding.

At a distance, surrounded by a dense wood, I thought I
could perceive the walls of some grander edifice than was
about us.   I pointed it out to Macklorne, and asked him what
it was.

"That is the castle of the graf. He is the owner of the

surrounding domain, and to him each cottager makes his returns." He continued, cheerfully, " ' Unto every one that hath shall be given:' but let me tell you, of all the souls that inhabit the grafschaft, he is the most unhappy. I know these poor peasants; there is scarcely a red-roofed cot within our view which has not, at one time or another, afforded me shelter; and I know the graf too; I saved his life—at least he says so—when lingering under a malignant fever. The peasant is happy—the graf is miserable; from him is ' taken away even that which he hath.' It is an excellent rule, it works both ways."

My companion went off upon some other topic, but I was impressed with the reflection, that even in this life the favors of Providence are dispensed with a more even hand than man is disposed to admit. · I had received a lesson from one who was drifting, a solitary waif, upon the world. How cheerful he was, how trustful, how ready to vindicate, how slow to complain. I began to love this Robert Macklorne.

I X .

We descended slowly toward the inn. Arriving there, we found a carriage before the door, with outriders and servants in livery in attendance. The new-comers were two ladies. They had alighted, and, as Macklorne ascertained, proceeded at once to a private apartment. Feeling no curiosity on the subject, I inquired of Catharine what room I was to have, thinking to rest a while before starting upon a short excursion, which my companion had proposed.

" We have given to madame and the fraulein the room of Herr Saint Leger," said Catharine, modestly; " it is but for an hour. It was our best chamber. Will the gentlemen step into the next one for a little while ?"

I willingly assented, and passed up the staircase to the apartment pointed out by the pretty hostess. The room occupied by "madame and the fraulein" was at the head of the wide staircase which I was to ascend. The door of the room was open; I mechanically glanced into it while passing, and beheld, standing in an attitude of expectation—Leila Saint Leger! Her face was turned toward the door, and she looked earnestly at me as I walked by, but gave not the slightest sign of recognition. Almost unconsciously I went directly past, and entered my temporary quarters. Here was a new dilemma. The door of my chamber was partly open, and led into the one occupied by Leila. I did not know what to do. At first I wondered why she at such a time should slight me; but then I reflected that five years had wrought a great change upon my person. My frame was developed, and I was larger and stouter every way. My hair, instead of being short, in the English style, was worn after the manner of a German student; and a respectable beard with mustaches, covered the chin and lips, where nothing was perceptible on the boy of sixteen.

X.

AND William Henry Saint Leger, do you recognise *your self*? Where is the earnest, believing youth, who, child like, prayed as his mother taught him, and who, though un happy, and ill at ease, believed in CHRIST? . . . . .

It was a momentary pang; it passed suddenly away.

XI.

I ceased to reproach my cousin for the imaginary wrong, and sitting down at a little window which overlooked the road, busied myself with watching all that was going on about the house. Leila paced up and down her chamber with an agitated step.

"Strange that he does not come," said she to her companion, whom I had not seen.

"My child," said the other, in a calm voice, "it is not yet time. You mistake the hour. Have patience."

"Patience—patience—have I not had patience? must I not have patience from this time henceforth? Do not chide me; think of my fate; think of this meeting, which I have nerved myself to bear, and oh!—think of Henry! Patience!"

At this moment the sound of horse's hoofs struck my ear, and looking out, I saw a horseman galloping down the road. He never slackened his speed till he came close to the door of the inn, when he brought his horse to a stop so suddenly, that it threw the animal back upon his haunches. He flung himself off, and at the sign from one of the liveried servants, ran hastily up the staircase. I had but a moment's sight of him. He was tall, well formed, with light hair, and an agreeable countenance. I had no time for a close scrutiny. The new comer dashed up the stairs, and into the chamber, and folded Leila in his arms. I could hear sobs and stifled groans, and then a kind voice in expostulation; it was the voice of the stranger lady, but it availed not—at least she appeared to think so—for in a moment or two she rose, went out, and left the lovers together. I do not think a word was spoken for a quarter of an hour. The signs of deep and painful emotion continued the whole time, and I began to find my situation awkward enough. I could not shut the door, for it opened into the room they occupied; I would not go out, because I wished to—stay in: so I kept my seat by the window.

"Oh, Leila!"—"Oh, Henry!" were the first uttered words.

"Great God! am I in my senses? Leila! for Heaven's sake speak, and tell me that I am dreaming! Is this the meeting at the trysting-place? On such a day you would return; on such a day we should meet here. Heaven! what has bereft me! The day has come; this is the place and here are we; you and I, are both here. Am I not with you, Leila?—do I not clasp this hand as I was wont?—does not my deep heart beat as always for you? And my angel! are you not here, and ——"

He spoke to dull ears. Leila Saint Leger had swooned in his arms.

Quick as thought he sprang to the table for some water, and sprinkling a quantity upon her face, she opened her eyes, and exclaimed faintly : " Henry, have you left me ?"

"I am here, dearest; I will never leave you—never, never—I swear that I will never be separated from you?"

" It is too late. 1 must keep my oath! I promised to meet you here, and I have fulfilled my promise, though 1 sink under it. But I do not think of that; I have confidence in my strength to *suffer*."

" Do you remember our last meeting, Leila ?"

"Oh, Henry, do not, do not speak of what has been! 1 can not recall the past. It is only for what is to *come* that I have nerved myself."

" And are you resolved ?"

" Immoveably !   Henry, we suffer—together.   I shall love you always, but we meet no more on this earth.   If you always love me, then, in eternity we shall be blest.   I have vowed that I will *wed* the Count de Vautrey ; nothing more ; I shall never be his wife."

The conversation, which was continued half an hour, I can not trust myself to detail.   It completely unmanned me.   At length Leila's companion entered the room and announced that it was time to return to Dresden.

How my heart ached for them !   It seemed as if I might do something ; I stepped forward, and entered the apartment. " So, Leila Saint Leger, you do not notice your kinsman, who is travelling the world over after you !"

She turned upon me a look full of wonder and terror.   " It is my own cousin William !" she suddenly exclaimed, as she clasped her arms about me ; " here is another sorrow."

I threw one arm around Leila ; the other I extended to her lover.   He pressed my hand in silence.   We understood each other.

" We must go, my child," said the lady ; and Leila rose to leave the room.   The young man approached slowly, and, bending over her, imprinted a kiss upon her brow.   He then turned and walked in silence to the window.   I saw that his eyes were almost blinded with tears, but he did not speak. I assisted Leila to the carriage ; her companion stepped in, and, accompanied by the servants and outriders, it rolled away.

I returned to the chamber.   Leila's friend stood where I had left him, gazing with a vacant eye into the distance.   I approached and laid my hand upon his shoulder.   He started, looked at me wistfully, shook his head, and turned again to the window.

"This will never do," I said, in as cheerful a tone as I could command. "I want to serve my cousin Leila. In serving her I find that I serve you."

"I understand you, but she is unshaken in her resolution. No persuasion can influence her."

A common interest makes a speedy friendship. We sat down together, and I learned the history of the love affair.

XII.

HEINRICH WALLENROTH was the son of one of the most distinguished nobles of Prussia, and resided at Berlin. Many years before, he had met Leila at the house of Madame de Marschelin, a noble lady of Dresden, related by marriage to the De Soisson family. Her husband had been long deceased, and Leila Saint Leger had lived with her from childhood, except when the father required her presence at St. Kilda. The connection on both sides was unobjectionable, and Madame de Marschelin did not consider that she was exceeding her trust to favor it, especially as the young girl would require, in the event of her father's death, a more efficient protector. The lovers had plighted their troth, and the years ran happily along, when Leila was summoned away. What followed I was already acquainted with, from her letter. She had but lately arrived in Dresden, and, strange as it was, I was witness to the first interview between the two. I inquired when she was to wed the count.

"The day after the morrow," said Heinrich, despairingly.

"Something must be done instantly." I exclaimed, "and what is done must be done with Vautrey."

"Think you that has not occurred to me?" said Heinrich; "but he is not to be found. I have searched Dresden through and through for him. By the Power that rules above us, could I meet him, (understand me, he should have an even field,) the question should be to the death!"

"You would probably be the victim. It is the way of such things. The villain is usually successful. And then, what would become of Leila?"

"What *shall* we do!" exclaimed Heinrich, impatiently.

"Would not Vautrey waive his privilege, provided Leila would relinquish to him a portion of her large inheritance— or the whole, if a part should not satisfy him?"

"I do not believe it. Still, it is worth the trial. But, even if he can be found, who will propose this?"

"I will, much as I dislike the office. You go to Dresden to-night?"

"Yes; without delay."

"I shall stay here. I will be in town by ten o'clock to-morrow morning. Where shall I see you?"

"I am at the Stadt-Prüssien."

"It is where I am to lodge myself. My luggage has already gone forward. In the meantime, find Vautrey, if possible."

"I begin to have a little hope. Adieu."

The next moment Wallenroth was galloping madly toward the city.

XIII.

I DESCENDED into the public room, and found Macklorne just rising from a game of chess with the host. He had been so much occupied with the play that he had not noticed my long absence. On the contrary, he apologized for letting the time run by until it was too late for our intended excursion, but proposed a short walk instead.

We sallied out, and taking an opposite direction from our previous stroll, were soon in the midst of new beauties.

I felt mysteriously drawn toward my *new* acquaintance, and resolved, if possible, to retain him in my company. I therefore narrated to him what had passed at the inn ; giving, at the same time, enough of the history of Leila Saint Leger to interest him in our plans.

"Now, my dear friend," continued I,—" for friend of mine I am determined you shall be—help us by your counsel. In the first place, I must be in Dresden by ten o'clock to-morrow. It is nearly thirty miles. In England it would be but a pleasant ride or drive before breakfast; here, in this deliberate land, it is an affair of half a day."

" Leave me to manage that," cried Macklorne, who entered into the enterprise with the glee of a school-boy. " Leave me to manage that. The honest herr has a very decent ' fuhrwerk ;' and although his horse is a quadruped of the last century, yet Catharine has a fine young ' klepper,' which I know she will allow me to drive to Dresden ; at any rate, I will try for it; and if the worst come to worst, we will set out to-night and walk the distance in seven hours. There now ! I will stay by you, my true heart, till the close of the play, and as much longer as you choose."

I took the hand which Macklorne in the warmth of the moment extended, and acknowledged my sense of his kindness by a cordial pressure. So strongly reinforced as I had been since the morning, I began to take courage.

XIV.

It was near sunset, and we turned toward the inn. The declining glories of the day gave a softened aspect to the landscape, and lent a new charm to what seemed perfect before.

As we approached the house I turned to take another look

at the prospect we had left. I beheld two horsemen coming at a slow pace down the road. Presently they overtook and passed us. The foremost was—Laurent de Vautrey; the other was the same sinister-looking wretch who was his attendant at Glencoe. Both master and man were soiled and travel-worn. The count had not altered as much as one would suppose, considering the lapse of years. His hair, long and black, hung as it was wont, and his countenance exhibited the same expression of secure indifference, coupled with that air of careless, quiet assurance, so generally acquired by a certain stamp of men of the world.

But without discussing his character farther—fiend, brute, devil or what not—there he was. With the servant the world had evidently gone harder. His appearance, though quite as sinister as ever, was considerably subdued; he was thinner and had a more hang-knave air. Perhaps he was in disgrace that morning and was trying to look contrite.

As they came up with us, Vautrey cast a searching glance, not at me, but at Macklorne. The latter returned it with an air of defiance. At the moment of passing, Vautrey muttered to him " Beware!"

" It is for you to beware, Sir Chevalier," returned Macklorne. " I am upon your track again."

A grim look of hatred was the only return, and the horsemen passed on.

" Do you know that man ?" said I.

" Yes, it is the Chevalier Montbeliard, the most abandoned, the most unprincipled, the most unscrupulous roué in all Europe. He hates me because I rescued a simple-hearted girl from his clutches before he had accomplished his object : it is a long story, at another time you shall hear it."

" Macklorne, that is Count Vautrey, the affianced of my cousin Leila Saint Leger."

"Now may GOD forefend!" exclaimed my companion: "Go, cut him down; kill, murder, assassinate—perish yourself, perish all of us—but arrest that awful doom for the innocent! Not a moment should be lost; away, let us ——"

Just then something pulled Macklorne sharply by the sleeve. We both turned, and I saw an object the most hideous and repulsive I had ever set eyes upon. The creature—I can scarcely call it human—was in the last stages of destitution. His body was covered with rags; his hair had apparently been unshorn for years, and hung in matted locks upon his shoulders, mingling with his grizzly beard; his head rested upon his breast; his frame was absolutely bare of flesh, and the nails upon his fingers had grown to be like bird's claws.

"So, so, my poor fellow, we have met again!" said my friend, soothingly, to the being who had thus suddenly and silently stolen upon us. "You look famished. Deutschland does not agree with you. I wish I could spare you enough to make you comfortable; here—it is the best I can do;" and he drew out a few groschens from his pocket.

"Let me see if I can not do something," said I. At the sound of my voice the object raised his head; I was relieved to find that he could raise it; and peered at me with the smallest, keenest, most intensely infernal fiery-black eyes I ever encountered. And yet, all this may have been the effect of misery and want.

No sooner had he set those eyes on me, than he uttered a cry and extended his hand eagerly to receive the promised alms. I drew out my purse and extracted some silver. But he shook his head impatiently and pointed to the road, as if in haste to get on. I gave my purse another turn, and a guinea and two thaler pieces rolled out. The wretch clutched them as if with desperation, and springing past me rapidly, made a wild gesture to Macklorne, and setting into a sort of trot, was soon out of sight.

"How our friends accumulate," said Macklorne. "Do not look so surprised. In this section, transformed and deformed and devil-formed creatures are common enough. The devil-formed on horseback and the wretch on foot. I have a story to tell you about this too; but not now. I must go and provide for our morning's conveyance; we must set off by five o'clock.

XV.

THERE are certain periods when events seem to hasten to their consummation.—I say seem to hasten, for though it is but short work to reap the field and get in the harvest, yet how slowly did the seed germinate, the leaves sprout, the blossoms put forth, and the fruit mature. The consummation is sudden nevertheless.—And at such periods how rapidly the scenes change, how swiftly one after another the actors glide across the stage; how strangely circumstances tend to concentrate everything upon some one hazard; aud how irresistible is the force which concentrates!

XVI.

THE toll-gate that day had been the neutral ground. What a singular grouping—had the several characters chanced together. But they were not thus to meet. Another act of the drama remained. A last scene in which all these should assemble: the kind-hearted but complacent matron—Leila and her lover—Vautrey ana the beggar—Macklorne and I.

XVII.

"ALL ready for a start," was the summons, twice repeated, in the clear cheerful voice of Macklorne, which awakened me from a refreshing sleep, but a few minutes, apparently, after I had fallen into it. I sprang up, and for a moment was lost in that bewildering unconsciousness of time, and circumstance, which often attends the slumberer when suddenly roused in a strange place. I looked around the room; the curtains were drawn across the windows, so that it was quite dark; I put forth my hand to grasp the nearest object; I strained my eyes to discern a familiar one. "Sleeper—sleeper—almost five o'clock—a hot cup of coffee ready, and no time to be lost—come, come!" brought me to my senses and out of the bed at the same instant.

"I will be with you in five minutes," cried I.

"You shall have ten," replied Macklorne, good-humoredly, as he made his way down the stairs. I stepped to the window, and, drawing aside the curtains, threw it open and looked out. The air was cool and fragrant; the dawn was perceptible by a few faint lines which streaked over the east; everything was still, except that there were occasional signs of returning animation among the inhabitants of the poultry-yard, while the bark of a dog, from a distant cottage, was answered at intervals by the mastiff of mine host.

At the door of the inn stood the "fuhrwerk," before which was harnessed the smart "keppel" of the kind-hearted Catharine.

XVIII.

I dressed myself quickly, and hastened down to the public room, where the table was already laid for us, with boiled eggs, rolls, and fresh butter. I found my companion in as cheerful a humor as ever, enjoying, with great zest, the idea of our morning's expedition. In two or three minutes Catharine herself entered with the coffee, her natural German quietness entirely forsaking her, under the excitement of this novel enterprise. We soon despatched the morning meal; and, after parting salutations with the young hostess, we drove off.

I found that Macklorne had perfected all his arrangements, for in the bottom of the wagon nestled an urchin, who was to take the conveyance back from Dresden.

XIX.

We went on for a little while without a word being spoken. At length Macklorne broke the silence: "What is your plan?"

"I have matured none," said I. "I am to meet Heinrich Wallenroth at the Stadt-Prüssien as soon as we get to town; in the meantime, I would advise with you."

"Well, then," he said, in a half playful, half serious tone, "let us resolve, in the first place, that Montbeliard, or Vautrey, as you name him, shall not marry your cousin; and, secondly, let us discuss the various means to be adopted to carry out the resolution." Suddenly changing his tone, he continued: "I *know* this Vautrey; he is the only human being toward whom I have a settled and unalterable feeling of abhorrence. It would be a charity to plunge a dagger into your cousin's heart, rather than give her up to him."

" But if Leila is determined, in consequence of ——".

" I care not for that," interrupted Macklorne. " She must oe forcibly prevented; then she can not reproach herself."

" How shall we find Vautrey?"

" I will find him in two hours after we get to Dresden," returned my friend.

" And what after he is found?"

" I should be tempted to destroy him," said Macklorne, " but that must not be. Let us see what you can effect with your cousin; after that we will turn to the count. And remember, I hold myself bound to you, as knight or squire, as principal or second, against one or against a thousand, in single fight or in the melée, rescue or no rescue, unto the death."

The conversation was carried on with animation, and with that peculiar confidence produced by congenial feelings, and a unity of purpose.

X X.

In this way we drove along; the road was familiar to my companion, who often turned aside into pleasant lanes and by-paths, in order to shorten the distance. At first, the inhabitants of the cottages were just rising as we passed; after a while, we witnessed, through the windows, active preparations for breakfast; farther on, they were partaking of the meal, and soon were seen commencing upon the labors of the day.

A few minutes before ten we reached Dresden. We stopped at a small inn before we came to the better part of the town. Leaving tne lad to procure refreshment for himself and horse, and return to the halfway house, we walked on together a short distance, when Macklorne, after giving me general directions by which I could find the Stadt-Prüssien, and, promising to be with me in two hours, crossed over, turned down a narrow street and disappeared.

XXI.

I PROCEEDED to make my way to the hotel, which I reached after a walk of half a mile, having once or twice missed the direct course. Wollenroth was standing on the steps, anxiously gazing at each person who passed. He greeted me as if we had been friends from childhood; but dejection and despair were in his look.

"She will not see me," he said; "My friend, what can be done? From this day, life has no charm—death no terror. Do not desert me; I put myself in your hands; only act—*act*, for Heaven's sake."

We went into a private room, and sat down together; he became more composed, and informed me that Leila feared another meeting would be more than she could bear, that he had taken neither food nor rest since he left me, but had walked up and down the streets the whole night, and only came to the hotel to meet his appointment.

XXII.

FOR a few moments I felt altogether at a loss. Heinrich seemed to depend entirely upon me, and I found myself, as it were unconsciously, falling back upon Macklorne. I began to think over the whole affair with seriousness. I tried to survey it in a practical, matter-of-fact way. How should I act? What could I do? How far ought I to interfere? Leila was the betrothed of Vautrey by the solemn appointment of a dying father, and who could tell what might depend upon the fulfilment of the troth? On the other side, the conviction that it was obtained by fraud; the absolute abhorrence of Leila to the count, and her repugnance to the union; the complete sacrifice it would effect of two young spirits, made me consider almost any course justifiable to relieve them. I thought of the interview I had witnessed between Leila and Vautrey in St. Kilda; of the scorn with which she then dismissed him from her presence; of his threat, and of her proud defiance. A chill ran through me as I contemplated the end. My visit to St. Kilda, my interviews with Leila, our relationship, her apparent fate, crowded tumultuously upon me. Must one so young, so fair, so noble, be destroyed without an effort in her behalf? What if she conscientiously insists on keeping the promise to her father—shall those not bound tamely witness the sacrifice? I was roused also to attempt something, by the resolute tone of Macklorne. The careless, cheerful, but honest and clear-sighted wanderer, on this occasion threw aside his humor, gayety, and indifference, for an unconquerable resolve. But I was a stranger in Dresden; I knew no one in the town save Wallenroth, who did not himself reside there; and so had to ask again: " What can we do?"

Wallenroth was really incapable of advising. The blow had fallen so suddenly that he was stunned. I repeated some words of comfort, but they seemed tame and commonplace. I assured him I would devote myself to the cause of Leila, but felt that my efforts were insignificant. I tried to cheer him, but only became myself the more dejected. At length I entreated him to seek repose. This he refused, until I suggested that he would need all his strength to carry out the plan we were to consummate, when he took some refreshment and attempted to sleep.

XXVIII.

I HAD sometime to wait before I should meet Macklorne, but I could not occupy it.

I had anticipated pleasure on entering the brilliant capital of Saxony. Here was a check to every feeling like enjoyment. How different my thoughts from those I indulged in but the day previous, when, enchanted with the idea of throwing myself upon the world, I set out from Leipsic, and climbed with Macklorne the vine-clad hills with an unbounded sense of freedom in the prospect. My life-motto came to my mind :

Sed mihi res, non me rebus, submittere conor.

" I will not yield to the circumstance," I exclaimed, aloud ; " it may effect my course of action, but myself—never. Courage ! our cause is a good one." Before the time expired for Macklorne's appearance I had regained my equanimity, and was ready to act with resolution.

XXIX.

MY friend had been as good as his word. He had discovered where Vautrey lodged, but evaded my inquiry when I asked how he had done so. I told him briefly what had passed between Wollenroth and myself, and we concluded, as the only alternative, that I should visit the count, without delay, for we could decide on nothing until we knew the position he would assume.

XXX.

I DIRECTED my steps to No. — in the König Strasse. My last interview with Vautrey had been when interested for the safety of Glenfinglas, I went to request him to abstain from an affray. The last time I had seen him (except on the previous day) was when, after being hurled from the cliffs by Donacha MacIan, he was drawn up, bleeding and insensible.

I could not decide in what way to approach him. I thought it best to leave that until I should learn the nature of my reception. Arrived at his lodgings, which were in the finest part of the town, I sent my name to the count, and was presently waited upon by his old valet and requested to step into his private room. I found him in a rich dressing gown, in an easy chair; the room in disorder: having the appearance of preparation for a journey or removal. Articles of fancy, destined apparently for a lady, were scattered around, and everything exhibited an unsettled state of things.

As I entered, Vautrey rose and came toward me. Holding out his hand, he said, " This is I presume the Mr. Saint Leger I met in Scotland, although I should not now recognise you. We are older—both of us—than we were five years ago. I remember there were words between us. I will say, let them be forgotten. I suppose you come to be present at the bridal. You have lived some time in Leipsic, I believe."

This was spoken naturally and without effort, while he retained my hand which it was impossible for me not to have extended to meet his own. " But sit down," he continued, " Miguel, some wine. When have you heard from our Scottish friends; do you fancy that bewitching Ella as much as ever, or have you lost your heart here, where maidens are more amiable, if not more captivating. Seriously, how are your friends at home, and how are you ?"

I was mastered at the outset by the careless freedom, ease, ready appreciation and cleverness of this profound dissimulator. His practical world-knowledge seemed an over-match for the book-wisdom of the student. I felt that there was a force brought into the field, against which I had none similar to oppose ; and that I was in danger of losing the day, not from want of strength to conduct the contest, but from loss of the vantage ground. A straight forward course was the only one for me to pursue. As soon therefore as Vautrey paused in his inquiries, I replied, quietly, that my friends at home were well, that I had not come to Dresden to attend the bridal, but to see what I could do to prevent it, and to that end had in the first instance called upon him. I went on to say (Vautrey showing no signs of impatience), that I believed the proposed union would make Leila miserable, and that I trusted, unpleasant as the truth might be, he was incapable of destroying the happiness of so lovely a creature by insisting on the fulfilment of a promise made to soothe the last moments of a dying father.

He listened with composure, until I finished. I had expected to be interrupted but he had learnt the lesson of absolute control. "Saint Leger," he now said, "you expect to see me angry — most men would be so — at this unwarrantable interference between Leila and myself; for I can not presume that you have her sanction in calling upon me;" I shook my head; "but," he proceeded, "I am not angry; I have lived too long to be angry; besides I take what you have said in good part, believing that you are honest. I will be equally frank with you. I have lived in the world and have had my pleasure in it; I have gratified my senses, I have pleased my tastes; what wealth could purchase or health could enjoy I have possessed; I have never missed my aim, nor been cheated of desired revenge; I have been successful with women and have defied men; the world has been my minister and it has served me faithfully;—for all that, at six-and-twenty I am sated—these things no longer attract or pleasure me. I seek some new life, I search for a new enjoyment, and I would find it with Leila Saint Leger. . She is mine,"—and his eyes glistened with triumph, in spite of his cool manner—"mine, by everything that can make oaths binding. Through life I have pursued her, and now she shall not escape me. Do not think, however, that I would sacrifice her. I know the sex. She will at first resist my approaches, she will be unhappy, she will not love me; but time will cure all this. You do not taste your wine—come, drink to my happy union with your cousin."

"Excuse me, count, but as I have broached a disagreeable subject, let me finish it. What you say does not alter my opinion, that Leila's happiness is now irrevocably at stake, and that, as a man of honor, you should release her from the promise that binds her. I perceive you will not yield. Are there no considerations which I could urge to change your decision?"

"What mean you?" he asked, quickly, while a slight red spot glowed on either cheek.

"Your fortune is ample, count, as you have said; but it might be doubled."

"By Heaven, you shall pay for this!" he exclaimed, starting to his feet: "but no, there shall be no more violence," he said, in a lower tone, as he resumed his seat. "I understand you, Saint Leger, but you do not understand me; you have had little opportunity to know me, and I acquit you of intentional insult. Others may call me what they will; unscru-

pulous, abandoned, a debauchee, a villain; but in this business
I have, as I said to you, a new purpose, a new hope. I tell
you, I have set my life upon this venture, and with my life
only will I abandon it. Say no more to me. Leila, I know,
does not authorize this application; you can not get her consent to your interference; but I give you credit for good purposes, else I had not listened a moment. As it is, you must
be satisfied. I offer you my hand again; I do not ask you to
pledge me in the glass; let the wine remain untasted, if you
will have it so, but—you are the nearest relative Leila has
upon the continent—will you not be present at the ceremony? It will take place to-morrow evening at seven, precisely, in the cathedral."

"I will be there, count. Good morning." I turned and
left the room.

XXXI.

On the way to my hotel I revolved this interview, to discover a clue to the unexpected conduct of Vautrey. I came
to the conviction that he had, in a manner, spoken truth with
regard to himself. He had run so completely the round of
pleasures, that they sickened rather than gratified: his life
nad been so continually spent in making enemies, and in opposing them, that he was tired of strife, and longed to be at
peace. It was especially undesirable to provoke a quarrel at
the present time, when his plans were about to be realized
and particularly dangerous to excite *me* to further opposition.
Such being his feelings and position, his conduct—taking into
view his adroitness to adapt himself to occasions, without
scruple—was easily explained.

Although foiled in my object, I was not deceived. But,
without some assent to our action from Leila, what, after all,
could be done? As it was, she was resolutely determined to

prevent any interference in her behalf. And so, thought I,
Laurent de Vautrey triumphs at last! this is the reward of a
life of wickedness! after he is satisfied with everything the
senses can enjoy; after years of debauchery and violence, he
is to lay hold on the only happiness that remains, and to possess the only object he desires. A thoughtless reproach of
Providence was about to escape my lips, but I restrained it.

XXXII.

LEILA, then, was to be sacrificed. How little really did
Vautrey know of woman's nature; how mistaken was he in
supposing his had been the school in which to learn it. Before reaching the Stadt-Prüssien, I had formed a new design;
I would make an effort to see my cousin, and try what persuasion would do. Taking a carriage, I drove to the house
of Madame de Marschelin. She was at home, and I thought it
best to obtain what information I could from her. This lady
was one of those fortunate persons with whom the world always goes smoothly; though kind-hearted and amiable, she
had not soul enough to suffer from any occurrence that was
likely to happen. She could not understand the calamity
which had now fallen upon the lovers, or the agony it brought
with it. I found little satisfaction in my conversation with her.
She was distressed that Leila was so unhappy. She wondered
how her father could have been so cruel; but fathers *were* cruel
sometimes; at least young girls were apt to think so; not that
Leila thought so; she was a sweet creature, a pattern of obedience; she loved her as if she were her own child—she was
sure she did. Who could tell but it was best so? Count Vautrey was of a noble family; he was said to be too gay; but
doubtless, he would reform. I grew faint under this good
natured exhibition of heartlessness, and without attempting to

prolong the interview, asked if I could see my cousin. Madame de Marschelin regretted that it was impossible, " Leila, poor child, would see no one." At length I prevailed upon madame to take to her a note, in these words :

" Leila, I must see you before the ceremony. I claim this as your kinsman and natural protector."

In a few minutes she returned, with the following :

" It is impossible — do not urge it."

" I knew it would be so," said her guardian : " Dear child, how firm ! well, I suppose it is all for the best "

XXXIII.

It was late in the afternoon ; sick at heart, exhausted by fatigue, weak for want of food — having tasted nothing since my early breakfast at the halfway house — I returned to the Stadt-Prüssien. There I found Macklorne and Wallenroth, impatiently waiting for me. The former had evidently been exerting himself to sustain his companion, and, in so doing, assumed a cheerfulness which he could not feel. I gave a report of my own movements, which seemed to take away what remained of hope — yet Macklorne would not despair. There is another day left. Providence will not desert us; let us hope yet. An ample dinner, prepared by the considerate directions of Macklorne, was in readiness ; and after it, overcome by fatigue of body and mind, we all retired.

XXXIV.

Through the night I was oppressed with dreams and nightmare. At one time I was at home in Warwickshire, listening with a heavy heart to the arguments of De Lisle ; then suddenly transported to St. Kilda, where, losing my footing, I seemed falling from the cliffs of Conagra into the foaming abyss below; next I was at Glencoe, bending over the wounded Glenfinglas, while fierce black eyes glowered at me from the adjoining thicket; and then I was walking in the professor's garden, with Theresa Von Hofrath, and while enjoying her companionship, Leila came running down the walk pursued by Vautrey, and implored my protection. The violence of the appeal awoke me. Starting up, I discovered that it was not yet day. But, I could sleep no more. The leaden weight that had oppressed me when a child now sat upon my heart. Memory, of all the faculties, was most wakeful. I revolved the scenes of my childhood; I thought of my mother and her gentle counsels; I essayed to repeat the little prayers she used to teach me; and Conscience then whispered that I had sinned against God, and my own soul, but I controlled myself and was calm. I resolved not to yield to nervous fears or to be miserable without a cause. Then, I thought, I would commend myself to God and summon Faith to my assistance. I tried, and—could not. At length I remembered where I was, and for what, and my mind sought relief in thinking what might yet be done for Leila. Thus occupied, I lay till it was quite light, when I rose, dressed, and went down.

XXXV.

MACKLORNE was up before me. Wallenroth, he said, after a most unquiet night, had just fallen asleep. At the end of considerable discussion we concluded we had done all which could be done, without Leila's assistance; but that we would be present at the marriage ceremony, ready to take advantage of anything favorable to our hopes. As a last expedient I despatched a note to Leila, stating our design, begging she would still reconsider her decision, and giving assurances that at the last moment even, we should be ready to rescue her. I, myself, knew too well her resolute spirit to believe anything could alter her determination.

XXXVI.

THE time passed gloomily. We did not separate; but continued to discuss one project after another, with feverish excitement. We walked about the town, we visited the cathedral, we went up to the altar, and stood where Vautrey and Leila were to stand. We even selected the place whence we should ourselves observe the ceremonial; Heinrich acquiescing, as one to whom everything had become indifferent. Afterward, restless and impatient, we paced up and down the street.

XXXVII.

THE day was spent. The hour arrived which should give Leila Saint Leger to Laurent de Vautrey. A few minutes before this, Wallenroth, Macklorne, and myself, had taken our places by a small chapel on the left of the altar. The immense wax candles around it were burning; they emitted no cheerful light, but added to the gloom which pervaded the cathedral. After a few minutes two carriages drove up, and presently Leila entered, leaning upon the arm of Madame de Marschelin, followed closely by Vautrey. Several attendants on either side waited at the door within the church.

As Leila advanced, my eyes were fastened upon her. 1 endeavored to mark some sign of wavering purpose, but could not ; her face was very pale, but her step was firm, her form erect, her air composed and dignified — she would do nothing even in appearance to violate the spirit of her prom ise. Vautrey, too, bore himself with an easy elegance, which, under other circumstances, would have challenged my admiration. An anxious furtive glance thrown around the gloomy chapels and recesses of the cathedral, however, gave evidence of some perturbation of spirit. They approached the altar together. For an instant I turned to look at my companions. Wallenroth seemed stupified, and was gazing vacantly on the scene; Macklorne, on the contrary, was excited to an almost incredible degree; a frown was upon his brow; his eyes shone with fierceness; his form was dilated; his breathing distinctly audible. The sound of the priest's voice brought my attention back to the parties; up to this moment I was calm; now a tremor seized me, a giddy sensation oppressed me, and I leaned against one of the columns for support.

XXXVIII.

THE ceremony went on—the moments to me seemed ages; the responses had been demanded and were made by Leila, in a firm unwavering voice; and the priest had taken the ring in order to complete the rite. At this moment, a moan at my side caused me to turn; Wallenroth had sunk down insensible. The priest paused, startled by the interruption; gesture from Vautrey recalled him to his duty; but now a slight disturbance was heard, proceeding from the entrance; the noise increased—the priest paused again—when a hideous creature with the aspect of a fiend, darted swiftly forward, and before one could say what it was, lighted with a single bound upon the shoulders of the count. I saw the glitter of steel aloft, and flashing suddenly downward; I saw Vautrey fall heavily upon the mosaic—*dead.* His executioner crouched a moment over him, with a brute fierceness; then drew the dirk from the wound, and as drops of blood fell from its point, sprang quickly toward me, shaking the weapon with a wild and triumphant air, and exclaiming "Tat's petter dune." The truth flashed upon me—I beheld in the repulsive wretch before me the creature we had encountered at the toll-gate—the wild savage seen at St. Kilda —the fierce cataran of the highlands, the leal subject of Glenfinglas—*Donacha MacIan.*

XXXIX.

It is impossible to describe the suddenness with which all this took place. A scene of confusion ensued; the party about the door ran in and secured the miserable Donacha, who indeed made no resistance.

Macklorne rushed forward and bent over the body of the murdered man; Wallenroth's senses returned and he was at Leila's side. She herself, though nearly overcome by the horror of the scene, looked as if breathing grateful thanks to Heaven.

Madame de Marschelin was for a moment in bodily terror of the assassin ; that removed, she became composed and remarked that it was an awful visitation of Providence. The priest was nowhere to be seen; he had fled into a private recess, and did not appear till satisfied all danger was past. For myself, I stood and surveyed the spectacle. All that I had ever known of Leila and of Vautrey passed, as a single thought, through my mind; another seal was set to a life-impression. What was man, proud man in the hands of the Almighty? How futile his plans—how vain his hopes— how mysterious his end!

I went up, and with Macklorne attempted to raise the body of the unfortunate Vautrey. Calling to the attendants who now approached, we succeeded, with their assistance, in placing it in the carriage which we accompanied to his late apartments.

Macklorne undertook to convey information of the catastrophe to parties named by Madame de Marschelin as business agents of the count. Friend or relative he had none

X L.

THE next day, impelled by a curiosity I could not restrain, I made inquiry for Donacha and was told that although placed, as was supposed, in secure confinement, he had managed to escape from prison and could not be found. I learned afterward that in a very short space of time he presented himself to Glenfinglas at Kilchurn Castle, and holding up the blood-stained dirk, fell at the feet of his master and expired; illustrating the nature of his relentless spirit and the fierce and indomitable passions which sustained him to the last.

X L I.

IT is time to pause.

Leila is happy in the arms of Heinrich Wallenroth. Francis and Margaret Moncrieff are both agreeably wedded. Hubert and Ella, gay and light-hearted, are satisfied with the world. At Bertold Castle time passes serenely and without drawback.

For myself—what? Theresa, I hasten to you—no, I must not. The resolution is taken. . . . .

Come, Macklorne, let us out into life.

THE END.

www.ingramcontent.com/pod-product-compliance
Lightning Source LLC
Chambersburg PA
CBHW021532110726
47902CB00004B/851